Bottom Dog Press

Salvatore and Maria

Finding Paradise

Gale,
our family stories are little
bricks of history.
Best wishes
Paul Gentile

Paul L. Gentile

Harmony Memoir Series
Bottom Dog Press
Huron, Ohio

ISBN 978-1-933964-95-9
Bottom Dog Publishing
PO Box 425, Huron, Ohio 44839
http://smithdocs.net

First Edition

General Editor: Larry Smith
Cover design: Susanna Sharp-Schwacke
Cover photo from Paul L. Gentile

Acknowledgements

There are many people to thank for helping take this book from an idea to a reality. I'd like to start by thanking all the family members who cheerfully gave information when asked. Thanks to Melissa Van Otterloo of the History Colorado Center in Denver. To Brad for his technical assistance and Gail Borruso for her photo genius. I'm indebted to Mimi and Sal Tripodi for their careful readings and thoughtful suggestions and to Barbara Ardinger for keeping me grammatically correct and coherent.

A special thank you to Larry Smith, my publisher and editor, for his patience and guidance through it all.

As in every challenging time and adventure, Joyce, my moral compass and wife, unselfishly guided me through the whole process. To everyone connected to this work, I am eternally grateful.

Preface

When I was young, I loved to visit my grandparents. They lived on what we called a farm, even though it was only three acres. There was something exotic and magical about that farm. At home, there were chores and rules, whereas at my grandparents' farm, we kids were free to run, play, and explore. My grandfather was a model of calm and pleasantness, singing and talking to his dog constantly by his side. I never saw signs of anger, never heard a harsh word. My grandmother would be in the kitchen baking delicious bread or making polenta, pastas and braised meats that were ordinary at home but indescribably mouthwatering at her table. Grandma died when I was ten, and so Grandfather Salvatore took over her work with sage advice and great cooking.

As I grew older, married and had children, I continued making regular visits to my grandfather, sitting in wonder as he told stories of his past, which seemed more exciting than anything at the movies. Grandpa Salvatore hadn't stepped out of a Norman Rockwell painting. He was deep and complex. Living in what we pictured as the Wild West, he had actually known Indians, Mexicans, armed guards, adventure, and violence. He had survived two world wars, the Great Depression, poor working conditions and labor disputes, and the loss of his loved ones.

The more I heard, the more I realized that this humble man had led an incredible life filled with adventure, hardship, and sometimes despair, loss, and sorrow. And yet, he had somehow balanced it all with peace, contentment, and brief periods of happiness. Born into poverty, as a child of 13, he was sent alone to a strange country where he didn't know the language, sent to America to work and send money back to his family. His aim was not to get ahead, but to merely live and try to beat starvation for himself and for his family.

In his great new country, he found prejudice, deplorable working conditions, and wages too low to feed a family. He had endured constant struggle, yet I never heard him complain, never heard him criticize, nor wish evil on anyone. He was always singing and showing a wonderful sense of humor, voicing a simple, practical philosophy of life in his stories. I best see him raising a glass and thanking God for his good fortune.

His is a common story, yet one in danger of being forgotten. Its lessons must not be ignored. Many families started as immigrants most often in or near poverty. Most families have faced what seemed to be insurmountable odds against moving up the socioeconomic ladder. It has taken three generations for my family to get to a level of comfort where I might sit in my suburban world and see this story as entertainment rather than as life lessons. I fear we Americans may be beginning to lose the hard-gained position that earlier generations made possible. And so I must tell his story.

Although Grandma died far too young, this is also her story, for she and my grandfather were partners through it all. It is a love story. They met at a young age and spent their entire lives together, working out solutions to all their challenges, and through it all, openly and honestly showing love and affection for each other.

This is a true story. Every incident actually happened. While my grandfather's stories were vivid and factual, he never complained about our questions, and gave informed answers. I had to do a great deal of research to find often shockingly depressing details to be able to write and recreate actual conditions and events. My wife and I traveled to every location mentioned in this book. We visited every village in Italy where my family lived and all the locations in Colorado and western Pennsylvania. I interviewed strangers and relatives, read books, articles, and newspaper accounts, scoured census records, and did extensive library and Internet research.

In addition to my grandfather's stories, I spent countless hours listening and taking notes as my mother recounted episodes of the family through her eyes. And my uncle Leo, idled by emphysema later in life, wrote pages of family history, and we talked on many occasions about his perspective. I also appreciate the willingness of my aunt Marge and cousins who shared their recollections.

While I changed a few names, most were not altered, and every person is real. The incidents and conversations actually took place as told to me. Some dialogue relayed to me in paraphrase is my creation. The thoughts and reactions belong to the person voicing them.

I hope the reader will gain a better understanding of and appreciation for the plight of the immigrant, the coal miner, the steel worker, the family members that work hard, and strive for a better life for themselves and those to come after. Salvatore's story needs to be told.

List of Photos and Illustrations

Part I

A New Country, A New Life

(Pacentro, Italy)

The Atchison, Topeka and Santa Fe thundered into the station, black smoke billowing from its smokestack, steam hissing, brakes screeching. As it slowed to a stop, the conductor jumped onto the platform and set down the metal stepping stool. First, a lady and a gentleman walked off, still talking as they strolled into the station. Other passengers stepped down. Finally Salvatore struggled off the train, pulling behind him a bulky and battered wooden suitcase covered with paper to resemble leather. He was barely five feet tall, and his straight, shiny, black hair and olive face, soot blackened from riding for days looking out the open window, emphasized his large brown eyes and square jaw. He was dressed in the coarse black pants, bulky jacket, heavy work shoes, and soft cap of the Italian *contadini.*

The sign on the station read "Trinidad, Colorado," the same words that were printed on the note pinned to his jacket. The platform was empty, so he went into the station hoping to find Donato, his *compare* (godfather) and sponsor to the United States. Across the empty room, a thin, stern looking man sat at the ticket counter. He wore garters on his shirtsleeves, eyeglasses, and a visor that covered his forehead and shadowed his face. Salvatore noted the calendar on the wall behind the man. It was May 31, 1902. He found it hard to believe that he had been on this journey from his village for thirty days. There had been times when he thought he would never get to Trinidad, but at last he was here. And yet there was no one to meet him.

The man at the ticket counter looked up and gave him a disapproving look. He had seen hundreds of this kind come through: scrawny little foreigners, weak, poor, dirty, here to take Americans' jobs. He muttered a few words as he waved this new intruder away. Salvatore didn't know what he was saying, but he read the scowl on the man's face and the harsh tone of his voice. Nevertheless, he moved hesitantly forward. Only able to speak Italian, Salvatore tried to explain how he had gotten here and where he was trying to go. He showed the ticket agent the note bearing the names Trinidad and Donato.

"My name is Salvatore Ciccone," he said in Italian, "I am to meet my sponsor Donato. He will take me to this place, Starkville."

Without looking at the note, the man shouted angrily and made another jerking motion toward the door as he turned his attention back to his work. Salvatore didn't need to understand what he said. He was not welcome. Salvatore turned and walked, head down, out onto the platform.

He watched the workers finish refilling the train's water tanks. Soon it was ready for the climb over the Raton

Pass into the New Mexico Territory, and started pulling out of the station. In the renewed silence, Salvatore sat on his suitcase and began to look around at this place that would become his new home. It was a strange looking land, with streets of dirt and buildings of wood, weak looking, not like the solid stone buildings back home in Pacentro. Up ahead, beyond the station, the ground looked dry and dotted with small, scraggly trees and weeds. Beyond a few houses made of stucco or adobe lay a backdrop of a hill that was flat on top. Looking over his shoulder, he saw the dirt road dropped down to a stream and a wooden bridge. On the other side of the stream was a scattering of buildings, the business section of Trinidad, a hodge-podge of wood, brick, and adobe with wooden sidewalks. Beyond them lay another of those strange hills with flat tops.

Trinidad sat at about 6,000 feet above sea level in southeastern Colorado, an area with a rich and often violent history. Archeological digs revealed that the area was inhabited by Native Americans as early as 8710 BC. The Spanish, moving north from their conquest of Mexico at the end of the sixteenth century, claimed the region for Spain. This trail served as a main east/west route, and during the late 1860s had been heavily raided by the Plains Indians in an effort to keep the white man from taking their land.

When coal was discovered in the mid-nineteenth century, the area opened to an influx of new, cheap labor from Mexico, Ireland, and the coal regions of the eastern U.S. In 1876 when Colorado Territory became the thirty-eighth state, the rough and tumble town of Trinidad was filled with gambling halls, saloons, and houses of prostitution, and there were gunfights on every corner. Bat Masterson had been through Trinidad when he was working on a crew building the Atchison, Topeka and Santa Fe Railway. The town leaders had hired him in 1882 to clean up the town. At the same time, Doc Holiday and the Earp brothers had arrived, too.

And now, just twenty years later, Salvatore was here, sitting on his suitcase, thinking about all that had happened to him in the last thirty days since leaving his family in Pacentro, Italy. His thoughts went back to the calendar behind the man inside the station. May 31, 1902. It was his fourteenth birthday. Dirty, hungry, and tired, frightened and alone, he looked around at this desperate place and began to cry.

Salvatore was the eldest of Antonio Ciccone and Francesca Tollis's seven children. Antonio was a sharecropper in the little, medieval village of Pacentro, which was perched on a hillside in the Majella Forest, midway between Rome and the Adriatic Sea. From the third century BC to the present, shepherds had moved their sheep through the forest and hills as part of the migratory grazing practice. Pacentro had long been ruled by a succession of aristocratic families who visited occasionally, usually for hunting. It was a feudal village whose residents worked to support the ruling family. Aside from the few members of nobility, professionals, and merchants, most of the population farmed as peasants or sharecroppers. Though the feudal system had been officially ended by King Joseph Bonaparte in 1806, it was still practiced in Pacentro, and Antonio was required to supply a quota of what he grew as determined by the *padrone* of the village, hired by the ruling family. He was usually more tyrannical than the aristocrats.

Antonio and Francesca lived in a modest stone house attached to others and fronted against a cobbled lane that wove up the hillside surrounding the great fourteenth century castello. How well Salvatore knew the ground floor of the house which had a dirt floor and housed their cow, gardening tools, and bins for storing the yield from Antonio's garden. The second floor was an open space dominated by a fireplace for warmth and cooking. A ladder led to a loft that was divided into two sleeping areas, one for Antonio and Francesca, and the other for the children.

Salvatore had been nine years old when Antonio told him he would have to quit school and help take care of the cow. But Salvatore was a good student who loved school and was a quick learner. He pleaded with Antonio to let him stay in school, but as in many of the hill towns in Italy, there were only two grades in Pacentro's little school, and it was necessary for pupils to go to the city of Sulmona, thirteen kilometers away, to continue their learning.

Antonio explained, "Salvatore, we have no money to send you to the city. You know I must spend more time growing the crops. All the land here I need for more vegetables, and so you must take the cow up past the *castello* for grazing."

Handling the cow daily took all of the time that Antonio needed to work the garden to meet the increasing quota of vegetables required by the *padrone*. Francesca felt sad for the boy and tried to console him, but Antonio became angry and told her, "Eh *signora*, you make the boy weak. He has no need for more school. To be a man he has to be out in the fields, working to put food on the table. Not sitting around with his nose in a book."

Salvatore's disappointment was softened when his teacher called on the family and gave him a few copies of a popular magazine about a hero named Ercolino. She said these magazines would help Salvatore improve his reading skills. She also said she would stop by periodically to help him with writing and spelling. Antonio thought, *This is crazy what you do.* But Francesca persisted, "If the boy must sit up on the mountain all day, it is better he reads than waste time and get into trouble." Not fully convinced by this logic, Antonio yet allowed it.

Francesca awakened Salvatore before sunrise and gave him a piece of old, stale bread wrapped in a cloth for lunch. Foggy headed, he slowly led the cow out of the village and up into the pastures of the Majella Forest for a day of grazing. He stopped at a spot along a gurgling stream where other boys were encamped with their cows. He set his cloth bag of bread in the stream and put a rock on it to keep it from floating away. Then he chained the cow and played with the other boys. By the time he ate his bread, the stream had softened it and transformed it into a delicacy.

He loved to play in the fresh air and drink from the bubbling stream. When the migrating shepherds passed through, he enjoyed singing folk songs with them and listening to tunes they played on their bagpipes. But he was still a young boy and sometimes got into the tight spots of youth. On one occasion, he had not chained the cow carefully, and while he was playing ball with the others, it got loose and ate the vegetables in a nearby garden. The owner marched Salvatore and the cow to Antonio, who agreed to pay for the man's loss, then promptly beat Salvatore, and made him work in that man's garden every day while the cow, safely chained, grazed.

Salvatore had grown to love this routine. He had felt that life could get no better. Up in that fertile pasture with its clear running water, surrounded by the beauty of the mountains, playing and singing with friends and the traveling shepherds, the boy felt like he was in paradise. Then the day came when his father told him things were going to change more than he could ever have imagined. He was now thirteen and considered a man. The oldest of the children, he would have to assume a greater responsibility in helping to support the family. Italy was suffering a severe depression at the beginning of the twentieth century, and the absentee owners of the *castellos* had stopped investing in their towns and villages. "There is no work for anyone in these towns. Our people are leaving in masses to seek their fortunes elsewhere—in America." Salvatore listened in anticipation and fear.

Their *paesano,* a man named Donato, had written to Antonio from America and told him that the Colorado Fuel and Iron Company was recruiting Italians and Greeks to work in their mines. A man could work in the mines if he was fourteen, but many who were only twelve were also getting work. If a person could pay for passage to Colorado, a job was guaranteed. Donato had been there for three years, and was sending money home regularly. There was one thing, he said, that they had to know: the government of the United States of America did not permit companies to recruit workers from other countries. Arrangements for Salvatore to go to Colorado would be made through Donato, who would act as the boy's sponsor. In his letter, Donato emphasized, "Salvatore must swear not to tell anyone of this job arrangement. He must always say that his *compare,* I, Donato, am his sponsor. If the officials find out a job is waiting, the Colorado Fuel and Iron Company will be fined, and Salvatore will be sent back to Italy in disgrace."

It was his responsibility to help the family. Salvatore had no choice but to go across the ocean. Even though he was sad to be leaving, he acted bravely and told his mother "Yes, I am happy to go." She knew it wasn't true, and she was heartsick. He promised to work hard in the land where those streets were paved with gold. "I will send enough money for you to eat well and keep our home and garden. One day I will return to buy you a larger house higher up the hill where the air is fresh and the sun bright."

Before he left home, Francesca packed him dried salami, cheese, and bread. She carefully sewed what little money they could spare into the lining of his coat, and gave him a little more for emergencies. His teacher came by and gave him a few more copies of the adventures of Ercolino along with her address. She told him, "Now you keep reading and write me of your adventures in this new land. I will write back to you, Salvatore. I promise."

At last, on his fateful morning, all the neighbors came out on the street to say goodbye. Salvatore looked at everything he had known all his life. His father cautioned him, "Listen, my son, do not trust anyone. There will be robbers in Naples. And no one is to be trusted in America. People will try to befriend you, but never let down your guard or they will rob you. Most important, and remember this, you should never do anything to disgrace the family name." His mother was sobbing as his brothers and sisters clustered around him. She touched his face and told him, "Be careful and pray to God for guidance." As she dissolved in tears, he kissed her, took one last look at the home he was leaving, and climbed onto the donkey cart of the merchant. He was taking the boy to Naples for a fee while making a delivery. Salvatore looked back through tear-filled eyes for as long as he could still see his mother crossing herself and praying as he rode out of sight.

Salvatore had never been out of his little village, and so the cacophony of Naples was overwhelming. He clung to his meager belongings as he struggled through noisy and confusing crowds to the even more frightening docks. Here he boarded the *S.S. Neckar* for the cross-Atlantic sailing.

The *Neckar*, a 409-foot, rusty tub from the North German Lloyd Lines, had been built to hold 750 passengers, but was carrying 1,080, with close to 800 of them in steerage. Salvatore was herded down narrow metal steps, lower and lower, into the cavernous, windowless, airless holding area called steerage. Here he would be spending nearly three weeks at sea among rows of bunks stacked three, and sometimes four, high. They were made of canvas stretched onto metal frames which were chained one above the other all the way to the ceiling and so close together it was impossible to sit up in one. Men, women, and children were mixed in these holding cells, and buckets were chained to the support posts to be used for toilet needs, though a small area in one corner surrounded by a flimsy curtain was designated for regular toilet use. People were packed so tightly there was no privacy, and the air was stale and rank from sweat and defecation and people throwing up right at their bunks, unable to get to the curtained area or the bucket.

Lying awake at night, too sick to sleep, Salvatore witnessed all sorts of degenerate behavior—people copulating, fighting, robbing each other—unthinkable acts.

Sweating and feverish, unable to eat or move around, he often thought death would be better than this suffering.

Finally, a little after nine in the morning of May 26, 1902, someone in the crowd shouted "Hey, we are pulling into New York harbor!" But Salvatore was not allowed up on deck to see the magnificent Statue of Liberty. Only those traveling first and second class had the freedom to walk about the ship. While disboardin and thanking God for the end to this misery, Salvatore surveyed the squalor and filth around him, thinking that he treated his cow better than this. Weak and shaken, he was hauled off the ship and herded into a cavernous hall that echoed with endless noise and the confusion of people being moved along roped-off lines to tables where they were physically examined and questioned. At one of these tables, Salvatore learned he was to be held at Ellis Island with no explanation.

He spent a fitful night there, afraid the whole time that he would be sent back to Italy with some of the others, who had been rejected for any number of reasons: the dreaded trachoma, suspected senility, insanity, or just for having the wrong papers. His fear was that the American officials had somehow found out that the coal company had guaranteed him a job, and he would be sent home. From 1885 to 1887 a series of laws called the Alien Contract Labor Laws had been passed, which prohibited any company or person from bringing foreigners under contract to work in the United States. Salvatore only knew that no one was to know he had the garantee of a job. He had answered all the questions just as he was told to, including no to the question did he have a guaranty of a job and yes his trip was paid by his sponsor. He revealed that he had thirteen dollars cash in his pocket and a train ticket to Trinidad. He was listed on the ship's manifest as a porter, and so all seemed to be in order. But before he could give Salvatore a good reason for the delay, the interpreter was taken away to resolve another problem, leaving Salvatore to be led to the holding area with some seventy-two other travelers.

Around noon the next day, he was among twelve of the detainees called back to the desk. His papers were stamped and signed, *Released to sponsor Donato Patrilli, Trinidad, Colorado, May 27, 1902, 12:20 p.m.* He was freed without explanation and put on a train that would take four days to reach Trinidad. At two stops along the way he had to change trains. Fortunately, someone always managed to read his tag and get him to the right place, but for him it felt like going through a maze not knowing what was next or where he was being led. He had no idea this new land was so big.

And now here he was sitting at the train station of this strange town that looked like it was out of one of his Ercolino magazines. Gaunt from the ordeal of his trip, he felt old and tired. May 31, 1902—his fourteenth birthday—and he sat exhausted and hungry and missing his family.

* * *

Amato was approaching from the houses behind the station, walking toward his saloon in town. When he saw Salvatore sitting alone, he walked over and greeted him in English. When the boy stared blankly at him, Amato, recognizing the clothing and look of a newly arrived immigrant, spoke to him, first in Mexican, "*Buenos noches*," and then in Italian, "*Buonasera. Come stai*?"

Embarrassed to be seen crying, Salvatore wiped away his tears—leaving streaks on his soot covered face. "*Buonasera*" he replied. "I'm fine, thank you."

"My name is Amato," the stranger said in Italian. "What is your name, and how can I help you?"

Relieved to find a friendly person who could speak Italian, Salvatore quickly told the man, "My name is Salvatore, and I come from Pacentro, Italy. I come here to work in the mines of the Colorado Fuel and Iron Company of Starkville." He shrugged his shoulders and added, "I was to be met by my *compare*, Donato, but no one is here."

Amato had seen many foreigners come through like this. Starkville was a little CF&I company town four miles south of Trinidad. He knew that by this time of evening Donato would be at one of the six Italian-owned bars in Starkville, that crude mining town of 2,000 people. He explained to Salvatore that no one was there when he arrived because all the men would have been working in the mine. He motioned to Salvatore, "Come with me to my tavern and I will give you something to eat while I try to contact your Donato." That sounded wonderful to Salvatore. He was starving, for he had eaten all the dried salami and cheese his mother had packed for him long ago. He had been paying for train station food, but was afraid his money would run out before he could get his first pay.

They walked down the dirt road, over the wooden bridge, and up the street to the saloon. Here Amato sat Salvatore at a table in the back of the room and started telephoning the saloons in Starkville. On the third try, he called the saloon owned by Joe Mainello and learned that Donato was there now. He then learned that Salvatore was to have arrived a day or two earlier, but Donato hadn't known of the delay in New York. He knew only that Salvatore had not arrived when expected, but would come in due time. Receiving the call at nightfall was unfortunate, because the jitney that ran from Starkville to Trinidad had made its last run, and Donato was in no condition to go anywhere. Tomorrow was Sunday, his day off. He would leave on the first jitney in the morning.

Amato told Salvatore all this and offered to let him spend the night in the chair for free, or, for twenty-five cents, he would give him some chili and bread and a cot to sleep on for the night. Salvatore chose the meal and cot, paid Amato, devoured the food, and went to the cot in a back room, only to find he had to share it with another man. As tired as he was, he lay awake fully clothed all night, thinking about the money his mother had sewn in the lining of his jacket. On the ship, he had seen people robbed and even murdered for less. He wasn't going to take any chances with these strangers.

In the morning Donato arrived and hugged him, then the two of them took the jitney to Starkville. It was a four-mile ride, the first two miles uphill to a halfway house, the last two downhill. The jitney had little power, and as it approached the crest of the hill, it went slower and slower until the men had to jump off, push it over the crest, and then jump back on as it resumed speed.

Starkville, first called San Pedro, had been founded in 1879 as a stop on the Atchison, Topeka and Santa Fe Railway before the trains ascended the Raton Pass and went into New Mexico. It was a rugged, frontier rail stop until Albert Stark opened one of the region's first coal mines. By 1900, the town's name had been changed to Starkville, it had a population of 1,500, and passenger trains no longer stopped there.

The town stood in a broad valley defined by the Raton Creek and rail lines that paralleled each other and ran through the middle of the town. A main street on the high side of the stream was referred to as *La Plazzita*, with a cluster of businesses: a bank, a post office, the train station, some stores, saloons for the white people, the Congregational Church, and a few houses of a better quality than others in town. These were the houses of the mine superintendent, school principal, justice of the peace, and the wealthier merchants. On the other side of the tracks ran a dirt road lined with lesser-quality frame houses. A branch of this road dropped down to the creek and ran over a wood-plank bridge to a patchwork of ramshackle wooden or stucco houses, a number of bars, and a little wooden Catholic church that had once been a Mexican mission church. The church was now occasionally serviced by an itinerate priest who traveled among the mining camps. For major events, the Catholics had to travel to Trinidad. This odd collection of mismatched buildings created the section of town that was home to most of the Mexicans, Italians, and Slavs. Their houses were close to the mine tipple and coke ovens and got most of the soot and noise that rained down on the town.

Donato walked Salvatore through the town, down across the bridge, and into the lower town where the Mexicans and others who didn't speak English lived. There the boy would live with Donato and three other men.

They approached a small wooden shack whose roof looked like its coat of coal dust was all that was holding it together. A small wooden stoop with no railings provided access to a door that opened into a filthy room swarming with flies and smelling of dirty clothes, body odor, and rotting food. It had a dirt floor, and in the center stood a wood-burning stove for cooking and heating, a table, two benches, and two chairs. Although there was electricity in the mine, there was none for the workers' houses. A kerosene lamp hanging from a chain in the ceiling provided the only light after sundown. At this time of day, however, sunlight peeked in through a single, grimy window next to the door. The window had a gunnysack hanging over it as a makeshift curtain. Bunks lined two of the walls, and a door in the third wall opened into another small, dirt-floored room containing a dresser, a chair, and two more bunks. A back door opened to an outside workspace where a table with a washbasin and the privy which consisted of a few boards and a sack nailed together around a two-foot hole in the ground were located.

Since this was a company house that was costing the men two dollars a month per room, Salvatore was told he would have to pay his share of the rent for one of the bunks in the main room. However, because he was not yet bringing in any money, he would be responsible for cooking the meals, getting the firewood, and keeping everything clean. Each of the men was responsible for buying certain food items at the company store. The company used a scrip system of issued notes replacing legal currency, so Salvatore could begin buying his share immediately. The store manager would keep a running tab, and what he spent would be deducted from his pay. Donato told him to store his suitcase under his bed and begin to clean the house before preparing the meal. The men were at the saloon celebrating their only day off for the week and would be hungry when they returned. After pointing out the supplies, Donato was off to join the others and catch up on drinking time that had been lost going to Trinidad.

Salvatore looked around the room, shook his head, sighed, and then slowly walked outside to familiarize himself with his new home. Beyond the privy, which was too close for proper sanitation, and in the center of a cluster of five or six houses were a well shared by those five or six houses and an outdoor oven made of adobe brick and mud and called a *horno* used for baking bread. He walked over to the well, pulled up a bucket of water, and carried it to his table, where he stripped off his shirt and washed his hands, face, and chest. The sun felt good and he sat quietly for a while, taking in his new surroundings. Looking up the hill beyond a few more rows of company houses, he could see parts of the massive tipple, plus the scales, washery, and coke ovens. Beyond them, rose Fisher's Peak, a 9,600-foot mesa, the funny-looking, flat-topped hill he had noticed in Trinidad. While it looked imposing from Trinidad, here in Starkville it was barely visible as he strained to see through the smoke, soot, and general ugliness created by the mine and the coke ovens.

Small patches of land between some of the houses had been sectioned off by makeshift fences of sticks shoved into the dirt. There wasn't a blade of grass, just dirt that blew about in the wind and became a sea of mud in the rainy season. Contained within those stick fences everywhere except here where the men lived were small vegetable gardens.

Salvatore noticed a woman hanging laundry out to dry. She paused, and as she tucked some falling hair behind her ear, she noticed the boy and smiled as she turned back to her basket. Another woman was pulling freshly baked bread out of the *horno*, and two more women were getting ready to cook. They looked at Salvatore and laughed, probably guessing the origin of this newly arrived greenhorn. A few children were running through the yards and chasing each other with sticks.

Salvatore soon realized that the men who were not working were in the saloons. With another sigh, he stood up, walked back into the house, leaving the doors open to air the place out. He washed off the table and the food-encrusted dishes, then began to look for something to make for dinner. The first things he found were a big box of pasta and a can of tomatoes for sauce. He thought of the countless times he'd watched as his mother made pasta, and so, even though he didn't quite know how to cook, it would be pasta for dinner.

Frank, the first miner to return, was a short, dark man in his early twenties, he had also immigrated from Pacentro around the same time as Donato. Staggering into the house, he mumbled something at Salvatore as he passed through to the back room and collapsed on one of the beds. Not long after, Big Mike and Little Mike sauntered in. They dropped into chairs at the table and, after a slight nod of acknowledgement, rudely called out, "So, greenhorn, where is the food?" Little Mike was actually the larger of the two, but he was called Little Mike because he was younger. Salvatore was tossing the pasta when Donato came in. They all sat down and devoured every morsel of a mushy spaghetti.

The minute they pushed their empty plates away, the other men fell into their beds and immediately began snoring, belching, and farting. Salvatore cleaned the table, washed the dishes and pots, and put everything away for the night. He then took one of the chairs out on the front stoop to sit alone and look up at the stars as he thought about his family and his home in Italy, both of which he feared he would never see again. *What is next*? he wondered.

And how long will I have to endure this misery before I can go home? Crying silently, he went to bed.

At five in the morning, while it was still dark, Big Mike awakened Salvatore by shouting, "Well, where the hell is my coffee?" After some really terrible coffee that everyone complained loudly about, the new cook was told, in no uncertain terms, that the coffee had to get better and it had to be ready for them when they woke up.

As they walked up the dirt road past the other houses and across the tracks that carried the railcars to the mine tipple, Donato began instructing Salvatore, "When we get to the office," he said in Italian, "I'll do all the talking."

"Do the men in the office speak Italian?" Salvatore asked.

"No, clearly not," Donato replied.

"Then you'll do all the talking," Salvatore replied, still in Italian.

"Look, smart ass," Donato said, "I'll do all the talking and you listen to me and do as I say. What these people expect is hard work and respect from you. You give them what they want, see, and you start earning your way."

With that, they were at the office, where Salvatore signed some papers and received his work assignment, badge, and instructions, all of which Donato interpreted for him. There was some confusion, however, as the paperwork was being filled out. Rather than trying to spell "Salvatore" correctly, the clerk decided to simply write "Sam" on the form. From that day forward, he would be Salvatore to his family and close friends, but Sam to everyone else.

"Donato," the clerk said next, "take Sam to the supply shed. Get him outfitted, and he'll go into the mine with you today."

They got "Sam" outfitted with shoes and gloves and cap, then Donato and he jumped into one of the wooden coal cars of the electric tram that took the miners deep into the earth under Fisher's Peak. Here young Sam began his first twelve-hour day of picking and shoveling. It was the start of a new life.

Salvatore saw that the tram ran on a double track at mine entrance, called the drift portal, about six and a half feet high and fifteen feet wide. Another tram already loaded with coal passed them on its way out to the tipple where young pickers separated the coal from rock before it was weighed.

Salvatore looked about, wide-eyed with wonder, as they smoothly glided into the yawning mouth of the mine and descended at a slight grade through the drift shaft into total darkness. Lights mounted on the miners' caps provided the only illumination, and the shadows gave the tunnel a haunted, sinister look. As they descended, the mine became noisier and noisier. They passed networks of alleyways on both sides of the tracks, alleyways that branched out like underground tentacles, each smaller than the main tunnel, each filled with the activity of augers drilling holes into which charges were loaded to blast the coal loose from the rock. Salvatore also heard the thuds and chipping of picks and shovels and the rattle of smaller coal carts being pulled by donkeys out to the main track. At the main track, these carts were unhitched from the donkeys and attached to the electric train that had carried the men into the mine. The newly-dug coal would be carried out to the tipple.

At first, Salvatore felt a chill as the damp air gradually changed to a stifling lack of air. The deeper they went into the mountain, the more oppressive and dust-filled the air became. In the smaller side tunnels where workers were shoveling and chipping with their shirts off, he could see their bodies covered with sweat and grime.

About one mile into the hillside, and nearly as deep under Fisher's Peak, Salvatore and Donato jumped off the tram and walked down a side tunnel labeled Fourteen Left. The way became darker and blacker with each step they took. The tunnel itself, as they could see with the lights on their caps, became smaller and smaller until it was impossible to stand up straight. Finally, Donato showed Salvatore how to begin chipping and pulling chunks of coal out of the wall so that Donato could shovel them into the small, donkey-driven, wooden cars to be taken out to the drift shaft. As short as he was, Salvatore had to stoop over, and in some places he had to lie on his side to get at the coal where the vein went down to just two feet. As he worked through the day, his muscles burned with pain, and he felt as if his back was breaking. Working in this claustrophobic space, he found it hard to breathe. With every breath, he inhaled a choking mixture of coal dust and sweat. Soon he was gasping for air, so he took his shirt off because of the oppressive heat. For the twelve hours he kept a steady pace, stopping only to eat some bread and swallow a little water.

By the end of the day, he could barely straighten his body as he walked on wobbly legs back to the tram. His back, abdomen, and arms were covered with deep scratches from scraping against rock as he crawled deeper into the shallow crevasse, lying on his side as he chipped for coal. As the cars moved up the main shaft toward fresh air outside, the wind coming from the main opening chilled him, and he tried with all his might to conceal the convulsive shaking of his wet and bleeding body. The combination of colder air and overworked aching muscles almost did him in, but he was determined that no one would see any sign that he could not handle this work.

It was after six in the evening. The whistle had blown, and the tram filled with coal-dust-covered men rolled out of the mine shaft and stopped at the tipple, where the men poured out and walked down the hill. A few of the married men headed to their homes and their wives and dinners. Other married men and all of the single ones went directly to the saloons to "clear their throats" with a few drinks before heading home. Salvatore did not drink, and he would not waste money he didn't have on liquor, so he went directly to the house. He had never been so tired and sore in his life, but pride prevented him from showing any signs of the pain or the despair he felt.

His loneliness and misery surged over him as he stepped into the empty house and looked around. He was all alone. His childhood had been abruptly stolen from him, and he knew his life would never be the same. This was not what he had expected America to be, and he hated being underground. But here he was, and here he would survive. He choked back his tears. Shaking off his self-pity, he went out back, where he drew some water from the well. After heating it, he scrubbed viciously, but in vain, trying to clean the coal dust out of his pores and the scratches that covered his arms and chest. The water and harsh soap burned the scratches and his hands, which had first become blistered, and then filled with burst blisters after hours of the pick handle.

One of the neighbor women standing in her yard was watching him go through this routine. She shouted over, "Hey, boy, now you look like a man. But don't waste your time and the water on that dirt you'll never get out of your pores." Ignoring her taunts, he finished washing and went inside to cook dinner. When the others arrived, they ate together, after which he washed the dishes before dropping, exhausted, into bed. No sitting out on the porch that night.

After a few days into the job, Salvatore was working by himself in a different side shaft. He had just finished filling a car when a driver backed his tram up to Salvatore's car to connect it, but as the two cars bumped, their hooking mechanisms jammed. As the driver was pulling on the mule's harness to get it to move forward, Salvatore climbed up on the coupling and began jumping up and down to dislodge the jam. Suddenly the lamp on his cap hit the overhead electric cable and it knocked him unconscious.

He was brought back to consciousness by the driver, who was slapping his face and shaking him. Martin Bowden was sixteen years old. Not much taller than Salvatore, he had kind eyes and a pleasant smile. He introduced himself while helping Salvatore to his feet and warned him, "Tell no one what happened or the boss will surely dock your pay for an unsafe practice."

Even though Martin was speaking Italian, Salvatore had a difficult time understanding him. "*So che parla Italiano*," Salvatore said, "*Ma non capisca quello che dici*" (But I don't understand what you say.) Martin laughed. He was using the Abruzzese dialect. "I am *Piemontese*," he said, "from up north, *Alta Italiano*. But I understand you because many people from your region live here and we all speak a little of each others' tongue."

With no time for socializing, the two were quickly back at work, for there was still much to be done before the end of the workday. At the end of the shift, Salvatore and Martin walked together as far as Salvatore's house. He told Martin he was newly arrived from Pacentro. Martin said he had been born in France and had come to America in 1887 when he was just one year old.

"Is your family French?" Salvatore asked. "Bowden is not Italian."

"No," Martin replied. "Our name is Baudino. My uncle came to this country first and changed our family name because Italians were not liked where he lived. When my father came to this country he stayed with my uncle, and everyone called him Bowden, too, so he also kept it as his name."

"And there is a place in this country where people do not like Italians," Salvatore murmured as he shook his head in disbelief. The two boys bid goodbye, and Martin continued toward his house as Salvatore entered his to begin making dinner for the men.

All too soon, the other men were careening home from the bar and devoured Salvatore's fried sausages and potatoes. Then the men had some time on the porch for smoking and belching and farting while Salvatore again washed the dishes and cleaned the eating area before dropping into his bed. Salvatore soon settled into this routine of gathering firewood, carrying water, cleaning, and cooking while still somehow finding time to get acquainted with the manager of the CF&I general store and the owner of Starkville's Italian *groceria*. Salvatore could speak in Italian at the *groceria*, but not at the general store. Other than a very few words (which were neither kind nor polite), the owner and his workers spoke no Italian, and so the neighbor ladies came to Salvatore's aid.

* * *

Finally his first payday arrived. On the way out of the mine, the men stopped at the office to receive their pay envelopes. Thinking of how much he would send home to his mother, Salvatore opened his envelope. Donato read the pay slip for him and explained what seemed to be very complicated. It was with shock and disbelief that Salvatore listened as Donato went through the details. The miners were not paid a daily or hourly wage. They were paid straight tonnage: forty cents for every five-ton car they filled. Each miner had to blast the rock, pick and shovel his own coal into the cars, then send them to be weighed. At the weigh station, pickers went through the load and threw out anything that wasn't coal. Only clean coal was weighed, not shale or rocks, and the company did not pay for prep time, but only the actual weight of the coal. Salvatore was told that the company men will cheat the miners at the weigh station. "The scales they use for paying us," Donato said, "are different from those they use for their customers. But you must never complain about it! If you do, they will send you down the canyon."

"What is this sending down the canyon?" Salvatore asked.

"My friend, they will fire you and throw you out of the house. Then you will have no work and no place to live. You will have to leave. When they throw you out like that, the people say you are sent down the canyon." Donato further advised him that there was nothing the men could do about either the cheating or the dangerous conditions in the mine. Salvatore should just keep his mouth shut and do his job.

In his first two-week pay period, Salvatore had shoveled an average of four five-ton cars of coal a day. For twelve days of work, that totaled forty-eight cars, or two hundred forty tons of coal, for nineteen dollars and twenty cents. But listed on his slip were deductions: for food, for the work clothing he had bought at the company store, for his share of two weeks' rent. There were also an eight dollar and fifty cents charge for the work supplies he was issued on his first day, fixed charges of one dollar for blasting powder and blacksmithing, twenty-five cents for pick-axe sharpening, and even a deduction toward medical expenses.

"But I haven't been sick," Salvatore protested. "What is this medical?"

"The company takes money out of every pay for the doctor, so when you need him there is no charge. But this guy we have, he is a drunk. Forget it. If you get sick, there is a woman in camp you can go to. The s*trega*. She will mix up something to make you better."

What was Salvatore's pay for his first two weeks? At the bottom of all these deductions was a total of one dollar and five cents, out of which he still owed the *groceria* seventy cents. He had left thirty-five cents. He was never going to be able to send money home at this rate. Something had to change.

The very next day, Salvatore picked up his speed in the mine, not stopping to talk with anyone or even to eat. He also volunteered to work a seventh day every other week. By the next payday, he was loading six cars a day, which brought him up to twenty-eight dollars and eighty cents, and even more for the seven-day weeks. Of course, there were the usual deductions, and prices at the company store were being raised. What more could he do? He knew he could save some money if he made a garden like some of the neighbors. He dug up a patch of ground at the far corner of the property, and a few of the neighbor ladies gave him seedlings to get started.

He loved being in the garden. It reminded him of joyful days spent alongside his father, learning to garden and being out in the fresh air. But the long hours in the mine, the cooking and cleaning, and now tending his new garden began taking a toll on him. He had lost weight and soon had terrible, dark circles under his eyes. The neighbor ladies began to worry about him and told him he had to take care of his health or he would be no good for anyone and his family back home would see no money at all. Salvatore knew they were right.

One evening, he went straight home as soon as the whistle blew, made a big pot of stew, and then went out and sat on the porch to wait for the men to come from the saloon. When they arrived, he stood in the doorway and announced that things were going to change. He said, "Listen. I am no longer to be the only one doing all this housework." The men protested, but he stood firm, fists clenched and jaw set saying, "I pay my share of the rent and I buy groceries, just like everyone else. So from this day forward, the housework will be shared." He was no longer the cook, shopper, cleaner, water and wood carrier, and caretaker of the garden. Although he was only fourteen and small in stature, there was no mistaking his strength and determination. After some grumbling, the men agreed. They would share in the work. But Salvatore had developed into a good cook, at least a better one than any of them, so it was also agreed he would do most of the cooking, which he didn't mind.

Salvatore loved the outdoors and continued working in the garden whenever he could. Out in the warmth and fresh air, he often sang the folk songs he had learned from the shepherds back home. The neighbor ladies loved to hear him sing and encouraged him. In fact, they often joined in the singing as they worked in their own gardens. They also gave him cooking tips and helped him pick out the best produce at the company store. Noticing that he was being cheated at the store because he didn't understand English, they also started teaching him English.

When he found brief bits of time in the evenings, Salvatore pulled his suitcase out from under his bunk, took out one of the Ercolino stories, and read under the dim light of the kerosene lamp until the men began to complain and made him turn off the light so they could sleep. He also wrote letters to his teacher, making certain to include news for her to relay to his parents, who could not read. He thoroughly enjoyed the adventures of Ercolino, and after a few years, was able to save enough pennies to subscribe to the magazine.

Just as he reached a point where he was sending some money home, a strike was called at all the coal mines in Colorado. When Salvatore wanted to know why he could not enter the mine, the men explained that an organization called a union, *syndicate*, was trying to get the mine owners to improve working conditions. Even though it might be hard to lose the work, they said, he must show support by staying out of the mines until the union and the mine owners reached an agreement. He learned that the year before he arrived in Starkville, there had been a confrontation between the Western Federation of Miners, who were trying to organize in Colorado, and the mine owners over the length of the workday. After much debate, the state legislature had passed a bill to officially lower the workday to eight hours. It was submitted to the public for a vote in November 1901, and it passed by a seventy-two percent margin. However, under pressure from the mine owners, the legislature failed to enact the amendment. Now, to show some muscle, the union was calling a strike to force the government to act.

Soon the Colorado National Guard was called in to quell the strike. Major Zeph Hill was appointed commander of the militia of Las Animas County with its headquarters in Trinidad. A curfew was put into place whereby no person was allowed on the streets after nine o'clock in the evening, and all miners were required to register and be photographed. Salvatore learned that a group of men from the Berwind Mine, twenty miles away, refused to do this. They were arrested by the cavalry and marched to Trinidad. One man, who was ill, fell and was left by the roadside to die. More violence erupted. Everyone was cautioned to stay out of Trinidad.

During this time, there was no money for food. But Salvatore was resourceful. Besides, he didn't like to be idle. While the other men were going to the saloons and drinking on credit to pass the time, Salvatore said he was not going to waste his time or spend money he didn't have. He noticed that the baker always seemed busy and so he approached him with an offer to cut all his fire wood in exchange for bread. The baker agreed to this, and now the men had bread to eat.

The strike finally ended, as many did, in failure for the union. Everyone went back to work under the same old conditions, and in some cases with pay cuts.

* * *

On his occasional day off, Salvatore usually walked up the hill past the mine and up the slope of Fisher's Peak. There he sat and looked west, out toward the distant Sangre de Cristo Mountains whose jagged, snow-covered peaks reminded him of the Gran Sasso and Majellas back in Abruzzo. He remembered and dreamed of his village, where the gray stone houses with their barrel tile roofs were so close they seemed to hold each other up as they gleamed in the shimmering *mezzogiorno* sun. In his imagination, he could see his father working in the fields, the Majellas rising grandly behind him, and his mother baking bread and making pasta for his brothers and sisters. He could hear the songs of the shepherds as they moved their flocks along the pastures. When he heard his mother singing in his imagination, he began to weep. He so missed his home and his town and everyone in it.

Some of the miners went hunting on their days off, but Salvatore had no interest in hunting, though he knew it was important to them as sport but more because it was another source of food when there was no money to buy meat. Salvatore preferred the solitude of his walks up to the mesa, where he could remember and relive his life back in Pacentro with his family. For brief moments, he was transported away from the dirt, smells, and confusion of that squalid mining town.

Martin often walked home from the mine with Salvatore. He lived farther from the mine, down along the stream, and he didn't drink. Sometimes the two boys sat for a while on the stoop and talked about their lives. Martin had been born in Lyon, France, though his parents were Italian and had been married in a small village outside of Torino. Martin's mother had an exquisite singing voice. She had been training for the opera in Torino, but gave it up to marry Martin's father. Because of the lack of work in Italy at the end of the nineteenth century, the young couple had moved to Lyon, where Martin and his older sister were born.

In 1887, when Martin was a year old, his family had emigrated to America for the promise of a better life. They had another son and settled in Las Animas County, Colorado, where his father got work in the mines. They lived close to another Italian family, the Grossos, who had come from the same town in Italy, and in 1899 Martin's sister had married James Grosso. Martin's father had been killed in a mine explosion in 1901, leaving his mother a widow with no means of support, and so Martin and his brother were working hard to provide for her.

Sometimes on his day off, Salvatore went to visit Martin at his house. Martin's mother, Domenica, fascinated him. She was rather tall and thin, wore her hair swept up into a pompadour, and was always dressed in a neatly ironed, long, black skirt and a shirtwaist blouse. Wrapped in a black knitted shawl, she often sat in a rocking chair gazing out the window. Almost as if talking to herself, she spoke softly about the career in opera she had given up to marry her childhood love, only to have him leave her in this Godforsaken place, alone with nothing but her memories. Her husband had promised to buy her one of those new, cylinder gramophones, but he had died in that cursed mine before he could do so. Now her daughter was married to a miner, her boys were working under the ground, and she was alone with only her memories of her music. Who had any use for a poor widow? She sighed and began softly singing one of the sad arias learned during her musical training.

And as she sang, Salvatore sat transfixed, listening to the beautiful music made by this woman who was so out of place in a crude mining camp. Sometimes she encouraged him to sing a folk song or even to sing an aria with her. He had a good ear for music and soon acquired a repertoire that was a rich blend of Italian folk songs, American popular tunes, Mexican folk songs, and operatic arias. All of these he sang as he worked, sometimes drawing strange looks from accidental listeners in the tunnels.

* * *

A miner named Guy Garfolo often worked alongside Salvatore, and occasionally Guy gave him advice to improve his tonnage without working so hard. Guy, who lived beyond Salvatore's house and closer to Martin's, often walked with the two boys from the mine and stopped for a while on the porch to talk. "Salvatore, you look so pale," Guy said. "You must cut back on your chores. There is a Chinese laundry in Starkville, but their prices are too high. I got a girlfriend in the Grosso family here. I know their girls would do your laundry for half the cost. Think it over."

Salvatore talked to Donato, Frank, Big Mike, and Little Mike about pooling their cash to get their laundry done by the Grosso girls. At first the other men were reluctant saying they didn't see the need. But finally, after a little more convincing, they agreed to get their work clothes washed for a dollar a week. On the appointed day, Maggie and her younger sister Maria picked up the first bundle of clothing. The men were surprised when the black, smelly pile of rancid clothing was returned in a neat, fresh-smelling stack. "Salvatore," they said, "at last you do something smart." These were the first kind words he'd heard from his harshest critics.

While many of the houses in town were company-owned, some families had been able, through a bit of entrepreneurship, to earn enough side money to buy their own houses. The Grosso family was one on these. Pietro Grosso also owned three cows and a few chickens and had planted a large garden. He sold milk and eggs and some of his vegetables. The girls delivered the milk and eggs and did laundry for many of the miners. This extra money helped the family maintain their homestead. It was a lot of work, and Pietro and his wife, Margherita, had suffered much to arrive at this good fortune.

Pietro was a soft-spoken, gentle man with a bald head, a fair complexion, smiling brown eyes, and a large handlebar mustache. He declared he would not attend church because, like many in town, he felt the priest was in the hip pocket of the mine owners. But he read the Bible regularly and was active in the Masonic Order and reached the Thirty-Second Degree. This was highly unusual, as Catholics were not permitted to join secret societies and the Masons did not take Catholics. But Pietro was an unusual man. Salvatore was drawn to this close family in many ways then and to come.

Margherita was also fair, but with blue eyes. She was barely five feet tall and more serious than her husband. She was also a devout Catholic who made sure her children received all the sacraments and attended Mass regularly. Although small in stature, she carried herself erect and walked quickly and with self-assurance. She was inventive and often created clever ways to deal with the many challenges of domestic life in a mining community. She was busy from the time she rose in the morning until she dropped her head on the pillow at night.

The Grossos considered themselves to be fortunate. How had they arrived at this place in their lives? Pietro had been born in 1848 in the tiny mining village of Montalenghe in the northwestern region of Piemonte, thirty miles northwest of Torino, Italy. He and his older brother, Martin, were both coal miners. In 1874, Pietro had married Margherita Martelli from the neighboring village of Castellamonte. Just one year before, Martin had married Margherita's sister, Dominica, whom everyone called Minnie.

Mining in northwestern Italy was sporadic, and by the late 1870s the mines closed. Pietro searched everywhere, but could find no work. Hearing there was work in France, he moved with his pregnant wife to La Ricamarie in the Rhone-Alps region of France. Just three years earlier, there had been a serious strike there and troops had fired on the striking miners, killing thirteen, including two women. More than sixty miners had been put in prison. But the mines were now fully working and job prospects looked good for Pietro.

Margherita was sad to be leaving her family, but they had no choice. There were two year old daughter, Francesca, and the coming baby to think of—*And how could they raise a family if there was no food on the table?* When Pietro was hired at the mine they moved into company housing at La Ricamarie, where their first son was born. But good fortune did not come that easily. When he was just nine months old, the baby died. No doctor was available, and so they were never to know the cause. Within the next few years, Margherita and Pietro had two sets of twins, one boy and one girl each time. It looked like they were in France to stay. But Pietro was concerned that his children should have all the rights of French citizens. Even though the four babies were born in France, according to French law, they were not citizens because their parents were not citizens, and so Pietro applied for and became a French citizen.

Working conditions in France in the second half of the nineteenth century were brutal. In 1874, a law had been passed making it illegal for women or children under twelve years of age to work underground, although they could still work above ground as pickers or operate the tippler. Many mine operators ignored the new law, however, and continued to put women and children underground. Conditions were deplorable, and the wages were so low people were working and still starving. When the workers began holding rallies to organize a union, Pietro became active in this organizing effort. As a result, his citizenship was revoked and the family was thrown out of the company housing and sent back to Italy. They just couldn't get on their feet.

In the next few years, all four of the twins died, then another daughter died as a child, leaving only Francesca. Pietro was constantly in and out of work, and the prospects of the mines remaining open were always questionable. It was a difficult decision, but in 1882, Pietro decided to leave his wife and daughter to venture for work in America.

The mining industry in southern Colorado was experiencing rapid growth. The Starkville mine was newly opened, and in 1881, the first Bessemer converter for steel making was installed in Pueblo, creating a greater need for coal and coke. Pietro had arrived and easily got a job in the Starkville mine. By working regularly for a few years he was able to send money home. However, as always happens in mining communities around the world, good fortune is short lived.

Since the steel mills and the mines were owned by the same people, decisions were made to open and close the mines based on steel sales. When production slowed at the mills, even though a large amount of the coal mined was used for home heating, the mines were closed. Even when they were open, conditions were appallingly dangerous. Mine explosions occurred almost yearly killing dozens of miners. Although the workers accepted these explosions as part of the job, treatment of the miners as less than human by the bosses was not accepted. John Osgood, owner of one of the two largest mining operations in the region, first instituted a scrip system for paying the workers on paper that was only redeemable at the company stores. That they received no cash was only one of a long list of grievances the miners had that eventually led to a strike that spread throughout the region. Pietro thus found himself in the same situation that he had faced in France.

In response to the Colorado strike, the owners brought in a trainload of three hundred black miners from the Tennessee area as strike breakers or "scabs." The strike continued through the winter, but with the strikebreakers in the mines, the owners felt no need to either use the locals or concede to their demands. Alone, hungry, and miserable, out of work with no relief in sight, and now without his wife and children, Pietro decided that this was not the kind of life he had envisioned. He made the decision to return to Italy. As soon as he arrived back, he was hired into the mine, but work in the Italian mines continued to be very sporadic and there just was never enough money to raise a family. By now, France had legalized trade unions, but the mine owners reacted by closing the mines. There would be no work there either.

By 1885 the strikes ended in Colorado, and the strike breakers were sent back to Tennessee. Pietro's brother Martin decided he would try to make it in America. Leaving behind Minnie and their only surviving son, ten-year-old, James, Martin Grosso left for Trinidad. Within a year, the Piemontese mines would close again, and this time it looked final. Martin was working in Colorado, and now Pietro was out of work in Italy. He and Margherita discussed their situation. This time with his wife, ten-year-old Francesca, and infant Theresa, Pietro boarded the ship *Champagne* in Le Havre, France, and sailed to America, then journeyed to join Martin in Colorado.

In May of 1886, the family arrived in Starkville, found housing, and brother Martin moved in with them. They were only in their new home six months when baby Theresa died. It seemed they couldn't get a family started. And yet during the next two years, Matilda (Mattie) and Margherita (Maggie) where born. Also during this time, Martin Grosso was able to scrape enough money together to send for his wife Minnie and son James. He found a house on the high side of the stream and soon moved his young family into it. No sooner were the brothers and their families reunited when the mines again closed.

As seemed his pattern, Pietro became involved in the organizing movement. However, the Federation of Labor was having a difficult time getting a foothold in southeastern Colorado because the men seemed afraid to organize. When the organizers came to asked Pietro to go to Wyoming and get work in the gold mines in an effort to help advance the union cause they also said they would pay to get him set up. He thought, *Why not? It's a job.* There was no work in Colorado. Though Margherita didn't like the idea, she was not going to be left behind to make do alone with the girls, nor was she going to impose upon Martin and Minnie. The decision was made. Pietro and Margherita packed all their belongings and the three girls into a wagon and headed north.

Work in the gold mines of Wyoming proved harsher than the coal mines of Colorado, and tensions were even higher. The Comstock region including Nevada was rife with violence resulting from the movement to unionize the miners. There were periodic outbreaks of fighting between union organizers and mine owners. He was beaten more than once, and it was only a matter of time before something worse would happen. Pietro feared for the safety of his family, and said, "I really fear for you and the girls, Margherita, and nothing good is coming from this move here. It's time we packed up and went back to Starkville."

Because he had worked for a time as a mason in Italy, he was now able to get work at the coke ovens in Starkville. The pay wasn't any better than digging and picking in a mine, but it was safer to be out in the open air. In addition, Margherita was so happy to be back with her sister and the Italian friends in Starkville that she had come to know as family.

At that time, the women were all talking about Cathay Williams, an African-American woman who was a laundress in Trinidad and was gaining a great deal of notoriety because she had filed for a military disability pension. Cathay had gotten into the army by reversing her names and enlisting as William Cathay, and had served for two years without being found out. As a result of her claim being denied, Cathay could no longer run her laundry, and soon she became indigent. All the talk got Margherita thinking that she could take in the laundry of single miners for added income to help save for the house she and Pietro wanted to buy.

Life was progressing nicely, and their daughter Maria was born in 1893, the year that women of Colorado were given the right to vote. It was also the year silver crashed and the country entered into the worst depression of its history so far. Companies closed, the Starkville mine went idle, the coke ovens closed, and so there was no work for anyone. Southern Colorado was destitute. Pietro was once more approached to help with the organizing efforts of miners in other regions. He had no choice but to do this if he were to save his growing family from starvation. But the family was getting too big to be moving around, so this time the brothers decided that Martin would stay with the family and, because of the danger involved, Pietro would work on alone in his labor organizing, which was struggling for a foothold in Colorado.

Just before Pietro left Starkville, an itinerate photographer passed through town. When these traveling photographers came through, the people would put on their best clothes and pose for a photo to send to family members who lived far away and whom they knew they would probably never again see. Margherita wanted such a photo, and so convinced Pietro and quickly got the girls dressed in their best. She had Pietro put on his funeral suit, and she donned her church dress and apron, pulled out a broad brimmed straw hat, wrapped a ribbon around it, and stuck a daisy in the ribbon. Then the family trouped to the photographer's office. The photograph shows Margherita, stiff and not smiling, sitting in a chair with Maria on her lap, Pietro sitting next to her and the other girls clustered rigidly around them. Then Margherita insisted the photographer take a picture of Pietro by himself so that she would have his image to look at while he was away.

Shortly after the photo session, he was gone, and for the next three years travelling to Arkansas, Utah, and Nevada, going into mines as a worker and, once inside, setting the mood for unionization.

Margherita had been saving pennies out of her laundry money. When the photos arrived, she broke one of her rules and dipped into that reserve to buy an oval frame with a convex glass and put the photo of Pietro in it. She hung that photo on the wall so the four girls could see their father every day while she was alone with them. Her brother-in-law Martin was there, but he had his own family to care for and there was no work, so he could do little for them.

But Margherita had no time to brood. She was doing the work of both the woman and the man of the house: digging the garden, cooking, doing laundry, making clothing, repairing broken equipment, hammering, painting...she did it all. And as she was doing it all, she was also teaching the girls how to grow up to be adults able to take care of themselves and their homes. By 1896, Francesca was nineteen and could carry her share of the burden. She and her mother continued to do laundry for single men and also sold some of their vegetables. "We must get by," Margherita would say, "by eating less."

While Margherita was trying to keep their home together, Pietro was having his own problems. Being an organizer then was a dangerous business, and he was often "given the kangaroo"—code for a professional beating by company thugs—and eventually "sent down the canyon." When things got too dangerous, he would move on to another state.

Another Boudino family, relatives of Martin, moved to Starkville, and the son became captivated by Francesca's beauty and the fact that they both spoke the same Italian dialect. He had even come from Montalenghe, the same Italian town where she had been born. Rather than going out and drinking when not working, he stayed around their house, made conversation, and offered to help with the many chores. Francesca enjoyed his company and Margherita enjoyed the help.

There was more than enough work to go around, what with baby Maria and the other two girls needing her attention. Margherita was having trouble with her teeth and couldn't afford a dentist. Like many working people, she was trying numerous home remedies that were not working. The *strega* told her smoking a pipe would alleviate the pain, but Margherita just laughed at this. Yet she was constantly in pain, and activity around the house was always just short of chaos. Finally the *strega* came by one day with a corncob pipe and some tobacco, insisting she give it a try. That evening, after the children were asleep, Margherita went out on the porch, and sat down to smoke her pipe. She was amazed at the relief it gave her. From that day forward, she would smoke her pipe each night before going to sleep.

One day Francesca was in a hurry to deliver the laundry. She was distracted and not paying attention to what was going on around her. One of the men in town was working on a broken fence used to keep his cow in their property. He had taken down a section of the fence, and his son had unchained the cow to move it to a better place to graze when suddenly a loud noise, like a gunshot, spooked the cow. It knocked the boy down then ran through the hole in the fence and out into the street. People were shouting, but Francesca was paying no attention. The cow ran her down and tread on her leg.

People rushed to her aid and carried her home. The doctor was sent for and ministered to her, but the damage was severe enough that the leg would never heal properly. For the rest of her life, Francesca walked with a limp. The Boudino boy was very attentive during her recuperation, and their relationship became more than casual as they sat and talked for hours. Homesick and unhappy with living in Starkville, he talked endlessly about Montalenghe. Even though she had been just eleven when she and her family had left, Francesca could remember many things about the place, including many family members they had left behind. Their time together grew into a deep bond and so they decided to marry.

Margherita got word to Pietro. Because of his union organizing, it was dangerous for him to be seen at home, so he had to sneak into his own house the night before the wedding. Yet he proudly gave his daughter away the next day, and was gone again. Shortly after he left, Francesca and her new husband returned to Italy, where they would remain for the rest of their lives.

Out of town alone again, Pietro decided this was no way to live. His oldest daughter was married, and now he would never see her again. His other daughters were growing up without a father at their side, and now Margherita lost an important helper. If he continued this way, he was either going to be killed or—worse—become a liability to his family. Unable to return to Starkville until things calmed down, he moved on to California, where he spent some time as a migrant farm worker. When he finally returned home, the mines and the coke ovens were working. Life would once again be as normal as it could be. During the next three years, Pietro and Margherita's last two daughters, Phyllis and Virginia, were born.

Through all the hardship and strife, the families of the two Grosso brothers were reasonably happy and close. Living near each other they could pool their resources to get by and thrive. Pietro and his family bought an old adobe house on the lower bank of the Raton Creek that had once been a stagecoach stop and later a tavern. Martin and his family lived on the other side of the stream on higher ground. The brothers built a rope bridge across the stream to connect the two properties. Life flowed back and forth across that bridge as the two families lived almost as one.

* * *

Over the years, as Salvatore matured into a young man, he learned much about his community. In the mining towns of Colorado at the turn of the twentieth century, the various ethnic groups were often suspicious of each other, and the mine owners used that suspicion to keep the miners from sharing and organizing. By putting workers from the same country together in housing clusters, they created ethnic neighborhoods or ghettos where the families would speak their native languages and not try to learn English or the languages of other miners. The rationale behind this strategy was if the men couldn't speak a common language, learn each others' customs, or get to know their families, they would not be able to organize. However, in the mines themselves the owners mixed miners of different nationalities and exchange happened naturally around work.

Until the turn of the century the largest population of miners had been cheap Irish, Scottish, and Welsh labor. During the strikes in 1902 and 1903, agents working for the Colorado Fuel and Iron and American Victor companies began importing large numbers of Italians, Slavs, Greeks, and Mexicans to break the strikes. Now, with all these diverse groups living in close proximity, the Irish, Scottish, and Welsh miners, who could speak English and had been there longer, held the supervisory and better jobs. Most resented the Mediterraneans as interlopers. Sadly the Italians didn't like the Greeks, who didn't like the Slavs, and no one trusted the Mexicans.

In Starkville the Anglos lived on the high side of the stream, in the *Plazzita*, with their own church, stores, and saloons. Most of the Italians, Greeks, Slavs, and Mexicans lived on the low side of the stream, which often flooded with the spring thaw and rains and was closer to the mine. However, they were grouped in their own ethnic neighborhoods, and each enclave had its own taverns, dance halls, and social clubs. While this division might have seemed to be serving the owners' purpose, the actual result was that very tightly knit subgroups of people with like backgrounds and cultures were forming lasting friendships and alliances.

One of these groups was Italians from Pacentro in the Abruzzo region. A larger group from the northwestern corner of Italy, the Piedmont region, had its own community. These two groups, while both Italian, spoke different dialects, had different customs, and typically stayed in their own groups. And the migratory chain grew as they sent for relatives back home and enlarged their numbers. The common threads were working in the mines, shopping at the same stores, and drinking and worshiping together.

Thanks to milk and laundry deliveries, young Maria Grosso was able to meet Salvatore often, and even though he was not Piemontese, they soon developed a casual friendship that included brief conversations with each laundry delivery. Maria was only twelve years old, and he was seventeen by then, but she was almost as tall as he. With light brown, almost blond, hair and brown eyes, she held a lively spirit. Though she had to quit school after the fourth grade to help with the work of the house, she was bright and eager to learn everything. A bit of a tomboy, she also liked to play baseball and was a practical joker.

Salvatore thought she was beautiful and had the brightest smile he'd ever seen. But more than that, he had fun with her and enjoyed their talking together. He wrote home admiring her spunk, quick wit, and playfulness. "I feel younger when with her, like a child," he told Martin. Maria could speak Italian, but in the Piomontese dialect, which he was learning from her and Martin Bowden. He was also trying to teach her some of his dialect. More importantly, he was working on his English and tried to use it to impress Maria. She often helped him when he couldn't find the right word, though not without a little teasing. A close group like an extended family developed with Martin's sister, Phyllis, married to Maria's cousin James, Guy courting her sister Maggie, and Maria and Salvatore becoming close.

When Maggie Grosso and Guy Garfolo were married in 1905 Salvatore was invited to the reception held in the lower town's dance hall. The next year, Salvatore's cousin, Tony Ciccone, came to Starkville and moved into the house. Salvatore rejoiced to have Tony there because they had been very close back home in Pacentro, Italy. Both felt they were more like brothers than cousins. Tony's mother had died when he was very young, and so Salvatore's mother had raised him, always treating him like a son. Tony was seven years older than Salvatore, though no taller, and they shared the family's features and coloring. They also shared a quiet, thoughtful temperament. The cousins could work as a team and send money home to family. But work continued to be sporadic in Colorado.

Martin Bowden, who worried about his mother, was now spending less time with Salvatore and Tony. His sister Phyllis had given birth to a little girl named Minnie after both grandmothers. While this should have been an occasion of joy for Martin's widowed mother, she remained despondent. She lived so close by that she could have helped with the baby, but nothing seemed important to her. Although several men in town were interested in pursuing her, she would have nothing to do with them. She was just not going to let herself become a widow to the mines again. Martin even took a job at the coke ovens to ease her mind from worrying about him in the mine.

"John and I bought her one of those new cylinder gramophones from an Edison catalog," he told Salvatore. "She's been talking about it. First, she yells at us for wasting money that we don't have, but now she does nothing but sit at the window listening to these two opera cylinders again and again. She just sits there listening over and over, and crying the whole time."

Now, because Martin and Salvatore were working in different locations and Martin was hurrying home every day, the two no longer walked together. Cousin Tony liked to stop at Joe Mainello's tavern with the other men after work. One evening he coaxed Salvatore into the bar. Mainello's was a large room with a coal stove in the middle for heat and kerosene lanterns hanging from the ceiling for light. A pool table was at one end of the room, the bar ran along the other end, and there was a scattering of tables around the room. On a shelf behind the bar stood a stuffed stork, a proud sentinel, the origin of which had long been forgotten. Some men were always playing cards, others were playing pool, and a number talking at the bar. One man had his dog with him. In the corner, a man named Rocco was playing the accordion with his three-piece band. After looking around, Salvatore sat at a table opposite the band and listened to the music, while Tony went immediately to the bar. After downing several shots, he called, "Salvatore. *Vieni qui.* Come here. Drink with us."

Salvatore shook his head. "No. I do not want anything. I would rather listen to the music."

"You like the music? Then sing. Sing! Hey, Rocco, play something from the old country so my cousin Salvatore can sing with you. He has a good voice."

Rocco nodded and began playing an old song that Salvatore was sure to know. When he invited him up to sing along, Salvatore shrugged as if to say, "Why fight it?" He crossed the room and began singing. Hearing his voice, the men stopped talking and listened, some with tears in their eyes as they thought of loved ones back home. When the song ended, the men clapped and cheered. Someone shouted. "Salvatore, sing 'O Campagnola Bella.'" Which he did. Then, "Hey, how about 'O Sole Mio'?" And so it went on for a while until he waved them away, "Please, thank you, but I finish now."

Soon, Salvatore was enjoying stopping at the saloon after work on the nights the band played, not to drink, but to sing. Joe and others offered him drinks, but since he didn't drink, Joe started giving him fruit or candy. Salvatore saved it all to give to Maria when he saw her. Although Salvatore and Maria were never alone, they were becoming a real couple. Rocco sometimes asked Salvatore to sing with the band at the dance hall, and one day Rocco asked him to join the band, which was planning to go on the road to perform in the neighboring camps. "Come, I will teach you to play guitar," Rocco said.

"No," Salvatore refused, "I do not want this kind of life. I need roots."

For a few days Big Mike seemed unusually quiet at the saloon, and then one night he went directly home from the mine, not stopping for a drink, complaining of a headache and stomach pains. He even went to sleep without eating dinner, saying he was too tired to eat. In the morning, he had trouble getting out of bed and said his stomach pains were killing him. He was shaking, and the men thought he had a fever. There was no way could he go to work, and so Donato said they had to go, but he would tell the boss that Big Mike was too sick to work.

Arriving home that evening, Salvatore found Big Mike still in bed, shaking and talking strangely, like he was out of his mind. Salvatore ran to get the doctor, who diagnosed Mike's shaking and delirium as typhoid fever. He ordered the house to be quarantined and told the men to wash Mike often and feed him plenty of liquids. It was no wonder he'd contracted typhoid. The sanitation in the miners' town was horrendous. The privy was too close to the well, and the air around the houses was thick with soot from the coke ovens. The doctor cautioned the men that it would take several weeks to a month for complete recovery, and then he quickly fled afraid of becoming ill himself.

But there was no way the men could miss work to give Mike the care he needed. They also knew the doctor would hit the bottle as soon as he got home and forget to report the incident. They kept Mike secluded, reported him sick every day, but never said it was typhoid. The mine's manager didn't pursue it. He knew there were plenty of men eager to work, and Mike was easy to replace. He would have been more concerned if it was one of the mules. They were valuable, and they would cause hardship if not able to work.

A few days later, Salvatore awoke feeling weak. It was difficult for him to work that day, and on the way home he felt chilled and suddenly had a terrible headache. By the time he reached their house, he was shaking uncontrollably. Tony ran for the doctor, but found him too drunk to be of any use. From the doctor's house, he ran to the Grosso house, where he told Maria about Salvatore. She rushed across the foot bridge over Raton Creek to get her older sister Mattie, living with her husband in the little compound on the high side of the river. Mattie had a special talent for ministering to sick people and often served as midwife. She went to the men's cabin with Tony. As soon as she saw Salvatore, she knew it was typhoid fever. She immediately began nursing both men. Soon Maria came, and the two women scrubbed everything. They also made the men take baths, aired out the house, and fed their patients broth and boiled water. This went on for several days, even when it seemed that the two patients might not survive. Then the fevers finally broke. Because he was worried about no money coming in for so long, Salvatore forced himself out of bed and to work only a few days later. But the fever had taken a toll on him. He had lost a great deal of weight, hair had fallen out, and large sections of skin on his face and chest had blistered, leaving him looking scarred.

For weeks after returning to work, Salvatore went directly home and slept before seeing to dinner. When he went out, he wore a hat until his hair grew back. One day Guy turned to him as they were walking home from the mine. "Salvatore," he said, "you're looking much better. Come and join us on our day off. Panfilo and I are going hunting with a few other men up near Fisher's Peak. It'll be good for you to get some fresh air. Getting some good rabbits will put meat back on your bones." After a little more friendly coercion, Salvatore decided to go.

Early in the morning of their next day off, he climbed into a wagon with six other men. They went up into the wild lands behind Fisher's Peak. It was a successful hunt, and as they got into the wagon in the late afternoon to ride back down the mountain, Guy jumped up front with the driver and another man. The rest of the hunting party sat in the back. One of the men was wiping down his rifle when the wagon hit a bump. The rifle went off, and Guy was shot in the back. By the time they reached town, he was dead. When the men reported the accident, the constable arrested all five men and held them in jail overnight. The next day they were all set free.

Guy's young wife Maggie was widowed with her one year old daughter. Devastated by Guy's death and with no income for food or the rent Maggie had to move back home and return to helping with the laundry and selling eggs and milk.

Salvatore began noticing that on days the laundry was to be delivered, Tony always walked home with him instead of stopping at the saloon. He also had washed, shaved, and put on a clean shirt. When Maggie and Maria arrived with the laundry, he would be sitting on the stoop, eager to begin a conversation with the young women. Soon Tony was studying to become a citizen. When Salvatore asked him why he was in a hurry for this citizenship, Tony replied, "If I am to be a good family man, I must be a citizen."

Salvatore couldn't help but tease his cousin. "A family man? Who would be interested in an old man like you?"

Tony's face turned red and he changed the subject.

* * *

One evening as Salvatore was singing at the saloon, an intense card game started. Suddenly there was a commotion at the card table, where the heated game had drawn a small crowd. A man named Gino Patino had won, but another player, Alfredo Ganucci, had been losing heavily and now accused Gino of cheating. The music stopped as all eyes went to the loud argument at the table. Alfredo pulled out his gun, but before he could shoot, Gino swung around, grabbed his miner's pick, which he had leaned against the wall, and in one swift move stuck Alfredo in the neck.

Blood flowed everywhere. As Gino ran out of the building, everyone gathered around Alfredo, lying on the floor. One man checked his breathing. "He's dead," he said.

Too drunk for sound reasoning, and fearing jail or worse—losing their jobs—the men who had been playing cards, along with a few others decided the dead man was a bachelor with no family they knew of, so therefore he would not be missed. They picked up the body, rushed out the back door, and threw the body down a well. Then they all went home.

The next day, while the men were at work, a girl who lived in one of the houses served by that well went out to get a bucket of water. When she drew her bucket up, it was filled with red water. She ran home to show it to her mother. Within minutes, several women were going to the well to discover the source of this red water. They found the dead man. Apparently he had not been dead when the men had thrown him down the well. He had tried to climb out and died hanging onto protruding bricks on the inner wall. The men involved were taken to the jail, questioned, and kept. After a fruitless search for Gino, it was determined that he had fled the area. The men were released without charges.

A few evenings later, as Salvatore was coming out of the mine he saw Martin Bowden waiting for him. After a greeting and a little talk about the card incident, Salvatore noticed that Martin seemed different, as though something were on his mind. "Martin," he said, "you act like you got something you want to say. What is it?"

"I have some news to tell you. My mother has consented to marry Matt Tessitore." This was a man who had been able to save enough money to buy a farm outside of Hoehne, which was fifteen miles away. "When she marries him," he said, "I and my brother John will move out to the farm and work together." Martin was happy to leave the mines. He had just quit his job at the coke ovens, he told Salvatore, and wanted to give his friend the news so that he could try for the now open job.

Salvatore thanked his friend and headed to the mine office to ask the foreman for the job. Salvatore said, "I am a good worker and promise to work hard. You will be so be happy with me working these ovens." It took some convincing, but the foreman finally agreed, and Salvatore was at last to be working above ground. Salvatore missed his good friend Martin, but he would not miss working in the mines.

Salvatore was happy to be working out in the open air, even though it wasn't the crisp, fresh air of the mountains. The ovens, however, were hot, and the work was hard and dirty. 190 beehive ovens at Starkville provided coke to the steel mill in Pueblo. Each oven was about fifteen feet in diameter with a hole at the top for the smoke to escape. Salvatore's job was to shovel coal into each oven through an opening in its side. Once the coal was loaded, he had to brick up the opening and fire the coal. When the coal reached the proper temperature, he had to break down the bricked opening and rake the coke into a wheelbarrow. Then he had to wheel the heavy load up a ramp and dump the coke into the rail cars. It was dirty, hot, back-breaking work, but it was outside. Salvatore could see the sky.

Each man had to have his own wheelbarrow. Buying his was a setback in sending money home, but Salvatore was working hard. And then one morning he discovered his new wheelbarrow had been stolen. He couldn't afford to buy another one. The supervisor was unsympathetic and said, "You get yourself a wheelbarrow or you're through." He was walking along the stream in despair when he noticed something in the brush. It was the parts of a broken wheelbarrow that had been thrown out along the bank. Salvatore picked up the pieces and found old pieces of wood to patch them together. Then he took the wheelbarrow to the blacksmith to have the metal parts repaired.

He was back to work, loading hot coals, when a very large Mexican man walked up to him, pointed at his wheelbarrow, and said, "That is mine, and I'm taking it." Salvatore said he had found it in pieces on the stream bank and paid to have it repaired. It was his. For all he knew, this Mexican was the one who had thrown the broken wheelbarrow into the bush. He could even be the same man who had stolen his wheelbarrow. Salvatore was small but strong, and though he was slow to anger, he was quick to defend challenges to his integrity. When the man tried to take the wheelbarrow, and they got into a struggle, Salvatore picked up the man and threw him onto the hot coals. The man jumped up and ran away screaming. Soon he returned with the supervisor and a company guard. He wanted Salvatore fired. When the supervisor saw it was Salvatore, however, he laughed and told the man not only was Salvatore one of his best workers, but the accuser was twice his size and should be ashamed that this little guy should beat him so badly. The guard escorted the Mexican man away and Salvatore went back to work.

That evening, while they were sitting out on the stoop after supper, Donato suddenly announced, "My friends, I am going back to Italy. I have been away from family too long. I tell you I am at a place in time where I can afford to go back." This meant not only that Salvatore was losing another friend, but the rent would now have to be shared by one less person.

In 1907, Donato returned home to Italy and regaled the people of Pacentro with stories of his adventures in the American Wild West. He wrote to tell Salvatore of how he held his neighbors spell-bound as he exaggerated the beauty of Starkville and the friendliness of the people, made up adventures with the Indians, and told everyone about the boundless opportunities to make money in the United States. He had told Salvatore's father, Antonio, that the mines were doing better because John D. Rockefeller had bought out John C. Osgood and now owned the mines and steel mill. Rockefeller had expanded the steel mill in Pueblo and opened another shaft into the mine at North Starkville. There was work there.

Antonio listened intently and with a bit of jealousy to Donato's accounts of his wonderful life in Colorado, while he (Antonio) had stayed behind, laboring in the fields of Pacentro. All his hard work and still his family was in danger of losing its home. If there was as much as Donato said there was, why, he asked himself, wasn't Salvatore sending more money? He must be wasting it on women and drink. Giuseppe and Pasquale, Salvatore's two younger brothers, were too young to go to America. Antonio started thinking: *Giuseppe has already taken over the cow. Francesca could do the gardening.* Antonio decided, "I, the father, will go to Colorado."

Salvatore was thrilled to get the news that his father was coming. Having him and Tony present would be almost like living at home. There would be family again. Thanks to his excellent work record and the favorable working conditions, Salvatore was able to get a promise of a job at the coke ovens for Antonio. He could spare his father the hardship of working in the mine, and they would once again be working outdoors alongside each other.

Over the next few months, Salvatore worked hard to prepare for his father's arrival and thought of little else. He talked to Maria about his plans. He wanted to make this a good experience for his father. In seven years in America, he had many accomplishments. He had learned English, cleaned up their living quarters, planted a garden, gained a good reputation at the mine. He was sought after to sing at events, knew his way around the merchants in town, and had a beautiful girlfriend and many friends. He was taller now and muscular from all the hard work. He presented a good figure. His father would be impressed.

The day finally came. Salvatore got the house spotlessly clean, including a special area for his father. Then he washed, shaved, slicked back his hair, and put on his best church clothes. He took the jitney to Trinidad and met Antonio with a warm embrace and a kiss as he stepped off the train. On the ride to Starkville, Antonio's conversation was mostly complaints about the voyage and the tiring train ride. He said all he had seen of America was desolation and dust. He had no idea the country was so big and bare. Stepping off the jitney he looked around and had just one word to say. "*Brute.*" Ugly. When he walked into the house, he quickly surveyed the room. "This is where we live!" he asked. "It's a shack for chickens. Floors of dirt? Our animals live on the ground with floors of dirt. We have warm rooms above them. You have me living like an animal!"

Salvatore's heart sank, but he tried to put on a bright face as he pointed out the garden he had made, which he was certain would please Antonio.

The other men living in the house welcomed Antonio, but they soon joined in, complaining about their living conditions and the unforgiving mine. Salvatore tried to be more positive. First, he pointed out that his father wasn't going into the mines, but had a better job at the coke ovens. The men only scoffed. As they and Antonio continued to complain about this dusty, God-forsaken land, Salvatore finally gave up and quietly walked out to the stoop. After a while, Tony came out and tried to cheer him up with some banter, but he could see and feel Salvatore's obvious pain.

In the morning, Salvatore took Antonio to the mine office to fill out the paperwork and get him started. He interpreted for his father as Donato had done for him. Each man on the crew had his own ovens that he was responsible for, so Salvatore showed his father what to do and where he was assigned, then he went to his own ovens to work. Once he had the openings bricked up and the fires going, he was able to take a break and went to check on his father.

Antonio sat with his head in his hands. "The work," he moaned, "it's too hard and too hot for a man my age. What were you thinking?" He had hardly done anything since Salvatore left him. Salvatore hastily worked on his father's ovens to bring him up to speed. He ran back and forth between his ovens and Antonio's all day.

Things did not get much better as the days passed. Antonio caught on to the routine, but he still worked too slowly, so Salvatore had to continue running between his ovens and his father's. He knew that if the foreman found out how slowly Antonio was working, they could both lose their jobs. Antonio did, however, like working in the garden, which took some pressure off Salvatore at home. Eventually they got into a passable rhythm of work at the ovens and at home.

Salvatore's main pleasures were singing at the dance hall, quiet walks with Maria, and sitting on the porch with Maggie and Tony. He no longer sang as often at the saloon because he wanted to be at the dance hall when Maria was there, and she was only occasionally permitted to go when there was a function for the girls, and then she and Maggie went together. Sometimes, if she could find the time, Margherita accompanied the girls and sat on the side, knitting, until she decided it was time for the three of them to go home. On evenings when the girls were going to the dance hall, Tony suddenly developed a dislike for the saloon and joined Salvatore at the dance hall.

Maria and Maggie danced with each other, which was customary for single girls. Salvatore did not dance but watched as Maria loved to dance, even if it was only with Maggie. She smiled proudly every time she heard Salvatore sing and people praised his talent. She thought he had the most beautiful voice in the world.

Other times, when he wasn't singing and had a little time, he would steal away to spend time at the Grosso home. This became difficult, however, because Antonio refused to go with him and resented the time Salvatore spent away from him. "They are not your family," he protested, "Why do you not stay here with me or we go to the saloon together?" Maria and Salvatore were growing closer and closer. With her he lost track of time and forgot all the unpleasant parts of his life when he was with her. She was always cheerful and uplifting. Somehow, he could talk and talk and talk about anything with her. He told her how much he missed his mother and brothers and sisters. How he missed Pacentro. How he would like to take her there someday. He talked about what he wanted out of life. "Paradise," he said, "would be a farm with animals, an orchard, and clean air." She gazed at him while he was talking as if no one or nothing else existed.

"I love to hear you sing," she often said. "I love to hear you talk. You have such a good heart. You're a good man, Salvatore."

"Me? I'm no different than anyone else."

"No! You're a hard worker," she said, "and you're kind. You do more than your share of the work, but I never hear you complain, or talk bad about anybody." She smiled at him. "I think you don't like it when people call you Sam, but you never correct them."

"Is no problem," he said in still broken English. "To me is, how you say? Nickname? I think maybe is a word of friendship. People feel to be not so...*formato*, they have nickname for me like we are friends."

She smiled at his logic and said, "I too am your friend, Salvatore. I'll call you by a nickname, but not Sam. That is too harsh, so you may be Sam to a lot of people, but to me you will be Salie. That's it. You'll be my Salie."

"Sally—girl's name?"

"No. Not Sally like a girl. You are *Salvatore*. That's too formal. You'll be my Salie. It could be just Sal, but I like Salie." She smiled and nodded her head for emphasis. "Yes, you'll be my Salie for always."

The next morning as he and his father were walking to work, he wanted to tell Antonio about his feelings for Maria. But Antonio was in his usual foul mood, already complaining about how much time Salvatore was spending with her. So they walked along in silence.

* * *

Around ten in the morning of Saturday, October 8, 1910, Salvatore thought he heard a loud, rumbling noise and felt the earth shaking under him. Within seconds, the sirens began blaring—an accident at the mine. Not even dropping his shovel, he ran toward the mine entrance. Workers were running from every direction, all of them carrying picks and shovels. Hearing the siren, women and children began running, too. All knew what the siren meant. Everyone stopped at the mine entrance. Smoke and dust were billowing out of the opening. The first workers on the scene tried to enter the shaft, but turned back from the poisonous air choking them.

The women stood quietly watching and began to pray. Who would come out? Whose husband, father, brother, or son would be taken by another of these too common mine disasters?

Then many of the men went in again, and soon some walked back out through the cloud of smoke carrying men who were unconscious but alive. They carried these survivors to a medical station set up to deal with the disaster. Some women cried out in relief and ran to their men as soon as they saw them. Others bowed their heads in prayer. They knew that with every man carried out, the chances grew that their man would be one who did not survive.

The cause of the explosion could not yet be determined, yet it had been powerful enough to tear up the tracks and destroy the wires. A cave-in blocked deeper access into the mine until the ruble could be removed. This was done by hand, rock by rock, until the rescuers could crawl past the debris. But the men could stay in the drift shaft for only minutes at a time before they came staggering out, coughing and choking for air. As they came out, others ran in, creating a constant rotation. The rescue teams worked through the long night.

Maria was there late into the evening with her mother, sisters, aunt, and cousins. One by one as their men emerged, the women helped them walk back to their homes in quiet relief that they had survived another disaster. Maria held Maggie's hand tightly, knowing how worried she was about Tony. And even though Salvatore had not been working in the mine, she worried about him. Another explosion or collapse could come while he was in the mine helping with the digging. Or he could be overcome by the foul, gassy air.

Finally Maggie spotted Tony. He was alive! "*O Dio mio!*" she cried and rushed to him as he was carried out into the fresh air. He was taken to the temporary station to be checked by the doctor, then sent home. Most of the family had gone home when her mother said, "Come, Maria. Our people are all out, safe and sound. These people need their time alone. Salvatore will be fine. The danger is over."

Reluctantly Maria followed her mother home, but Salvatore and the others continued working through the night.

The next day Sunday, October 9, the women gathered at church in a prayer vigil while Salvatore and the men not injured or overcome by fumes continued their search of the mine. In one of the Starkville side tunnels, a cut was made into the wall of the neighboring Engleville mine, and a portable fan was set up in the Starkville drift shaft to pull fresh air into the mine. At the same time, fans in the Engleville mine were set to pull the gaseous air out and let fresh air in.

On Monday afternoon, around four o'clock, the first ten bodies were found in a chamber 12,000 feet from the mouth of the mine.

Big Mike was among the first to be found. He was still sitting upright at the throttle of the tram; his right hand on the controller; his left hand on the brake. Apparently he had been taking the tram out of the mine when the force of the explosion killed him instantly and overturned the cars behind him.

Conflicting reports were issued daily. The October 10 issue of the *Telluride Daily Journal* reported that State Mine Inspector John Jones had announced the mine was non-gaseous and explosives were not used for any purpose.

The October 12 edition of the *Steamboat Pilot* reported that a special car carrying government mine experts and miners trained in first aid and rescue work had left Seattle, Washington, for Starkville to aid in the rescue effort. In the same article, it was stated that the explosion of gaseous dust had occurred because the mine was not sprinkled, a federal requirement that had been ignored by the mine superintendent in spite of repeated warnings.

By Saturday, October 15, the bodies being found were in such horrible states of decomposition or so badly charred that they were unidentifiable. Some were identified by the metal work checks, which the miners attached to carts to identify their work, found in their pockets.

Not until the end of October was the last body found. The mine had not been worked for nearly a month, and even though the men worked tirelessly every day on the rescue effort, they were not paid for this time. By the end of the month, they were exhausted, in poor health, and destitute. Those who weren't prepared for an emergency would starve without work. Many were forced to leave and hunt for work at other mines in other towns.

Thirty-two men had been injured by the blast and flying rock, and another ten had to be treated for smoke and gas inhalation. When the digging was completed and all bodies removed, a formal report was issued by the Colorado Fuel and Iron Company: *On Saturday, October 8, 1910, an explosion of gas and dust caused by an arc from a runaway trip at the Starkville mine killed 56.*

It was an extremely short report, almost insignificant, but tensions were building again over the inhumane conditions of the mines. The workers could handle the hard work, the long hours, the poor pay, and the less than adequate living conditions, but these explosions were happening too often and killing too many men. Preventive measures could easily be taken and the men wanted action from the owners now.

This had been a terrible disaster, but not an isolated one. In fact, as union papers reported, it was commonplace for men to die in mine explosions across the country. Just three years earlier, in 1907, nearly five hundred men had died in the worst mine explosion in United States history at Monongah, West Virginia. Conditions in the mines hadn't changed. Explosions kept killing good men. In January 1910, seventy-five men were killed in an explosion of gas and dust at the CF&I Primo Mine. In November, seventy-nine died in the Victor-American Mine. Less than a month later, ten more men died in the Leyden Mine.

The Colorado state legislature had passed a law back in 1884 requiring mining companies to report their accidents. Over the next twenty-five years, in Colorado alone, 1,700 miners had died in accidents at a rate of three times the national average. But the mine owners escaped major criticism or financial loss by claiming in their accident reports that the accidents had been caused by human error. That way, they did not have to pay hospital expenses, compensation for workers who were permanently maimed and could not work the rest of their lives, or funeral expenses of those who died.

At the Holy Trinity Church in Trinidad, a funeral was held for Big Mike and other Catholic miners from the Starkville mine. Big Mike, a bachelor all his life with no family in the area, had only Salvatore and the men of the house as his mourners, though many members of the Grosso family attended the funeral and joined in the procession from the church through town to the Catholic cemetery.

On December 1, 1910, the newspapers ran a story about an inquiry into the explosion that found CF&I responsible for the explosion. But no penalty was attached, and on December 20, an inquiry into the Delagua explosion, which killed seventy-nine miners, found the Victor American Company blameless. The Starkville mine couldn't reopen until the end of December. During these months Starkville was quiet and somber as men returned from the hospital in Trinidad and many of the injured who were not hospitalized waited to return to work.

There was nothing to do but wait. Salvatore busied himself working around the house and spending time at Maria's helping Pietro with his animals. Most of the other men idled at the saloons, drinking on credit. Tempers flared and fights broke out. Morale was at a terrible low and the mood of the whole area was ugly.

* * *

After agonizing over how he would broach the subject, Salvatore finally made an opportune decision. Antonio and he were sitting alone on the front stoop after dinner when he announced to his father that he had asked Maria to marry him.

Antonio's only response was an angry, "What's the matter with you? Go back to Italy and find a nice Italian girl to marry. Not this French *puttana*."

"Papa, I don't want to marry a girl from Italy. I want to marry Maria. And she is not a *puttana*. She's not even French. Maria is a good girl and a natural-born American, but her family is Italian. Why do you talk like this?"

With a shake of his head and a dismissive wave of the hand, Antonio replied, "Eh! That family, no Italian. They are French and the French are all *puttani*. And you say she is American? You think this is better? Eh, the Americans are worse than the French!"

"Papa, I tell you again, they are not French. They're Piedmontese."

"Eh, Piedmontese. French. What's the difference? Those people don't know what they are. And she goes up and down the street with her sister selling milk and vegetables and God knows what else. You need a good Abruzzese girl from the heart of Italy whose father doesn't let her out of his sight until she's married. Not one out on the street selling and going into miners' houses with clothes to wash."

Salvatore knew his father was deeply unhappy in America and tried to be patient. "I'm going to marry Maria," he said, "and that's it. I want your blessing, Papa, but I will marry her with or without it. And we will have no more ugly talk like this about her or her family. Give respect, Papa, as you would want for yourself. I tell you I am marrying Maria and that is it!"

"That is it? That is it!" his father repeated. "You've been in this country too long. You talk like an American with no respect for your father." Antonio picked up his chair and walked back into the house, leaving Salvatore to sit outside and cool his anger.

As time went on, Maggie, her baby Margaret, Tony, and Salvatore and Maria became inseparable. The men spent more time at the Grosso household. On special occasions, Salvatore and Maria took the jitney into Trinidad to see a new silent movie at the Isis Theater, but it was too expensive to go very often. Mostly, Salvatore liked to help Pietro with the garden and the animals. Antonio not only refused to go there, but when Maria had to walk past his house to deliver her milk, if he was sitting out on the stoop and saw her approaching, he always picked up his chair and went into the house, slamming the door behind him. As soon as she passed, he came back out, set his chair back on the stoop, and sat with his arms crossed over his chest like a stubborn child.

Finally Salvatore and Maria, and Tony and Maggie decided they would get married the same day in a double ceremony. That would save money for Maria and Maggie's parents, because they would only have to prepare one wedding meal. The Grossos were delighted with the idea. Pietro made an offer to the four newlyweds. They could live in the family house, and he, Margherita, Phyllis, and Virginia would move across the stream into the house Dominica had vacated when she married Matt Tessatoro and moved to Hoehne. Mattie and Panfilo already lived on that side of the stream near Pietro's brother Martin and his family. The entire Grosso clan would be together, with the newlyweds just across the rope bridge.

As the wedding day drew nearer, Antonio said he would not go to the wedding because he had no suit to wear. But Salvatore was determined to do what he could to make it happen. He took Antonio into Trinidad and bought him a blue suit and pair of dress shoes, and so Antonio agreed reluctantly to go to the wedding.

With no money for wedding gowns, Margherita offered to make new dresses for both girls. Maria, always the practical one, decided she could not get much use out of a white dress. She would have a navy blue wedding dress and low heeled shoes, which after the wedding would be her good dress for church and special occasions. Although Salvatore had grown to his final height of five foot seven, Maria was nearly five foot six and in high heeled shoes looked a little taller than him. Because this was her second wedding, Maggie decided she could wear her best long skirt if Margherita would make a fancy new blouse. She was near Tony's height and, like Maria, decided to wear sensible shoes. "We can dress everything up with flowers," said Maria. Margherita wove wild flowers into a headpiece for each girl and they carried small bouquets of carnations and fern. Each groom wore a sprig of carnations and fern on his lapel.

On July 15, 1911, Maggie and Tony, and Salvatore and Maria were married by Father Salvador Persone, Pastor at the Holy Trinity Church in Trinidad. Each couple was also best man and maid (or matron) of honor for the other. Antonio attended, and Pietro gave both girls away. After the ceremony, Pietro surprised the two couples by taking them to the Elite Photography Studio in Trinidad for formal wedding photos. They had no idea how he had found the money to pay for such a luxury.

Except for Margherita, the other women in the family stayed in Starkville during the wedding ceremony and prepared the wedding feast, which was held in the dance hall. They cooked large tubs of polenta sprinkled with pieces of chicken that Pietro had butchered for the special occasion. They also made salads and roasted vegetables picked from the garden, and set out the breads and pastries the women had been baking for weeks. Joe Mainello offered some wine and beer from the saloon, and Rocco's band played as a gift to Salvatore. Everyone enjoyed the big Italian feast and had a grand time.

Martin Bowden came in from Hoehne to attend the wedding with his mother, stepfather and brother. Afterward, he told Salvatore that he loved the open country and was purchasing a 160-acre ranch out on the rim of the Purgatoire Canyon, about forty miles northeast of Trinidad. He had come across the land while hunting and through time had developed a friendship with the owner, an old man who told Martin that living on the rim of the canyon was a tough life and he was thinking of giving up the ranch and moving back into town. Martin decided to buy it. He and his dog would be moving out there, all alone, which suited Martin just fine. He had lived with his mother long enough. Her new husband was a good provider, so she no longer needed him.

After the wedding, Salvatore, Maria, Tony, Maggie, and her daughter Margaret all moved into the house along the bank of the Raton River. Their new sturdy home had been built as a way station for the stage line. It had been used as a tavern before Pietro bought it. The eighteen-inch walls of adobe brick were covered with stucco, and it had three by fifteen-inch floor joists and a solid stone foundation that made a basement room ten feet high, which had been used to store the tavern's wine and supplies. There was a little land along the side of the house for a small garden. However, each spring the river flooded so high that crops were destroyed, and the basement often flooded, too, and so Salvatore and Tony chose to work in Pietro's garden on the high side of the river.

Antonio was invited to live with them, but he refused, still not accepting Maria or her family. Never happy living in America, within the year he decided to return to Italy. Around the time of the wedding, he had fought with Salvatore over money. He had told Salvatore that he should continue to send money home to Italy, but Salvatore protested, "No, Papa, I have a wife now and will have my own family to support." So Antonio decided it was time to return home. Salvatore's brother Giuseppe, now fourteen, would come to Colorado and take his turn working in the Starkville mine.

* * *

The year 1912 was a busy year. Antonio returned to Italy, and Salvatore and Maria became parents of a beautiful baby girl. As was the custom, the first-born girl was named Francesca after Salvatore's mother. Maggie and Tony also had a baby, and new sister for Margaret, whom they named Mary. And so that former stagecoach stop/tavern was now a vibrant home filled with a close and happy family of seven, soon to become eight.

Salvatore had received a letter informing him that brother Giuseppe would soon be arriving in Trinidad. Determined that his brother would not arrive to an empty station, Salvatore made preparations. On the day of Giuseppe's arrival, Salvatore left early for Trinidad and was waiting on the platform when a shy and handsome young man with brown hair and rosy cheeks stepped off the train. Choking back tears, Salvatore took his younger brother in his arms, hugged him, and whispered in his ear, "*Mio fratello. Benvenuti a casa nostra.*" They hugged again and cried, then they talked all the way to Starkville, Salvatore asking about everyone and Giuseppe answering as fast as he could.

Unlike Salvatore's lonely arrival, when they got to town, the entire family was at the jitney stop to meet them. Maria held out her arms, kissed and welcomed him. Then it was the turn of Maggie, Margherita, and all the girls. Tony was so happy to see him that he grabbed him and swung him in the air like a rag doll. Giuseppe blushed and smiled shyly as he was introduced to each member of the family, then they all went inside for a great meal. Exhausted after all the celebrating, the newcomer dropped into his welcome bed and slept soundly all night.

Soon after, Salvatore decided to fence in the side yard so they could get some animals for additional income. He, Giuseppe, and Tony fenced in the area along the river where the garden had been, then built a pen and a shed. Pietro gave them a few chickens and they pooled some money to buy two pigs, eventually adding two cows to their holdings. Their plan was to sell eggs right away, and soon be able to sell milk. When they slaughtered a pig to feed the growing families, they had a few extra cuts left over to sell. Salvatore,

Tony, and Giuseppe worked their shifts, and then hurried home to work in the garden across the bridge. Before crossing the bridge, they took care of the animals. Even with the new babies, Maria and Maggie were able to maintain the household, sell eggs, and continue doing laundry for some of the single miners.

Everyone had to pitch in to keep the extended family healthy and vibrant. There was also unspoken concern for the well-being of Pietro and Margherita because, of their thirteen children, only the six girls had survived into adulthood. That meant they had no boys to work in the mine and support them as they aged. Although he would not admit it, breathing was becoming more difficult for Pietro. After all the years of breathing coal dust, his lungs had become hard and stiff, and he fell into fits of coughing and spitting up black phlegm. It was something no one would speak of, but everyone secretly worried about.

One night, after Salvatore and Maria had finished a full day of work and fallen into bed, they were awakened by crying. Francesca, now thirteen months old, fussed and cried all night. Salvatore had to leave for work early in the morning, but his daughter was in his thoughts all day. *What was causing her discomfort?* She cried all that day and again through the night. They sent for Mattie, but she could find nothing wrong. She gave the baby some herb tea and sponged her head, but nothing calmed her. The next morning, Salvatore told Maria they had to send for the doctor, but he could not sense the source of her discomfort. On the third day, when Salvatore came home, the silence was deafening. He found Maria sitting at the table, quietly crying. Maggie, Mattie, Phyllis, Virginia and Margherita and Minnie were gathered around her.

Maria looked up at Salvatore. “She’s gone, Salie. Our little one is gone.”

He bent down next to her, holding her head against his chest, softly calling her name and stroking her hair.

"Twice today a bird flew into the window," she said. "That means death is coming to the house. Twice today. Into the window. And now she's gone."

Still not knowing what caused the baby's death, they buried her and then went through the motions of their daily lives. But Salvatore couldn't pull out of his blues. In only a short time he had known the joy of having a child and then the inconsolable agony of losing her. He felt sorrow and guilt, plus an emptiness inside. He said to himself, *If I had provided a better living place for my daughter, she would surely be alive today instead of lying alone under the cold ground.* Salvatore would be bricking up an oven and begin to cry. He'd be walking home from work and begin to cry. After dinner he'd go out to sit on the stoop. Maria would go out to see what he was doing and find him staring into space with tear-filled eyes. They would sit holding hands and cry together. On his day off, he walked all the way to the cemetery in Trinidad where he stood over Francesca's grave and cried.

Then one day as quickly as it had started, the crying stopped. It was his day off, but he didn't go to the cemetery. When Maria asked if he was going he just said, "No. Not today. I have too much to do here," and he went out to work in the garden all that day.

That evening, when they were sitting outside before going in to bed, she took his hand and said, "I'm glad you stayed home with us today. You are my strength, Salie. I need you here with me and talking to me."

"Maria," he said, "you know I cry and I cry. Then last night, baby Francesca, she come to me in my sleep, and she tell me she cannot rest because my tears are falling on her grave and burning her face. She tells me I must stop so she can rest. And so I stop."

Not long after this, Maria was pregnant again. They were happy and would continue to grow their little family.

Brother Giuseppe adapted quickly to the work in the mines. As had happened to Salvatore on his first day at work, the boss couldn't deal with the Italian name and so he renamed him Joe on his record, so before long, everyone began calling him Joe, including all of the family. Except Salvatore. Giuseppe just smiled and said, "So I be Joe." He was a gentle, easy-going young man, very handsome, though slightly lighter in complexion and hair color than Salvatore, and, at age fourteen, already taller than his older brother. A little awkward and bashful, Joe blushed when he talked and looked down at the ground, which made a loose shock of hair fall over his eyes. His youthful zest kept the house alive with joyful chatter.

Giuseppe had been only four years old when Salvatore left for America. He revered his older brother and was constantly trying to please him and Maria. He played the harmonica and often in the evening would start to play an old song from home, which Salvatore joined in singing. Maria loved music. There were many nights when they all sat on the stoop, enjoying the music and each other. Soon Joe developed an interest in Maria's younger sister, Phyllis. She was his age, and although he didn't say much, it was clear the young pair enjoyed each other's company.

* * *

While Salvatore and his family were thinking good times were returning, these were not good times for miners in southern Colorado. Mounting casualties and inhumane working conditions had made the area ripe for another attempt at unionization. The United Mine Workers of America decided the time was right to focus on the CF&I mines. The Rockefellers' mines had the highest casualty record, and their mining camps were in deplorable condition. Following investigations of the high number of explosions and mine accidents, state laws had finally passed requiring an eight-hour work day, an end to the scrip system, and the enactment of child labor laws that were being totally ignored by the management.

The UMWA declared a strike in September of 1913. Salvatore knew men who went on strike and were promptly evicted from their homes. In anticipation, the UMWA had leased land near the mouths of the canyons leading to the major coal camps and built tent colonies, which were tents built on wooden platforms with cast-iron stoves. These tents were offered to the homeless miners and their families.

Next, the mine owners demanded protection by the state militia, which they said was necessary to keep the miners—portrayed as lawles—in line. Acts of violence were soon being reported in the papers. The governor approved the order for militia, and a trainload of thugs—fresh from fighting miners in Bluefield, West Virginia, and now hired by the Baldwin-Felts Detective Agency—rolled into Trinidad and Walsenburg. They took to riding through the tent colonies, shooting randomly into the tents.

Beatings were followed by evictions, or worse if a man was found to be involved in the unionizing effort. If the miners tried to pass the guards and go into the mines, they risked rough action from fellow workers. All the women were worried about their men. Margherita was worried about Pietro, who had become so weak from coughing and his stiffening lungs that he was unable to be active in the fighting. But he was still a vocal union sympathizer. Eviction was not a problem since they owned their own house, but harassment and violence were a constant threat.

Salvatore, Tony, and Joe were idled by the closing of the mines and coke ovens. No money was coming in, and it was too dangerous to venture out very far. Everyone stayed close to home and away from Trinidad, now a hotbed of discontent and violence. The volatile mix of the guards and angry strikers was fueled even more by the arrival of Mrs. Mary Harris or "Mother" Jones, a teacher, then a seamstress who, after losing her iron-molder husband and four children to the yellow fever epidemic, took on her husband's union activist role. Now eighty years old, she had just been released from prison in West Virginia for the role she had played in the Paint Creek-Cabin Creek coal strike.

For this struggle, Mother Jones mobilized the women and children, and marched on the Cardenas Hotel in Trinidad, where Governor Ammons was staying while visiting the area to "determine the extent of the violence." She announced to the flock of newspaper men who were covering the activity that since their men were being shot down if they tried to speak up, the women and children would take to the streets. "Let the militia try shooting at women and children," she called out to their faces. When they took to the streets, the militia did fire on them, causing the women and children to scatter, and Mother Jones was arrested again.

The violence escalated. Roaming bands of Baldwin-Felts guards shot at men on the road solely for standing there. Retaliating miners shot at the guards. The men couldn't go into the mountains to hunt for food because they would be shot for carrying guns, so they stayed close to home and lived off their gardens.

The governor activated the Colorado National Guard, who were ordered to ride through the Ludlow tent colony and shoot into the tents. Some of the miners had dug pits under the wooden tent floors so their women and children could hide and not be hit by flying bullets. In their enthusiasm, the guards rushed the tent colony again, this time setting the tents on fire. When the fires were extinguished, four men were found to be shot before they burned, and the bodies of two women and eleven children were discovered in the pits.

Maria and Salvatore were shocked to get the news that the Petrucci family had suffered tragic losses at the Ludlow Massacre. After Frank Petrucci, who had roomed with Salvatore, had married and moved to Berwind, they hadn't heard from him. Now they learned that he and his family had apparently gone to Ludlow, and Mrs. Patrucci and her children were hiding in one of the pits. While Mrs.

Petrucci survived the fire, all three of her children—aged four years, two and a half years, and three months—had suffocated in the pit. The bodies of all the victims were taken to Trinidad, where they were held at a mortuary pending further investigation. "And this is America?" lamented Maria to her equally forlorn husband.

The miners promptly retaliated with ambushes of guardsmen and by setting fires at some of the mines. Mass arrests were made. The family kept a low profile through all this violence. Salvatore and Tony stayed close to home and spent most of their time caring for the animals. Joe would go to the bar looking for company and to get the news. The miners couldn't afford a newspaper, but barkeep Joe Mainello always had one at the saloon.

They would read how Rockefeller, the owner of the mines, was being advised that his public image was suffering for him and his companies, and so had hired Ivy Lee, a pioneer in the public relations field, to conduct a pro-CF&I/ Rockefeller campaign. Bulletins were quickly sent out to all papers claiming the women and children had died from an accidentally overturned stove, and the newspapers were filled with positive stories about Rockefeller, portraying him as compassionate, deeply religious, and philanthropic. At the same time, Lee sent out negative stories about the miners and strikers, portraying them as shiftless, illiterate drunkards and their families as filthy and adding that they were all living in self-inflicted squalor.

The men would gather around, and as one of them would read these unbelievable stories the rest would swear and scoff at the audacity. Joe would go back to the house and report. They were thinking life would never get back to normal when the announcement was made that the investigations had been completed and the Ludlow victims were allowed to be buried.

Maria, Maggie, the Grosso women and a group of women from Starkville wanted to attend the burial services of the Petrucci children. Salvatore didn't think it wise but understood, "I know respect must be paid. But you all stay together, go there and come back as soon as you can." The women were frightened, but felt they had to do it. Walking hand in hand and afraid someone would recognize them and retaliate against them for being there, they passed through a gauntlet of armed guards. They honored their fallen friends, then hurried back to the seclusion of their homes.

Some men were eventually called back to work, but many were not.

During all this chaos, Maria gave birth to their second daughter on June 19, 1914. They named her Francesca in honor of her grandmother and departed sister, but would call her Frannie. Some said it was bad luck to name a baby after another child who had died, but they waved away the idea, saying she was named after her grandmother. They felt good about having healthy, beautiful Frannie in the house. But the mines were idled and there was no money, so while they had vegetables from the garden, milk from the cows, and eggs from the chickens, things could not go on this way for long. What they ate, they couldn't sell, and what they couldn't sell meant no money to pay the taxes on the house. The violence was continuing and the federal troops continued to occupy Las Animas County.

* * *

In these desperate times word came that there was work at the Phelps-Dodge Corporation's Stag Canon mine in Dawson, New Mexico. The number two mine, which had been idled the previous October by an explosion that had killed 263 miners, was reopening and they were hiring. The men talked about this and Salvatore decided that he would go to Dawson for the work. Baby Frannie was too new for safe travel and Joe would be able to help with the garden and the animals. Tony would assume family responsibilities and help care for Pietro and Margherita.

With the violence still going on around them, it was important that men were in the household for safety.

Maria lamented his leaving but accepted it. Maria didn't want the life her mother had lived, with a husband always traveling from mining town to mining town, but she also knew she could not be traveling with a new-born baby, nor could they afford to leave the homestead. Salvatore promised he would return as soon as things died down and the local mines were back to full operation.

It was a sad evening before he departed. Salvatore, Maria, and baby Frannie stayed in their room on their side of the house. Tony, Maggie, and the girls stayed on their side. Each family sat in silence, Salvatore holding Frannie, then sitting on the bed with his arms around Maria. There was nothing to say. Joe lay in bed, unable to sleep and listening to the quiet sobbing of two families about to be separated.

Early the next morning, Maria put on a brave face as Salvatore began his journey over the Raton Pass into New Mexico, through the town of Raton, and then southwest to Dawson, on the banks of the Vermejo River. Although Dawson was bigger than Starkville, the influx of men looking for work created a shortage of rooms. The mine operators converted empty railroad cars into sleeping accommodations for the single men, and it was in one of these cars that Salvatore found his new home. There was neither ventilation nor heating in these cars, no water nor electricity. They were just parked on a siding along the tracks. The men had to wear all their clothing to be warm at night and jump down into a trench alongside the railcar and go behind the bushes for calls of nature. The filth and odor in the dormitory cars were unbearable, and every man had to be constantly on watch to guard against robbery. These squalid living conditions were worse than they had been in Starkville, and the work at the mines was dangerous.

Among the miners were large populations of newly arrived Italians, Greeks, and Mexicans, none of whom were welcomed by the locals who resented foreigners coming into their area, taking their jobs, and overrunning their towns. Few of the newly arrived miners trusted anyone. Because of the unbearable stench in the dormitory cars, Salvatore spent a great deal of his time off in saloons, where fighting and stabbings invariably broke out. Salvatore learned to always take a seat with his back to the wall. He didn't like spending so much time in the saloons, but it was better than the thought of returning to the foul smelling dormitory cars, where he had to sleep with one eye open in fear of being stabbed and robbed for his shoes.

Salvatore was learning to speak Spanish and to drink beer. Still, every chance he could get, he would write to Maria. He tried to be light and cheerful about conditions, but it really didn't work. Maria could see through the false gaiety to the loneliness. He also put the money he had earned into the envelope with each letter and mailed them home. Then it was agony waiting for her letter acknowledging that she had received the money and hearing of all that was going on back at Starkville. Though he was always depressed after reading the news, that did not stop him from reading them over and over.

In every letter, Salvatore asked if there was news of work picking up at the Starkville mine, but conditions remained unchanged. It was still not safe to go into Trinidad, and one even had to be careful in Starkville, for the guardsmen continued to make vigilante-style swings through town, breaking into saloons to make certain there was no talk of organizing and stopping people on the street for identification. The organizing effort had failed. The UMWA was out of money and had called off the strike and pulled out of the area. But the owners persisted in running the area like a detention camp.

The situation got so bad that Maria wrote to Salvatore telling him Tony and Maggie decided to move with the girls to Koehler, New Mexico, which was further east and south of Raton. They had to get more money, and Joe could handle the work that needed to be done around the family households. In due time, Salvatore got word from Tony that sounded like conditions in Koehler were safer, the living conditions were better. He added that a *paesano* of theirs from Pacentro, Frank Lucci, was there with his family and had gotten word to him that they were hiring.

Salvatore couldn't believe the news. Frank was a distant relative; someone from home. It would be good to see him again. Salvatore decided to join Tony and his family, and move on to Koehler. Once at Koehler, he was hired to work in the mine and moved in with Tony and Maggie. Life and work were both better at Koehler. He was with family.

Salvatore and Tony connected with Frank, and he and his wife Mary were happy to see them. Frank had first come to America in 1900 and settled in Colfax County. After Salvatore had left Pacentro for America, Frank had returned and married. In 1904, he, Mary, and their newly born son had returned to Colfax County, then had moved to Koehler in 1906 when the mine first opened. Their family, having grown to five children, was cramped in the small company house, but Mary made a happy home and now they were reunited with old friends and family.

Salvatore, Tony, and the family were to spend many days off with the Luccis, reminiscing about Pacentro and the people they knew. This new living and working arrangement made Salvatore's separation from his family a little more bearable, but when he saw the Lucci children playing with each other and smelled bread baking, and saw Maggie with her daughters he became even more homesick.

Back in Starkville, Maria and Joe were doing their best to keep the household together. Phyllis was spending more time at the house helping out, and Joe was becoming quite attached to her. As they had long talks, she began feeling they were becoming close friends, whereas he was feeling something more. He often pulled out his harmonica and played for everyone, but the music often ended when Maria began crying.

More months passed, and finally, in late 1915, Salvatore got the letter he had been waiting for. Maria had written that the mine was open again and working full force. Now the operators were looking for workers to replace those who had been killed or moved away. The war in Europe had created a great demand for weapons, which the United States were selling to England, Italy, and Germany. This increase in production created a greater need for steel, meaning more coal and coke to make the steel. There was work for everyone.

Salvatore was going back to Starkville, but Maggie was expecting another child, which would make the trip dangerous for her. The mines were working well in Koehler too, and so Tony and his family would stay back until everyone was able to make the move.

Mary Lucci made a going-away meal for Salvatore. She made polenta and sausages, a great salad and ended with wine and piazzeles. The adults were all gathered around the table and the children were playing on the floor. Salvatore began to sing and soon they were all singing. Then things got quiet, Mary and Maggie began to cry, and Salvatore said his goodbyes. It had been a pleasant evening, but all were sad to see Salvatore leave while they stayed behind missing family in Starkville.

* * *

Salvatore felt very fortunate to get his job back at the coke ovens. Joe had returned to the mine. Everyone was working and the family was healthy, with the exceptions of Pietro—whose lungs continued to harden and make him struggle for breath—and Margherita, who was having terrible bouts with what the doctor had diagnosed as kidney problems.

Soon Maria and Salvatore were expecting another child. They decided he had been in this country long enough, and now it was time for a responsible father to become a citizen. In December 1916, Salvatore officially became a citizen of the United States of America. Around the same time, Tony and Maggie returned from New Mexico with their three daughters; a third daughter Jennie had been born.

Joe was thinking he should study for citizenship too and was considering asking Phyllis to marry him. Lately as they talked, she had been mentioning another Joseph—a quiet, small, unassuming man, a talented sculptor who was creating religious artifacts for the church. While the church didn't pay near what his work was worth, it helped when the mines were down and he said he felt that he was doing God's work. Now this second Joseph was moving to Morely to work in that mine and on statuary for a new church. Phyllis admired his work, and that he was a citizen. If Joe were to compete with the sculptor, he had better get his citizenship before proposing to Phyllis whose attachments were growing for this sculptor.

Every day, Joe went straight from work to the English class conducted by a retired teacher. This class helped the immigrants prepare for citizenship. After class one evening, he was walking home, feeling pretty good about his progress. As he approached the house, he saw Salvatore waiting for him on the porch.

"Giuseppe, *vieni qui.* Come, sit. Have a little *cichette.*" As he handed Joe a beer, Salvatore explained, as gently as possible, that he would not be able to see Phyllis tonight or in the future. She was marrying the sculptor and moving to Morely.

Joe cried out, "I don't understand! What do you mean? She's not here? She's going with Joseph? But I can talk to her. I can stop her."

"Eh, Giuseppe; *Quietare! Quietare!* She's going to marry him. When they are married, they will live in Morely where he is working. She is gone. Keep your pride, *mio fratello.*"

Joe was dumbfounded. It was a terrible blow. He sat motionless. He had waited too long. He ran all the things he should have done through his head.

Maria and Maggie felt sad to have their sister move. Even though Morely wasn't far away, it might as well have been clear across the state with no transportation or time to travel any distance for a visit. It would never be the same as running across the rope bridge. Even though they were feeling their own loss, they tried to console Joe. Tony took him up to the saloon and got him drunk.

In the morning, Joe was up and out to work without talking to anyone. The family tried to cheer him up, but he remained unresponsive. He stopped studying for citizenship, stopped playing his harmonica or sharing any family fun. He just went to work in the mine and came back home to work in the garden.

This went on for quite a while until one day Joe announced to the family that he would be leaving. He had written to relatives who had recently moved to Youngstown, Ohio, where a new steel mill had been built and they were hiring. He had no idea where Youngstown was, but he was going there. Salvatore tried to convince him not to leave saying that he was still young. There would be other girls. He should stay with his family. But to no avail.

Maria and Maggie laundered and pressed all of Joe's clothes. They packed dried sausages and cheese for him to eat on the train. Early in the morning of his departure, the family gathered at the jitney stop to see him off. One by one, they stepped forward, kissed him, and wished him well. Maria hugged him tightly, held his face in her hands, pushed a lock of his hair back, and asked him to never stop playing the harmonica. She said there was a special girl in Youngstown who was waiting for him and his music.

When the jitney operator clanged his bell to signal he was leaving, Salvatore took Joe by the arm. As they walked to the jitney, the big brother tried to squeeze in all the advice he could. Just as his father had once told him, Salvatore told Joe to be on the lookout for clever men and women who would try to get friendly so he would let his guard down and they would rob him. He told Joe to write and keep them informed about everything he was doing.

Joe just smiled his shy smile and told Salvatore, "Don't worry about me. I can take care of myself." He said that he would never forget the kindness of everyone in Starkville. Then he jumped on the jitney, and stood waving as it rolled out of sight.

Salvatore felt like he had failed his brother, that in some way he was letting his family in Italy down. Brother Pasquale was now old enough to work in the mines, but he was unable to come to America because of the war. Even though he was only sixteen, he had been drafted into the Italian Alpine Ski Troops to fight at the Austrian front. The family was left with just the girls at home and with only Antonio to support them. Although he knew Joe would continue sending money home, Salvatore felt pangs of guilt. But he didn't have time to dwell on these feelings. Margherita was having more severe "kidney" attacks, and Maria and Maggie, in addition to their regular household chores, were sharing in the caring for her and the Grosso household.

In the saloons, talk was turning to the European war. Would the U.S. get into it? If they did, who would be leaving the mines to fight? Many thought the U.S. would never join the war, or if it did, the men would be needed in the mines to feed the steel mills that were so important to the cause. But no one knew anything for certain, and worry about the war to end all wars continued to grow. Regardless of what decisions would be made about who would go to war, Salvatore felt strongly that he was now a citizen and had an obligation to do what was right. In January of 1917, he registered for the draft.

* * *

Spring came, and with it came the thaw and the rains. When Salvatore and Tony got home from work one afternoon, they noticed that the river was rising too fast. Salvatore had been trying to gauge the level of the water as the storm became more threatening. Now they could wait no longer. The animals had to be moved to higher ground. As he and Tony moved the livestock up to Pietro's property, Maria and Maggie took the girls up to their father's house.

When everyone was moved, Salvatore stayed behind, fearing the worst for their house. When the full force of the storm hit, the river's surge was so violent he knew it was going to be devastating. He ran downstream to the saloon and dance hall, both of which sat lower than his house, and tried to roust the people out and up to higher ground. But they were dancing and singing so loud most couldn't hear him. Those who did hear him laughed and told him he was blowing it out of proportion. The saloon and dance hall were sturdy buildings. There was nothing to worry about, and he should stay to have a drink with them. They would just wait out the storm right there. When he realized it was futile to reason with them, Salvatore left for the high ground.

The river raged through town, taking with it some houses, the Catholic Church, and the saloon. For the next three days, bodies were being found along the river banks all the way to Trinidad. Salvatore felt terrible that he had been unable to get many of the people out, and the fact that he tried didn't soften the tragedy. However, his family was relieved to find their house standing. It was a really solid, substantial building. But the outbuildings were gone, and a large rock, about five feet in diameter, had been lodged midway through the basement wall. They decided to cement around it and leave it there.

The storm and flood were followed by a beautiful early summer. After work had been completed on rebuilding the pens and the debris had been cleaned away, a large group of family and friends packed food and beer into a wagon and went up Fisher's Peek for a picnic. The view of the Sangre de Cristo Mountains was beautiful, and from that distance even Starkville looked good. Everyone ate, drank, sang, and played baseball. It was a glorious sunny day.

Perhaps it was because of the bumpy ride back home, but that evening Maria announced to Salvatore that she was in labor. He awakened Maggie, and she ran across the bridge to get Mattie. When Mattie arrived, she took command, and soon a beautiful baby girl was born before morning. This one they named after Maria's mother, though they anglicized it to Margaret. But the baby's name complicated things in the household of two families. Sister Maggie and her daughter were both Margarets. As they were talking about who would be Margaret and who would be Maggie, baby Frannie began playing with her sister. All of a sudden they heard her call the baby Mauggie. From that day forward, the household had a mother Maggie, a daughter Margaret, and a baby Mauggie. The house was, in fact, getting too small for the limited names that were being repeated because of the Italian custom of naming the children after their grandparents.

Maria was just getting back to full strength when her mother fell seriously ill. Margherita had been complaining about pain and been unable to sleep, but now the pain was so severe she was doubled over. They sent for the doctor, but he said it was just a recurrence of her kidney problem and gave her a bromide to drink. In frustration, they turned to the *strega*, who gave her herbal teas, made a poultice for her stomach, and told the women to put cold compresses on her head. They took turns sitting with her day and night, but she couldn't lie down. She held her stomach and kept rocking side to side.

After a week of agony, on November 7, 1917, Margherita Grosso died. It might have been a burst appendix and gangrene, but there was never an official announcement. The doctor wrote "gallbladder" on the death certificate. The funeral mass was said by Father Hugh at Holy Trinity Church with burial at the Catholic cemetery.

Pietro and his family were devastated. They had lost their rock, the strong one who'd been there for everyone in every situation. She had been the one able to save and manage what little money they had to buy a house, cows, pigs, and chickens. She had taught her daughters all she knew, and now she was gone. Phyllis was too far away to help with the day-to-day work, and Virginia, at sixteen, was the only one left at home. Even as they were grieving, Mattie, Maggie, and Maria knew they would have to take a more active part in their father's life. But how would they manage without the wise counsel and direction from Margherita?

After the funeral, friends and family went back to the house, where the neighbor ladies had prepared a meal. As they were eating, one of the men from the telegraph office suddenly rushed past on his way to the mine with a message. He stopped to tell the crowd the awful news. There had been an explosion at the Hasting Mine, just north of Ludlow. It would be weeks, however, before they learned that the explosion had killed 121 men.

After all the strife, nothing had changed. The company immediately put out a press release falsely claiming that the explosion was due to human error. A worker had supposedly left a safety lamp open. In reality the Hastings Mine had been known for some time as the most dangerously gaseous mine in the state. The southern Colorado and northern New Mexico coalfields once again were filled with striking miners, and so again the militia was called into action.

In the winter of 1918, when CF&I closed the coke ovens, Salvatore was sent back to work underground in the mine. World War I had ended, and with it the need for steel to make the weapons, and so as orders for steel were cut, there was less need for coke. Even though coal was needed for home heating, the reduced need for coke at the steel mills meant a reduced need for coal. The mines were open or closed day by day as the need for coal rose or fell. Salvatore and the other miners walked to the mine each morning, where they were told either to go in and work or turn around and go home because there would be no work today. Many of the men went to the saloons.

One mild spring afternoon when the mine was open and Salvatore was working, Maria was hanging laundry and the girls were playing quietly in the yard. Suddenly the whistle blew. The women grabbed their children and ran for the mine. As they feared, there had been another cave-in. There was always a danger of gas explosions, but many of these cave-ins were simply a result of the men working too fast for the tonnage, and not taking time to use enough wood to safely shore up the ceiling.

It was the same story that day. Not enough posts and beams, the ceiling of the mine was inadequately supported, and the women were waiting to hear about their loved ones. Salvatore had been knocked down and his leg was pinned by fallen rock. After some chipping and shoveling, however, his coworkers were able to free him and carry him out. The doctor was too drunk to be of use, so they also carried him home. Mattie ran down from the house above and quickly washed and cleaned out his wounds. She then gave him a pan and told him to urinate in it. She washed the wound again with the urine and then wrapped his leg. He would not be able to return to the mine until the leg had healed well enough to take the pressure of walking and work.

The next evening, they had just finished eating when there was a knock at the door. Maria opened it to find two of Salvatore's *paesanos* standing there, dour expressions on their faces. She invited them in, offered them seats at the table, and brought out two glasses and a bottle of wine. One of the men was carrying a letter with news from home for Salvatore and Tony. Someone had died.

It was a tradition that when a member of a family in Italy died, they would send a letter to a *paesano* living near the relative in America. This man would pay a visit to deliver the news in person, to soften the shock of the news.

Now the bearer of the news began by telling Salvatore his brother Pasquale had returned safely from the war and was in good health. He had even received a decoration for bravery. However, on the heels of the war there had been a severe influenza epidemic that ravaged Italy along with most of the rest of Europe. Two of his sister Bombina's children had died from it. From the look on the miners' faces, Salvatore knew there was more. His mother, Francesca, had also succumbed to the flu. Salvatore cried out and buried his head in his hands. Now he would never make that trip back to Italy to see her. Never would he buy her all the things he had promised. Never would he see her face again, never see her smile or hear her voice or laughter. It was terrible being so far away at times like this, and he felt he had somehow let his family down.

Maria came around the table and put her arms around his shoulders. Maggie took hold of Tony's hand as he also began weeping, for Francesca had been like a mother to him. Her death was a loss for both men and a reminder they would never return to their homeland. As was the custom, the *paesanos* sat through the night with the grieving family. When Maggie went across the bridge and gave the news to the Grosso family, they all returned with her to spend the vigil together. Through the next few days, friends in town also came to the house to pay their respects. As soon as he was able to put weight on his foot, Salvatore and Tony took the jitney into Trinidad, to have a Mass said for Francesca and another one for Bombina's children.

But there was no time for the luxury of mourning. Things were not good in Italy. Things were not good in Starkville.

Salvatore was more concerned with missing work and having less money coming in than worrying about his injured leg. Maria was expecting again, and soon there would be another mouth to feed. He was able to put weight on the leg now, and besides, it was too depressing to sit around the house brooding over lost family members back home in Italy or lost money here in Starkville. He was worried about where they would get enough to eat and be able to hold onto the house. Salvatore had to go back to work.

He had, in fact, been thinking for some time that they could not keep going like this. People around town were starving. Many were forced to leave town and seek better work at other mines, but fewer miners did not help the miners left behind. The mines were closed more than they were open now, and when they were open, conditions were deplorable. Men could no longer pay to have their work clothes washed, which cut hard into Salvatore and Maria's income. Except for the babies, people were deciding they could do without milk or eggs. Salvatore's family could certainly eat what they were no longer able to sell, but no sales meant that the only income they had came from the mines, and they didn't know how long they could continue to pay taxes on their property. Without the money from laundry or milk and eggs, there was not enough to buy feed for the animals.

Though he was approaching seventy years of age, Pietro could barely breathe now, and the least bit of exercise would send him into a fit of coughing up that tar-like substance in his lungs, plus a little blood. He looked like a man in his eighties. He was no longer able to work.

Maria's youngest sister, Virginia, was now seeing a man named Dan Desantis regularly, and it seemed serious. Dan was young, tall (nearly six feet two), and very handsome. A strong, hard worker, he was also a very compassionate person. He promised Virginia that if they married, they would live with Pietro so that she could continue to care for her father. While this was good news, the family still worried because no one could rely on the mine to sustain the ever growing families. The entire family was pooling together to survive. Yet, how long could this go on?

About this time Salvatore received a letter from his cousin Christy, who lived in Aliquippa, a small town north of Pittsburgh, Pennsylvania. Christy worked as a janitor in the local bank and also helped Italian families by interpreting for them when they came to the bank. His news for Salvatore was that Frank Lucci was now living in Aliquippa. Frank had told Christy about the last mining strike and violence in New Mexico, which had driven the Lucci family to decide to leave. They had moved to Aliquippa to work in a fairly new steel mill, where newly completed construction had nearly doubled its size. And the mills were hiring. He suggested that Salvatore consider moving his family to Aliquippa. But neither he nor Maria wanted to leave Starkville. They were determined to find a way to survive.

One day when Salvatore came in from caring for the animals, he noticed that Maria was in pain. She had started into labor, but, thinking she had plenty of time, she didn't want to take him away from his work. Now her pains were too close together. The baby was coming, but no one was there to help. Maggie and Tony had taken the girls to Hoehne to visit Domenica and her family. Salvatore called for little Frannie, "Run up to the hill and get Aunt Mattie! Tell her the time has come. Your mama is having the baby."

Frannie ran out of the house and scurried onto the rope bridge. She was so tiny she could hardly reach the hand rope, and mid-way across she fell into the stream. Pietro happened to be outside, and hearing Frannie's screams, called to his family, who ran to the stream and pulled her out. Fortunately the water level was high enough to break the little girl's fall, but low enough that she didn't drown. Although she was soaked and freezing cold, there were no broken bones. Through all the commotion, as they were wrapping her up to warm her shaking body, no one was listening to what she was trying to say. Finally, Mattie shouted for everyone to be quiet.

"Mama's having the baby," Frannie cried. "Mama is having the baby!"

At that, Mattie jumped up, rushed across the bridge, and ran into the house just in time to hear the cry of a newborn baby. Salvatore, with a broad smile on his sweating face, was holding a baby boy. He had just delivered his first son. Mother and son, he told Mattie, are fine.

Within minutes, the whole family crowded into the house to share in the joy. As was the Italian custom, Salvatore wanted to name his first son after his father. He would be Antonio. As weak as she was, however, Maria put up a fight. Antonio had never treated her right, had never accepted her. Until the day he had gone back to Italy, he had never even spoken directly to her. There was no way, she said, she was going to honor him by naming her son Antonio. But Salvatore was not going to give in. It was going to be Antonio.

When the doctor came to the house to check the baby and make out the birth certificate, Salvatore and Maria still had not agreed on a name. The doctor assumed authority and said that since the baby was born on George Washington's birthday, he should be named George. He wrote that name on the birth certificate and left.

No one was happy with the name George, but it still was not going to be Antonio. Finally, on the baptismal day, Salvatore and Maria reached a compromise. Salvatore remembered the Italian hero of the adventure stories he had read as a kid. The baby's name would be Ercolino Antonio.

It was a long cold winter in 1919. Spring came late that year. With no more need for steel for the war, the coke ovens remained closed. CF&I decided to close the Starkville mine. They gave no indication when or if it would reopen. Another reality that was hard to face was the fact that the coal seam through Starkville was nearly played out now. Fewer miners would ever be needed

Salvatore, desperate now, wrote to his cousin Christy and asked if there were still any work opportunities in Aliquippa, Pennsylvania. That summer, he received a letter from Christy encouraging him to make the move. The Jones & Laughlin Steel Mill was continuing to expand in Aliquippa, and, yes, they were looking for workers.

Maria had to quit school after the fourth grade and had never traveled beyond Trinidad. "Salie," she asked, "where is this Aliquippa?"

"I'm not sure," he said, "but it is close to Pittsburgh. I passed it on the train to Trinidad." He added that he remembered being on the train for two or three more days after that.

"Oh Salie, you're asking me to leave my family and everyone and everything I know and travel for days on a train to a place I've never heard of. If I make this big move, I know I'll never see my family again."

"Maria, in nineteen and two, when I am thirteen years old, I leave my family in Italy and travel thirty days to be here. I never see them again. But now you are my family. Me and these children, we are your family. If we stay here, they starve. What can we do?"

"But Salie, it was so hard on the family when Phyllis moved to Morely, and now with Mama gone and Daddy in such terrible shape....What will happen if we leave too?" she asked through her tears.

"America is a big land, and we go far, but not across an ocean. My mama is gone, too. I never give her all the things I say I will. I know I will never cross the ocean again. But some day we can come back to Starkville. Some day." He took her hand and stroked it as he continued, "I know it will be hard for you. It will be hard for me, too, Maria. It is now seventeen years I'm here in Starkville. That is longer than I lived in Italy. This is my family, too. Everyone has been good to me. It hurts my heart to say we are leaving, but I think we have no choice for our children. And with us gone, the family will have less people to worry about feeding."

Reluctantly, through tears, she agreed. "I know," she said with a sigh. "You're right. But it will be so hard."

They sat quietly for a long time, not speaking, just holding each other.

Maria cried herself to sleep that night. After a few more days of talking and trying to find alternatives, they confirmed their difficult decision to move east. When they made the announcement, the sisters gathered around, hugged them, and cried.

Pietro sat quietly for a while, then said, "This is a decision you two must make for the good of your family. Many years ago, we had to do it, and your children will have to do it one day. You do what you must do."

And so preparations began and continued into fall. Maria and Salvatore sat with Maggie and Tony to talk about the house and the livestock. They would turn their share of ownership over to Maggie and Tony and leave them the chickens. Salvatore would sell the cows to get money for the trip and to hold them over in Aliquippa until he got work. They would butcher the pigs, and make sausages and hams, and ship the meats with a few meager belongings to his cousin Christy in Aliquippa. Maggie and Tony would keep the rest.

Salvatore and Christy continued to plan through the mail. Christy assured him there would be a job and soon said he had found a house they could rent.

It was time to say their goodbyes.

Very early one morning in September, Salvatore, Tony, Panfilo, and Dan climbed into the wagon and rode out past Trinidad along a desolate road until they came to a lone tree marking the beginning of a dirt lane. They bumped along this lane in the direction of the rising sun for twenty miles until it was barely a path. Eventually it disappeared altogether in the barren desert floor that was dotted with sage brush and an occasional scraggily tree. A herd of antelope scurried by, kicking up dust. Finally, the four men spotted the humble, low-lying cabin up ahead at the edge of the Purgatory Canyon and overlooking the thin line of the river weaving below. They were here to visit Martin Bowden and his brother John, who had moved in with him.

Inside this small adobe cabin, with its low timbered shed roof and sitting on the rim of the canyon were a sparsely furnished kitchen/sitting room dominated by a stone fireplace and two small bedrooms partitioned off to the side. The ceiling was low and almost cave-like because the only two windows were small to prevent the strong winds that swept off the canyon floor from entering the cabin. These winds made strange whistling sounds as they passed around the rocks, sounds that made people say the canyon was haunted. It was because of these eerie sounds that the Spaniards who passed through this vast expanse in the sixteenth century called it el Cañon de las Almas Perdidas del Purgatorio, the Canyon of the Lost Souls of Purgatory, which became Purgatory Canyon.

Martin was happy to see them. After a welcoming drink, he walked them around his land and along a path that ran down along the edge of the canyon wall, where he showed them some carvings he was making in the walls. He explained that while exploring his property, he had come across footholds, presumably carved by Indians, down the side of the canyon. He had climbed down these footholds and found pictographs the Indians had carved. Martin was a talented artist who had liked to draw as a child. He had also developed skill doing ironwork, but now he was working his farm with no interest in going into town for diversions. His discovery of the pictographs had made him think he would like to pass his time in carving pictures of the nature around him. The carvings pleased him, but they lacked something, so he had begun to have his nephews buy house paints and bring them to the cabin with other provisions when they visited. He would then mix colors and paint the carvings he'd made. He said the painting would eventually fade, but his carvings would live on, just like those of the Indians.

The men had an enjoyable visit. It was an opportunity for Salvatore to see his old friend, and to say goodbye before leaving for Pennsylvania. They had another drink and toasted to a safe journey. Walking back to the wagon, Martin put his arm around Salvatore's shoulder, "You are a good old friend and I will miss you very much. When you come back to Colorado to visit the family, you must come to visit me."

Salvatore shook his head, reached for a handkerchief and wiping his nose just sighed, "Eh, sure."

"You will come back," Martin said, "you will." The men embraced, said their goodbyes, and rode back to Starkville.

Finally Maria and Salvatore took the jitney to Trinidad and walked to the cemetery to visit their daughter for the last time. They also visited the graves of other family members and friends. This was extremely hard to do, but necessary to say goodbye to everyone.

It was late afternoon the day before they were to leave and the packing was all completed when there was a knock at the door. Soon neighbors and friends came streaming through the door to say goodbye, each carrying an item of food or something to drink. Pietro and all the family from above came in. Rocco and a few of the men in his band came in playing music. Everyone hugged and kissed Maria and Salvatore and wished them well. Then the party began. Salvatore sang, Maria danced, they all told stories, they laughed and cried and they talked about the time they would all be together again. That night, after the visitors had gone home and the house was still, neither Salvatore nor Maria could sleep. They walked out onto the stoop and sat in silence, looking out over the home they had loved and the town they might never again see.

On an early October morning in 1919, they were making their final preparations to leave, Pietro came down to the house and gave Maria the photos the itinerant photographer had taken of him, Margherita, and the girls when Maria was a baby. He also gave her the photo of him in the oval frame and another photo taken by a traveling photographer when she was a teenager. Maria, her sisters, and some cousins were sitting on their front stoop (p. 98). As he handed her the photos, he said, "The family will always be with you." When she began to cry again, he told her "Maria. this is not a sad time, but a new beginning for you and your family. Your true home is wherever you, Salvatore, and your children are." She smiled into his eyes. "The others you will always carry in a special place inside you." He embraced his daughter.

They walked outside together, Salvatore, Maria, their children, Tony, Maggie, their girls, and Pietro. They were joined by Mattie and Panfilo, Virginia and Dan, Uncle Martin and Aunt Dominica, and cousins James and Phyllis and all their children. Maria's sister Phyllis and her husband Joseph also surprised them by coming from Morley. Everyone walked with them up to the *Plazzita* and to the jitney stop, where all hugged and kissed each other again.

Then the young family of five climbed onto the jitney. Tony and Maggie rode into Trinidad with them. As the jitney pulled out, Tony held Mauggie, Maggie held Ercolino, Salvatore held Frannie's hand, and Maria stood holding onto the handrail and gazed back at the only home she had ever known and at the relatives that had been her whole life. She knew all the talk of visiting and of when she would return was just that—talk. She would never return, never again see these people who were her life. With tear-filled eyes, she waved and vowed to keep a picture of them in her mind forever. Soon the jitney eased over the crest of the hill and the little mining town was gone from sight.

At the railroad station, they said more tearful good-byes. Tony hugged Salvatore, called him his brother, and assured him the house would always be there for them if they should ever return. As Maggie and Maria embraced, Maggie said, "This house will be so empty without you, but I swear I will write you often." Maria couldn't speak. She just held on tightly until Salvatore gently eased her away and led her and the children onto the train. Standing on the back platform, the family waved as the train rolled out of Trinidad and into their new and uncertain future.

Business district of Trinidad, Colorado 1907

Starkville, Colorado housing 1900

1905 wedding of Guy Garfolo and Maria's sister Maggie. Left of groom are Pietro (P) Margherita (M), far left Salvatore (S), seated Maria (m).

Grosso family home in Starkville, Pietro standing, Maria holding baby Margaret, sisters Virginia and Phyllis next to her, 1906.

Part II

Starting Over

West Aliquippa, Pennsylvania 1980s

Maria stared at the changing scenery as their train sped away from Trinidad and its familiar terrain out across the flat, desolate plains of Kansas. She read the names of the towns they passed: La Junta, Coolidge, Garden City, Dodge City. They slept in their seats and fed the children from what they had brought. The baby was restless and hungry, so as they passed Topeka, she told Salvatore they were not going to have enough milk to last the trip. From the conductor, he learned that the train had a long stop at Kansas City, where many people would be getting on and off and switching trains. He would get off, buy some milk, and be back on before the train started up again.

"Oh, Salie," she said. "I don't know if that's a good idea. What if you don't make it in time? I have no idea where we are or where we are going."

"Don't worry," he said. "I have plenty time to do this."

Within minutes, the train rolled out of the Kansas plains and into the chaos of stockyards and freight yards. All the passengers could see were miles of track and trains. Maria had never seen so many people and so much activity. Union Station in Kansas City was a grand hub of activity. As people began loading and unloading their belongings, Salvatore jumped off the train and set off looking for a place to buy milk. Maria stared worriedly out the window as she explained to the girls, whose eyes were wide with fear. "Your Daddy is getting milk for Ercolino, and he will be right back."

Too soon the whistle blew and the conductor walked through the cars, announcing their departure. Maria was silently praying by now, searching the platform for her husband. She felt the tug of the engine starting to move the train. Just as the girls began to cry, she saw Salvatore running with all his might and cradling a bottle in his arm. He caught up to the train, grabbed the handrail with his empty hand, and jumped up onto the platform of the last car. Maria was trying to calm herself and the girls, assuring them that Daddy was on the train when suddenly he walked into their car, smiled as he sat down and said, "Okay, Maria, here is the milk."

Fort Madison, Iowa. Chillicothe and Jolliet, Illinois. And then the confusion of an urban sprawl that dwarfed Kansas City as the train approached Chicago, crawling through industrial clutter that Maria had never dreamed she would see. They finally pulled into Chicago's Central Station on the banks of Lake Michigan, a huge body of water that was another first for Maria. All she had ever seen were the river and streams around Starkville and Trinidad that might flood in the spring, but were shallow enough to walk across in the dry season. Maria was awestruck by this huge lake. She and Salvatore quickly gathered up their weary and frightened children and ran to change trains for the Capital Limited to Pittsburgh.

Holding Leo and the girls' hands, Maria and Salvatore walked into the cavernous station, which was buzzing with activity, in search of their next train. She and the girls looked around in a mixture of wonder and fear at the crowds hurrying off in every direction. They heard train arrivals and departures being announced over the loudspeakers, vendors shouting their wares, whistles blowing, and engines roaring. At last they found their train and soon were safely on the Capital Limited and on the move again.

Staring out the window, Salvatore and his family saw the scenery change from the flatlands of the lake area and gradually transform to rolling hills of eastern Ohio. When Maria spotted the wide Ohio River lined with steel mills, her heart sank. "Oh my, this country is so big and everything looks so different," she said to Salvatore. She felt as if she were in a foreign land, so very far away from Starkville, and deep in her heart, she knew she would never see her family and childhood friends again.

As the train crossed the bridge at the confluence of the three rivers, Maria could see the massive Heinz Foods plant. and cork and glass factories stretching up the Allegheny. Down the Monongahela, she viewed the Jones and Laughlin and U. S. Steel mills. Even though she had seen much through the windows of the trains, Maria was not prepared for the sight of the powerful mills crowding both banks of these rivers—and those giant smoke stacks belching clouds of smoke that blackened the sky, dark enough that lights had to be on at mid-day. At Pittsburgh's Pennsylvania Station, once more they had to change trains. This time they had to walk to the Pittsburgh and Lake Erie station across town. The children were wide eyed as they walked through the high-ceilinged dome of the Pennsylvania Station and out onto busy city streets of traffic, clanging trolleys, police whistles, and hordes of pedestrians running through a maze of tall buildings. They had to cross the Monongahela River, which was wider than any river in their part of Colorado, and they walked on a bridge so high it made them dizzy. The bridge had open spaces through which steel girders passed to the supports below. Salvatore carried Mauggie, Maria carried Ercolino, and Frannie—who remembered all too well her fall from the little rope bridge across the creek—clung to her mother's skirt. The parents were as fearful as the children, but they preserved their attitude of courage.

Finally, the weary family arrived at the Pittsburgh and Lake Erie Station. They followed a trail down the grand staircase and through an echoing, marble waiting room under its dazzling stained-glass dome; then they boarded another train for the final part of their journey past the point where the Ohio, Monongahela, and Allegheny Rivers meet. Finally they headed back up the opposite side of the broad Ohio River.

Once out of the city, the train passed more steel mills and train yards, then a little open land. The green hills, stained with industrial soot, rising on both sides of the river created a narrow passageway that widened into a broad valley. At last they spotted the sprawling jumble of belching smokestacks, roaring furnaces and mountains of slag that would be part of their new life.

The train came to a stop at a little wooden station with the name "Aliquippa" painted on the walls. Salvatore felt very much as he had seventeen years earlier when he arrived in Trinidad. But this time he was not alone. He had his wife and three children, his stomach was full, and his emotions were filled with the anticipation of a new beginning. *In this great land*, he told himself, *anything is possible.* At the station waiting to greet them stood Christy and his wife.

Before stepping off the train, Salvatore looked out over the town that was to be his new home. Eventually he would learn that the first cabin had been built here in 1769 on land previously farmed by the Iroquois Indians. It lay just downriver from where a small stream, Logstown Run, met the Ohio. Eventually a small village had grown up, and in 1878 the Pittsburgh & Lake Erie Railroad chose to build a train station here with an amusement park and a large dancehall in the village to encourage the people of Pittsburgh to ride the trains. The rail company chose the name Aliquippa and created the legend that it had been named after Indian Queen Aliquippa, who had met with George Washington at this very sight. In reality, Washington had met with Seneca Queen Aliquippa at the junction of the Youghiogheny and Monongahela Rivers south of Pittsburgh. It was a popular spot when the Jones and Laughlin Steel Company bought the land in 1906 and began construction of what would someday become the largest continuous casting steel mill in America.

In1919 when Salvatore was looking out over four pairs of train tracks, he saw below a village of mostly wooden houses on narrow lots spread over six streets running parallel to each other between the tracks and the river. To his right, he saw the gigantic blast furnaces and smoke stacks of the mill, which towered over this little piece of land on which nearly 3,000 people lived. The building that had once been the dancehall now housed the company offices; the amusements and grassy park were long gone. To his left, three smaller mills belonging to the Vulcan Crucible, Russell Shovel, and Kidd Drawn Steel companies hemmed in the cluster of houses and shops, which were just as covered with soot as the houses he had just left in Starkville. Here in Aliquippa, the roaring of the furnaces and the banging of steel bars being rolled and formed created a constant din that nearly deafened the newcomers but were unnoticed by their greeters.

*　*　*

These newcomers stepped off the train and were immediately surrounded by Christy's family. Christy seemed edgy, and, without delay, ushered everyone off the platform and down a set of concrete stairs, nodding solemnly to one of the ever-present police officers as they passed. The stairs took them into a tunnel that went under the tracks and served both automobile and pedestrian traffic as the only access into and out of the little town surrounded like an island on all four sides—tracks on one side, the river on the other, and steel mills at each end.

Together they walked up onto Third Street, a commercial street that ran perpendicular to the tracks and cut across the town's avenues until it ended at the river. On the corner of Third Street and Main Avenue, the other commercial thoroughfare, Christy's father-in-law owned a grocery store in a building where the entire family lived in rooms above.

As they walked, Christy explained their hasty exit from the station. In September, the American Federation of Labor (AFL) had called a strike against U.S. Steel. This strike had spread, and now 350,000 workers were striking plants in Pittsburgh, Chicago, Wheeling, Johnstown, Cleveland, and Youngstown. The Amalgamated Association of Iron Steel and Tin Workers, which had tried to organize the steel workers in the 1890s, had been devastated by the Homestead Strike of 1892 which had resulted in twelve dead workers and dozens wounded. The strike had been a failure with no concessions to the workers. Membership then dropped from 24,000 to 8,000. The AFL had decided to step in and work with the steel workers, but they were still asking for higher wages, an eight-hour workday, and recognition of unions. Mother Jones, a name Salvatore recognized, was a woman now nearly ninety years old, who had gone to the Monongahela Valley to rally striking workers and had been arrested and put in jail.

This news was sounding hauntingly familiar to Salvatore.

The difference here was the workers at Jones and Laughlin had not followed the U.S. Steel workers on strike, and the mill managers and town officials were determined that there would be neither organizing nor striking in Aliquippa. That was, Christy explained, why the police greeted each train that stopped there. If anyone getting off looked like someone they thought might be a potential organizer, that person was followed or taken aside and escorted back onto the train. Along the way, he added, a little accident, like a blow to the head, had been known to happen to the visitor. Christy was well known by the town officials because of the store and the fact that he worked at the bank and often acted as an interpreter for the Italian immigrants. He had, he assured Salvatore, talked to the police as they were waiting for the train to arrive and told them that his cousin was a good, hard-working man with no union leanings. He and his family were coming to live and work in Aliquippa as sound, law-abiding citizens. Nevertheless, Christy thought it best to make a hasty exit before any officer could change his mind and begin asking questions.

This news disturbed Salvatore for several reasons. He hoped this situation was not going to create a problem for his getting a job, and he was concerned for his brother, who was working in Youngstown and might have been involved in that strike. Lastly, he had left Colorado because the situation there was dire and dangerous for his young family. He did not want to be placing them into a sililar situation.

At Christy's family store, everyone went upstairs to the apartment, where Christy introduced them to the rest of the family. There were kisses all around and pleasantries about how good looking the children were, who they looked like, how Christy's family would have recognized Salvatore anywhere, how beautiful Maria is, and on and on. At last they all sat down to the first good meal of steaming spaghetti and fresh salad the weary travelers had eaten in three days.

Maria was awestruck by the signs of affluence in this little apartment. She was seeing things that did not exist in any house she had ever been in before. The living and dining rooms were separated by French doors with glass panels and crystal door knobs. The other doors had glass transoms above and crystal knobs, too. There was an ornamental fireplace in the living room and another in the dining room. They were sitting around a long mahogany table opposite a grand buffet covered by a delicately woven lace runner on which sat elaborately framed family photos.

For hours they talked, Salvatore and Christy reminiscing about family back in Pacentro. Christy was just two years older than Salvatore and had left Italy for America before him. Maria and Christy's wife were exchanging information about life in Starkville compared to Aliquippa. Finally, someone noticed it was getting late and the children were falling asleep.

Christy said he would walk them to their new home. Maria's spirit brightened slightly as they walked up Third Street, and turned onto Beaver Avenue, a long street of tidy little clapboard and shingled houses sitting on neatly groomed lawns that were small, but well kept. Along the street were rosebushes and flower beds, cheerfully painted picket and wrought iron fences with gates. A warm glow was cast over the street by the iron lampposts all along the sidewalks. Maria commented that they didn't even have sidewalks in Starkville. At this time of evening, people were sitting on welcoming front porches and greeting them as they walked by. Children playing in the street scurried up onto the sidewalk when they heard the clopping sounds of horseshoes on the brick pavement. It took the newcomers quite a while to move down the street as Christy stopped to introduce them to their new neighbors along the way.

But Maria's mood changed as they turned into an alley running behind Beaver Avenue and they walked up to number 503½, once a barn, now their new home. First they passed the outhouse and the water pump that they would be sharing with the house in front. Next they walked up the wooden ramp that had been built for the animals and entered a large, dark, nearly empty room adorned with a pot-belly stove, a table, a few chairs, a dry sink, and a Hoosier cabinet. Up a narrow set of stairs was the loft where the hay had once been stored; a single wall now separated it into two sparsely furnished bedrooms.

Christy explained that housing was very tight in Aliquippa and this was the best he'd been able find for them. He lit a lamp for them, then bade them well and left. Maria quietly washed and dressed the children for bed as Salvatore readied the bedrooms. Then he went back downstairs and built a fire in the pot-belly stove. Maria tucked the children into their little cots, kissed them goodnight, and went down stairs, where she sat at the table with her hands folded in her lap and began to cry. Salvatore came to her, sat down beside her, and put his arm around her. "It will get better," he whispered. "It will get better."

Because of the crashing and pounding of the mill and the strong smell of sulfur, an ever present reminder of where they were, they didn't sleep well that first night. People had said after a little while they wouldn't notice the noise and the smell, but this was hard to believe.

Salvatore was on his way before daybreak, anxious to get a job, fortunately not needing an interpreter this time. Out on Beaver Avenue, he encountered Mike Lucci, who had moved there from Koehler, New Mexico. Mike welcomed him with a hug and two cheek kisses. As they walked together to the mill, Mike advised him to keep a low profile—something Salvatore had done so many times before.

Maria had adjusted the fire in the stove and was just finishing feeding the children their breakfast when she heard a knock at the door. She opened it to find Mary Lucci and two other neighbor women holding buckets and mops. They introduced themselves, welcomed Maria, and immediately set to work. They cleaned everything, heating water on the stove, mopping floors, washing windows, and hanging curtains, all the while chattering about life in Aliquippa and Colorado.

Maria thanked Mary for her kindness to Salvatore while he was in Koehler. By the time the women left, Maria was singing. Out of her suitcase she took the pictures of her father in the oval frame and the two family photos and hung them on the wall. Then she started to prepare good food for her hungry man's return from a hard day's work.

* * *

One of the men waiting at the mill's gate with Salvatore was showing the others a flyer he had received from a relative in the Monongahela Valley, just south of Pittsburgh and loaded with steel mills. The flyer, titled "Wake up Americans!!" was filled with inflammatory claims that "Italian Laborers" were striking and threatening good workers who wanted to continue working. "These foreigners," it asserted, "have been told by labor agitators that if they would join the union they would get Americans' jobs."

Salvatore could only shake his head. Once again he was finding himself in the same atmosphere of suspicion and hatred aimed at those with different ethnic backgrounds, religions, or skin color. He shook his head in disbelief and said to himself, *Eh, another place in this country where people don't like Italians.*

That evening, as soon as Salvatore walked through the door, Maria knew all was not well. He had spent the day waiting to be called to work, but he had not been one of the lucky men. He was told that every day men gathered at the gate and waited to be called in. There was unrest and negative talk, and rumors of violence among the men at the gate.

Salvatore returned to the gate every morning and waited all day to be called. Finally, after a month of waiting, he was brought in, given a badge, and put to work as a brakeman on the locomotive crane. Nothing he had done up to this moment could have prepared him for what he found inside the mill. When he first came from the quiet fields in the mountains of Italy, he had marveled at the dark, damp conditions of the mines in southern Colorado, and then the heat and soot and backbreaking shoveling of the beehive coke ovens. But the massive size, deafening noise, and frantic pace of activity inside the steel mill made everything he had known before almost insignificant.

Everything in the mill seemed oversized. There were three Bessemer converters and a row of five open-hearth furnaces that were over a hundred feet tall, with five equally tall blast furnaces that shot hot air into the furnaces to heat the ore. This activity created flames that shot into the sky and lit up the night. It was the sight that as early as 1868 had prompted Boston writer James Parton to describe Pittsburgh as "hell with the lid off." Hell had not diminished in half a century. Alongside the furnaces stood mountains of raw ore that had been shipped upriver by barge or dumped by rail and were waiting to be fed into the hungry jaws of these monster furnaces. Huge cranes carried hot ingots to bloomers (massive metal plates and rollers) that hammered and rolled the steel, stretched it into bars, all the while spraying curtains of hot lava and molten steel chips over workers standing up to twenty feet away. Hydraulic shears, bigger than a worker's house, slammed onto sheets of steel and cut them into pieces to be shipped to fabricators.

Salvatore had to jump up onto a foothold on the side of a gigantic crane and hang on as it moved along railroad tracks to the spot where he assisted in braking it to a stop, jump off, and hook massive chains to buckets of molten steel. The crane then lifted the buckets and moved them onto railroad cars as sparks flew and mechanical anvils slammed with deadening thunder so loud that all communication had to be through hand signals. Whistles blew, machinery screeched and banged, and furnaces roared as steel was poured into molds, moved to rollers and pounded and stretched into shapes. Everything had been built on a massive scale, and the production line moved at a frantic pace with no safety measures in place. It was a dangerous job. Many workers were killed by a misstep or a bucket of molten steel breaking loose from its chains. Men looked like ants, scurrying around lifting, pushing, pulling, or shoveling as machines moved up, down, forward, and back in this potentially deadly ballet. Workers had to buy heavy, steel-toed shoes; thick, fireproof gloves; and hard-hats to protect themselves from the molten ash flying through the air. Even the metal rail which Salvatore had to grab to ride the crane was too hot to touch without thick gloves.

His shift started at seven in the morning, and as he was leaving his station at five-thirty in the evening, he was replaced by a man on the night shift who worked from five-thirty until seven the next morning. Men worked these long shifts six days a week, and some who held crucial jobs worked seven days a week. To make it worse, they worked in turns, shifting every few weeks from day and night turn. At the end of his first day, Salvatore returned home, soaking wet from sweat, filthy and tired with aching muscles and burn holes in his clothing. Maria didn't need to ask if he had been chosen that day. She filled a lead tub sitting in the middle of the kitchen with hot water and vigorously scrubbed his back with Lava soap and a scrub brush while he did the rest. Exhausted and still adjusting, he was at long last working, and there would soon be money coming in. They were happy.

Through that long month of waiting, the family had barely survived on the food they had shipped ahead. Vegetables and other supplies were given to them by Mary and the other neighbors to help them through this difficult time.

Mary told Maria that she knew what she was going through. She too had suffered the separation from her parents and homeland, knowing she would never see them again. Once acclimated to life in New Mexico, again she had been uprooted and moved to Aliquippa. Yet she assured

Maria that things would indeed be better here, "You are part of our family now." Aliquippa was a very tight-knit little community, inhabited by a few English, Irish, and Welsh families, but mostly by Italians, Slavs, Poles, Jews, and the one Chinese family that owned the laundry. This community seemed open and friendly, miles away from the labor and ethnic strife rampant at the mill. Living in such close proximity, the people learned the languages and customs of their neighbors. It was common to hear an Italian offer a greeting in Slavic to a neighbor of that heritage, or a Polish shopper use an Italian expression in an Italian market, or a Slovak utter a Yiddish sentence to a Jewish shop owner.

There were four houses of worship in Aliquippa: Roman Catholic, Greek Catholic, Methodist, and Jewish. There were two ethnic clubs, the Slovak-American Social Club and the Sons of Italy Club. Along the town's two main streets stood a line of businesses that included a bank, a shoe store, clothing and hardware stores, and a brewery. On nearly every corner was a small ethnic grocery store. All the residents' needs could be met without their having to leave town. Social life for Salvatore and Maria centered on their neighbors, the Catholic Church, the Sons of Italy Club, and the local shops. Along the riverbank ran River Avenue where some of the grandest houses were occupied by the doctor, a plant manager, and a few of the wealthier merchants.

Even though the police, the town's management, and some of the homes were owned and controlled by the company (as they had been in Colorado), the mill did not exercise the same level of control as the mine owners in Starkville. However, the Woodlawn Land Company, which was an arm of Jones & Laughlin, had built the housing in the town of Woodlawn, plus a large, five-story company store named the Pittsburgh Mercantile Company, which sold everything from clothing and furniture to food and garden supplies. This store also operated on a form of the scrip system, whereby employees charged their purchases and the company deducted those charges from the men's wages. However, the people of Aliquippa rarely traveled to Woodlawn to shop, and there were no company-owned stores in their little hamlet. Salvatore refused to get pulled into the scrip economy again. He proclaimed to his family, "We don't go to the PM store. There are plenty good stores in Aliquippa. And we don't buy with credit. We save until we have the money, or we go without."

Although the company held tight reins on the schools and the newspapers, the churches and doctors operated independently, and the shop owners were mostly residents living on the same streets as the mill workers.

Maria was soon settling into a routine. She could go to Mancini's Market just down Beaver Avenue for groceries and to Klein's for dry goods. She quickly came to know Mr. Mancini and other shop owners and their families. But, still, she missed her family terribly. In the evenings after the children were in bed and the chores completed, she sat at the kitchen table and by the faint light of the lamp wrote to her sisters. Most of her correspondence was with Maggie, to whom she wrote about her life as if she were talking to her. Sometimes it seemed as though she were keeping a diary with Maggie, while back in Starkville, Maggie was writing her. Maria could picture Maggie sitting at the table they had shared, though Maggie could only imagine Maria's environment from her descriptions.

Maria and Salvatore did not like living in a barn in the alley. Salvatore wanted to buy his own home and make a garden. But the lots were very small in Aliquippa, and most families wanted gardens, so in a good-will gesture, the mill management arranged to have two barges tied side by side in the narrow channel that separated little Crow's Island from the riverbank to make a bridge to the town. They rented plots on the island to the residents for a nominal fee for them to make gardens. Salvatore happily rented a space and planted some tomatoes, green beans, zucchini, onions, garlic and peppers.

One day Christy took Salvatore to the Woodlawn Trust Company, where he worked, and introduced him to the bank manager. That day Salvatore opened the first savings account of his life. During his early years in Starkville he had sent everything he could save back to his family in Italy. Once he was married, the erratic work at the mines made it impossible to save, and he was barely able to keep his little family fed. For the first time, he was now earning a steady paycheck, and even though it was meager, he insisted on putting something into savings each payday, even if it was only twenty-five cents.

And so he and Maria and the children were finding that their new life was pleasant in this little community. Salvatore bought a bicycle and rode it to work every day. The children seemed healthier, and Maria was getting involved in a warm group of close friends. Here, she could walk to church any day and not have to wait for an itinerate priest. Frannie started at the Washington Elementary School, and the girls began to make friends. Children played in the streets, which were paved with bricks, not the dirt that turned into mud when it rained. The children of Aliquippa seemed more carefree than in Starkville. They all spoke English, although most spoke a second language at home, and they often gave their friends nicknames. While Frannie stayed Frannie and Mauggie stayed Mauggie, the local girls had trouble with the name of little brother Ercolino. He soon became Leo, and that name stuck to him for the rest of his life. There was a lot going on in Aliquippa.

It took them a few years of hard work and saving, but soon they had enough for a small down payment on a house. This had not been easy, for Salvatore was only making twenty dollars a week for a seventy-hour workweek, and he had three children to feed. He and Maria used their ingenuity to manage food and clothing on next to nothing.

Their break finally came. Through gossip at the store, Maria learned about a house on Allegheny Avenue that had been empty for almost a year. Saint Joseph's church was at

404 Allegheny Avenue, and one Sunday after mass the family walked up the block to the house at 339. It had a front porch, a fenced-in front yard, and a back yard that ran all the way to the alley. A row of company-owned houses began next door and ran to the end of the block, but this house stood on its own with its own yard. It needed to be painted, and the fence was in need of repair, but they saw it as their place.

Salvatore learned that the house had been taken over by the bank after the death of the owner and then sold to the Union Brewery Company to settle the deceased's debt. But the brewery decided not to use it and had not been able to sell it, and so there it sat. Salvatore made an offer and was able to purchase the house for $2,500. Christy went with him to the bank again and helped him take out a loan. Though Salvatore hated loans, there was no other way to buy the house.

* * *

Their two-story shotgun house was brown, asphalt-shingled, with faux-brick. Its front door opened into the living room, which led directly into the dining room, which opened into the kitchen, where the back door led out to a small porch. Up a steep flight of stairs from the kitchen were three small bedrooms. The house had indoor water in the kitchen, but no bathroom. The outhouse was just steps away. To heat the house, there was a cast-iron stove in the kitchen and a smaller, more decorative one in the parlor. Both burned wood or coal, and vents were cut in the ceilings to allow the hot air to rise into the bedrooms.

Neighbors and friends joined in to move Salvatore, Maria and their family and helped to clean the house inside and out. Salvatore scraped and painted every piece of wood. He repaired and painted the fence. He cut back weeds and planted rose bushes in the front yard. He stopped renting a plot on the island and planted a vegetable garden in his back yard. Maria made curtains, and in no time they had a warm and cozy place they could finally call their own. She soon became good friends with Theresa Rubino, who lived across the alley. Salvatore considered himself lucky to be working regularly without the starts and stops he had experienced in the mines. They saved a little more money and eventually Maria was able to order a nine-piece dining room set from the Sears catalogue for $120.

The day the dining room set arrived was an exciting day for the family. Maria called to Salvatore, "Oh, Salie, at last we have a dining room!" and they put it together, then Maria sewed crisp new curtains and hung them in the window. She hung her father's photo in its oval frame on the dining room wall and placed the other family photos across the top of the buffet. Theresa came by to see the new room, and the children were so excited they had a hard time falling asleep that night. Once they were settled, it was a delight to sit on the front porch after dinner and visit with people strolling up and down the street.

On Sundays, Maria dressed the children in crisp, cleanly laundered clothing and proudly walked her family to the church, just a half block down the street. How pleasant to visit with friends after church, and see the children on the porch watching all the comings and goings of the various church activities. There were the processions to and from the church for weddings, funerals, and feast days. On holidays, they witnessed traditions they had not seen before, like the Slavs in their native costumes taking baskets of food to be blessed at Easter. Maria was feeling at home and growing to love this little village so full of activity.

Through the night, the mill would blow the stacks of the blast furnaces dropping soot all over the town until it looked like a storm of black snow had covered the town. Every morning, the women of Aliquippa were outside early, scrubbing their porches and their furniture. They called back and forth in conversation with other women scrubbing their own porches. On her way out, Maria took the card the ice man had given her, folded it to the proper colored section telling him how much ice she would need for the ice box, and set it in her kitchen window.

When she needed meat, she walked around the corner to Ogerizek's, where the smells of hams, slabs of bacon, sausages, and dressed chickens hanging from hooks mixed with those wafting up from barrels of exotic spices, creating a heavenly, meaty aroma. After a little conversation with Mrs. Ogerizek, who had just finished scrubbing the market floors and was spreading fresh sawdust over them, Maria walked back home with her purchase. Sometime later during the day, perhaps while Maria was doing the laundry, Mrs. Champion came by, her wagon loaded with fruits and vegetables. Maria picked out what she wanted that was not found in their own garden, then usually invited Mrs. Champion in for a cup of coffee. While they were visiting, Mr. Ariday often stopped his bread wagon to see if she wanted any bread. She never did because she always made her own. He surely knew that, but he always stopped anyway, perhaps for the coffee and a little pleasant chatter.

This socializing was a nice diversion, but Maria spent most of the day, every day, working—cleaning, doing laundry, sewing, cooking, gardening, and canning in season. By late evening, after everyone had finished supper and the dishes were washed and put away, Maria got out the Black Cat polish and rubbed with all her might to clean the cast iron stoves and polish them to a high sheen. Then she put the children to bed. It was only then, after everything was done, that she would finally sit down for a little conversation with Salvatore on the porch. Or she might sit at the kitchen table and write a letter to one of her sisters or read the latest one from Maggie. Finally off to bed she went, and her routine would start again in the morning.

Many of the people in Aliquippa had relatives living in Youngstown, Ohio, which Salvatore learned was only forty-five miles away. He had always felt bad that his brother Joe had moved there and wanted him back with the family.

He talked with Maria about it, and they soon agreed: Joe should be there with them. They had one bedroom, the girls had another, so Joe could share the third bedroom with young Leo.

Salvatore wrote to his brother that the mill was running at top speed and there would be a job for him. "Please come and join our family. You are my brother and we have been apart too long." Joe agreed. He would make the move.

When Salvatore arrived home from work one day, he was met by an excited Maria on the porch. "Salie, I got such great news today. You know that Daddy went to Montalenghe to visit my sister Francesca. Well, Maggie writes that Daddy is going back home to Starkville, and he'll be taking train from New York."

"Maria, yes, this is good news that he's coming back from Italy in good health, but why are you so happy?"

"I'm sorry. I'm so excited because Maggie writes in her letter, that his train back west is coming through Aliquippa. Daddy told Maggie when it stops to take on passengers, he will get off to say hello. Salie, that day should be Thursday! Just two days from now! I'm going to take the children to see their granddaddy."

"This is good, Maria, but the trains, they don't stop that long. You remember me getting milk in Kansas."

"Oh, yes, I know. But—just to see him! If only for a minute, that would be wonderful. Look, she wrote the time he's supposed to change trains in Pittsburgh right here. I'll go maybe two hours before that to make sure and be at the station when the train comes into Aliquippa."

She spoke with such a glow in her eyes that he just smiled and patted her arm. "This is good," he said.

All the next day, Maria busied herself washing and ironing the children's good clothes to look their best when they saw their Grandfather Pietro. She baked bread and cooked their meals, singing the whole time. She had a hard time sleeping that night and was up before dawn the next morning.

Today was her big day. She dressed the children, put on her wedding dress, which was now her church dress, and left early enough to allow for the children, who could not walk as fast as she did when she was alone. She carried Leo, and Frannie held Mauggie's hand. She had kept Frannie home from school that day so she could see her grandfather. They walked down Third Street, through the tunnel, and up the steps to the platform at the station, and as they walked, Maria kept asking Frannie if she remembered what Granddaddy looked like and telling her stories about Starkville. As they sat waiting for the train to arrive, Maria fussed over the children, straightening hair ribbons and adjusting stockings.

It was a long wait, but eventually she heard the whistle and saw the train approaching. Holding her children's hands, she cautioned the girls not to move forward. As they stood searching the windows of the passenger cars for Pietro's face, the train sped past. It never slowed. It just kept going, speeding by, and then it was gone. Maria stood there in disbelief. What had just happened? That had to be the train, but it hadn't stopped. At the speed it was traveling, she hadn't even been able to make out any faces in the windows. Had her father even been on the train? She went into the station and asked a worker if that was the right train.

"Yep, that was it all right," he replied. "But it don't stop here no more. The railroad changed the stop to Woodlawn 'cause it's a bigger town. Sorry, lady."

She walked back out to the platform, sat down on a bench for a while, and softly cried. Frannie and Mauggie put their arms around her and rested their heads on her shoulders. Frannie said she wanted to see Granddaddy, and then she began to cry, too. Then because Mama and Frannie were crying—and without knowing why—Mauggie started crying, and, eventually, Leo, too.

Once she had collected herself and calmed the children, Maria said, "Granddaddy won't be stopping today. But we're dressed so pretty, let's go visit Aunt Mary." And they walked to Mary Lucci's house to give a reason for an outing for the children and for some sympathy and consolation for Maria.

When she told Mary of her disappointment, Mary said, "Oh, Maria, I wish we'd known. I would have gone to Woodlawn with you and the children." This made Maria feel even worse. She began to cry again. *Why hadn't she checked at the station?* She had wanted to see her father so much, she was thinking only of that. Mary suggested that Maria could write a letter and explain what had happened. Perhaps Pietro had seen them as the train sped by, and that would be good. Then she poured Maria another cup of coffee. Mary's coffee was famously bad. She had a huge enameled pot into which she poured coffee, chicory, water, sugar, milk and egg shells. Then she boiled this concoction and left it on the stove all day. With such a large family (eight children), she felt that she didn't have the time to be making coffee throughout the day. Nor did she have the money to worry about who would want milk or sugar, so everyone drank the coffee as it was.

Maria sat at the kitchen table and gratefully drank her coffee, which calmed her. In passing, she mentioned that she had been having terrible headaches for quite some time.

Mary asked about the headaches, then said, "I don't like this, Maria. If there is no reason for these headaches, someone must have put the *mal'occhio* curse on you."

"That's silly, Mary. I don't believe in the evil eye."

"No, Maria. It's true. You have a new house and a beautiful new dining room. Someone is jealous of you and has given you the *mal'occhio*. You need to see Marra Geuzeppe. She's the *strega* here and can remove that curse from you."

Maria just laughed the thought away. Feeling better now she decided she should be getting home. She thanked Mary, gathered the children, and started for home.

The next day as she was working in the kitchen, there was a knock at the door. She opened it to find Mary standing beside a very strange looking woman who was slightly hunched over and had several teeth missing and a prominent wart on her nose. Mary introduced Maria to Marra Geuzeppe, who went to work as soon as they stepped through the door. She sat at the kitchen table and told Maria, "Get me a plate and some water." She poured water into the plate, took a little bottle of oil out of her bag, and chanted some incantations as she poured a few drops of the oil into the water. After a minute or two, she said "Okay, this *mal'occhio* it is now gone, and your headaches too will now be gone." She made a gesture with her hand of them vanishing then kept her palm open for a donation. Then she too vanished with Mary.

The town doctor and Marra Geuzeppe were not the only sources of health care. The neighbors often pitched in, too. Theresa Rubino, who lived across the alley, once asked Maria for help. Her son had badly infected tonsils. Dr. Miller had come to the house to check him and said they would have to come out immediately. He would operate in their kitchen. But Theresa couldn't bear to watch, so Maria came over to stand at the kitchen table and assist as the doctor laid the child and proceeded with the operation.

A few years later, when Leo was playing with friends, as the bread wagon rode by, they jumped up on the back for a free ride. But when Leo jumped off the moving wagon, he landed badly. Another boy following the truck on his bicycle came down on Leo, the handlebars hitting him squarely in the larynx. He was knocked unconscious. Mrs. Genario and the driver of the wagon carried Leo to his home and upstairs to his bedroom. Marra Geuzeppe soon arrived and she and Mrs. Genario helped Maria minister to her son. He lost his voice for a while, and when he regained it, he spoke hoarsely, as though he had laryngitis, something he would carry the rest of his life.

Because there was no bathroom in Salvatore and Maria's house, it was necessary to take baths in the lead tub in the kitchen. At bath time for the children, Maria filled pots with water from the sink, heated them on the coal stove, and poured the hot water into the tub. She started with Leo, and then each of the girls, after which Salvatore carried the water out back and poured it over his plants. One day when Maria was washing Frannie's hair, the kitchen door opened and the parish priest, Father Healy, walked in. Salvatore rushed up to the priest, took him by the arm, and escorted him out the door, admonishing him for walking in without knocking. "My wife is giving my girls a bath," he said. "What's the matter with you walking into my house without knocking?"

Obviously taken aback and red faced the priest blustered, "I'm the pastor of your church. I'm always welcome in my parishioners' houses. There is no need for knocking where I am concerned." He then explained that he had come to suggest they should have their new house blessed.

"I don't care if you are the Pope," Salvatore replied. "At my house, you knock."

After that incident Salvatore began work on enclosing their little back porch to create a little indoor bathroom. There would be no more baths in the kitchen.

The mood at home brightened when they learned that Salvatore's brother Joe was coming to live with them. On the day of his arrival, Salvatore met him at the train station with a hug and cheek kisses, then walked him home, introducing him to everyone they saw along the way. Maria, who welcomed him with a special meal, commented on how good he looked. He was a little heavier and taller than Salvatore, but no longer the shy boy they remembered. Joe had matured since leaving Colorado and was now a handsome young man. Salvatore rejoiced to have his brother back in his life.

During their special supper, Joe teased Frannie, telling her she had grown so much since he last saw her so that he didn't recognize her now. He also fussed over Mauggie and little Leo, then said in Italian, "*Che bella famiglia*, (what a beautiful family)!" With Maria and Salvatore he recounted his experiences in Youngstown. The strike of 1919-1920 had ended in dismal failure. The mill gave the workers no concessions. Many men had been jailed, and after everyone returned to work, wages had been cut back and hours increased. He was happy to be away from there and with his family. Maria asked if he was still playing the harmonica and was pleased when he pulled it out of his pocket and began to play.

The next day Salvatore took Joe to the mill and introduced him to the supervisor. A hard worker, Salvatore had been moved from brakeman to tapper in the tin mill. While the pay was no better, the work was a little less dangerous, and he went from a seven-day week every other week to a straight six-day week. He had thus built a good reputation, and so with his introduction, Joe was hired. The family was happy together and the men were working regularly.

* * *

Major social events which everyone in the family looked forward to were—the church festivals. The largest festivals were those of the saints' feast days. Every town in Italy had a patron saint whose feast day was celebrated with a festival and parade. When the Italians came to the U.S., they brought their saints' day festivals and other traditions with them, and each church might have several. The feast days started with a mass said in Italian, before which the officers of the festival committee carried a statue of the saint into the church on a decorated platform. They were preceded by an honor guard from the Knights of Columbus in their full regalia, and a musical escort provided by members of the Sons of Italy Orchestra. At the end of the mass, this entire delegation—now led by the priest and followed by members of the congregation—paraded out on the street and through town to the site of the celebration.

Excitement filled Salvatore and Maria's house this September morning because it was the day of St. Magno's Festival. St. Magno was the patron saint of Bugnara, a village in the Abruzzi region of Italy. There was a large contingent of immigrants from Bugnara in Aliquippa who were involved in this celebration. Enthusiasm had been building all week as members of the parish, the festival committee, and the Sons of Italy erected and decorated booths in the empty lot next to the Sons of Italy Hall. There would be food and game booths, speeches delivered from a grandstand, and a concert by the Sons of Italy Orchestra. Many of the children of the Italian families were expected to play a musical instrument, and being chosen to play in the Sons of Italy Orchestra was considered a great honor.

On the morning of the festival, Maria and the children sat on the porch to watch the procession, which passed their house, rounded the corner onto Third Street, then turned onto Main Avenue. The procession moved slowly, stopping to allow people to run up to the statue and pin money to its clothing. Every time this happened, a fire cracker was set off. By listening for these blasts, people throughout the town were able to gauge the progress of the group. As the procession started up again, the people who had pinned money to the statue and other onlookers joined in, making it longer and longer. When they reached the festival ground, the priest said a prayer and town dignitaries gave speeches officially opening the festivities. Then the orchestra climbed up on the grandstand and began their first song, followed by a mix of classical music, marches, and Italian folk songs.

After the procession had passed their house, Maria and Salvatore walked to Main Avenue with their children for a pleasant afternoon with friends and neighbors. Everyone played games, ate and drank, and socialized clear into the evening. Maria loved the music and catching up on local gossip. The children enjoyed just playing with friends and running through the crowds. The men indulged in a few drinks, played some *bocci* and enjoyed a few rounds of *morra*, a kind of Italian rock, paper, scissors game. Two men faced each other with closed fists. They next thrust fingers forward at the same time and shouted out what they guessed the total of extended fingers would be. The man to guess correctly was declared the winner, followed by another round of drinks.

Because of the Volstead Act of 1920, there was to be no alcohol sold at the festival. However, there was some confusion as to whether the Twenty-first Amendment allowed drinking of homemade wine if it was not for sale. The men always took some of their homemade wine to the club, and the police even enjoyed a few glasses. Of course, hidden under the bar, and served in coffee cups, bootleg liquor was available, of which the police conveniently never seemed to notice.

Joe had to work on the day of the St. Magno Festival, but by evening, after he had gone home, bathed, and changed into better clothes, he came to the celebration. Maria smiled as she saw him munching on a bag of *lupini* beans and chatting with a few young ladies who appeared extremely interested in what he was saying.

Late in the evening, Salvatore and Maria were holding Mauggie and Leo, who were exhausted. Joe offered to hold Frannie, but she insisted she was too old to be held, so he just held her hand as they watched the festivities come to a dramatic end with the traditional doll dance. Two men climbed inside two dolls, one male and one female doll, that were about ten feet tall. Supporting the weight of these dolls on their shoulders, they danced down the street and in front of the bandstand to the sounds of several folk songs played by the orchestra. Immediately following the dance, everyone walked to a section called North Beaver, at the opposite end of town, where fireworks, which had been set up in a large vacant lot next to the train tracks, lit up the night sky. Then came the long walk home, late at night with exhausted children, either sound asleep, or complaining about the walk.

* * *

Maria always busy baking, canning vegetables from the garden and sewing clothes for the children, was working harder now to do as much as she could before their fourth child was born. On the morning of November 13, 1922, after Salvatore and Joe had left for work, she went into labor. This time Frannie was in school, so it was Mauggie she sent across the alley to Mrs. Genario who told Mauggie to get Marra Geuzeppe, then she ran to Maria.

Later that day, with Marra Geuzeppe as midwife and Mrs. Genario assisting, their second son was born. Salvatore was happy to have another son, but now it was his turn to dig in his heels over the name. Just as it was the custom to name the first-born son after the paternal grandfather, it was also expected to name the second son after the maternal grandfather. Since Maria had refused to name Leo after Salvatore's father, Antonio, Salvatore would not hear of naming the baby Pietro after her father. Maria said since Salvatore had chosen his storybook hero, Ercolino, and they had used Antonio as the middle name she would do the same now. Except they would not use a storybook name. After some searching, they settled on Carlo, which was an ancestral family name, and Salvatore's middle name. They both liked this name, so it was soon agreed. The baby became Carlo Pietro.

Now that he had a name, it was time to have him baptized. Maria had become so close to Mary Lucci that she felt as though she was part of the family, not only in Aliquippa, but they also had that Colorado/New Mexico connection. The Luccis were distantly related to Salvatore's family, and so it just felt right. She and Salvatore asked Frank and Mary to be little Carlo Pietro's godparents. It wasn't long before the girls and their friends had anglicized the baby's name to Carl Peter.

A few weeks after Carl's baptism, Salvatore was working out in the garden behind his house, raking leaves and making compost that would ferment through the winter, when he heard loud shouting and a great deal of commotion in the alley. He stopped what he was doing and walked out into the alley, where several neighbors were watching the spectacle of Marra Geuzeppe chasing her husband out of their house and down the alley, swearing and hitting him on the head and shoulders. Wrapping his arms over his head for protection, the husband flew past them and down the alley, then turned toward Main Avenue.

One of the witnesses came over to the neighbors, laughing as he told the story. Apparently Marra Geuzeppe's husband had been complaining for some time that their bed was lumpy and uncomfortable. To surprise her, he had bought a new mattress, which had just been delivered that day. But she was not at home. He had told the men who delivered the new mattress to take the old one away. When Marra Geuzeppe came home and he showed her the new mattress, the surprise was on him. She went into a rage. For years, she had secretly been hiding money earned from her healing work in that mattress. He had just given away her life savings!

Salvatore went into the house and told Maria the story. Later, they found out that Marra Geuzeppe's husband had recovered the mattress...just as the men who had taken it away were about to burn it. He had convinced the men to take it back to his house, at which point Marra Geuzeppe made them take away the new one. A disaster had been averted, and the town had something to gossip about for a while.

* * *

There is always a mixture of the bitter with the sweet. On a blustery March day in 1923, Christy came to the house with sad news. Virginia had sent him a letter saying that

Maria's father, Pietro, had died in February. As if that were not bad enough, because he was a Mason and didn't participate in the church, he could not be buried with his wife in the Catholic cemetery. He had to be buried across town in the Masonic cemetery. In her letter, Virginia also told them she had married Dan Desantis and, now that their father was gone, they would be moving to Morley. The Starkville mine was down again, she explained, and Dan would be able to get work at the Morley mine where they could rent a company house next door to Phyllis and Joseph.

Maria took the news especially hard. Losing her father was sad and, compounded now with Virginia's moving, this meant the homestead would be gone. It was all too much to take in. Salvatore tried to console her by reminding her that after her father had breathed in all that coal dust for so many years, he was fortunate to have lived to seventy-five. The Luccis came as soon as they heard the news, and Mary used all of her best comforting words, but Maria was inconsolable. She blamed herself, first for leaving her father, then for missing him at the station when he passed through Aliquippa three years before. Everyone tried to convince her that she had done nothing wrong. After all, how could she have known where the train might stop? Of all people, they said, Pietro would have understood. But sorrow is personal, and Maria had to work her way through it in her own time and her own way.

Concerned that Maria was not coming out of her depression, Salvatore talked to Frank Lucci about it. Frank had seen an ad in the *Woodlawn News* that William S. Hart was appearing in a new movie, *Sands*, at the newly opened Strand Theater on Franklin Avenue. They agreed that Mary would watch the children while he took Maria to see the movie. It would be their first outing alone together since coming to Aliquippa. They took the bus to Woodlawn in early evening to see the new theater and the movie. Salvatore loved westerns, and Maria hadn't done something like this since they'd left Starkville. Movies always lifted her spirits.

Not just the movie itself, but the festive atmosphere inside the theater, and especially the music of the piano player that set the mood. The crowd cheered the hero and booed the villain, and sometime during these silent movies the film invariably broke, so the audience stamped their feet and shouted until the film was taped back together, at which point everyone cheered. Maria allowed herself to enjoy the excitement.

Never having the luxury of dwelling on her own problems very long, she was soon dealing with the next family crisis. While riding his bicycle to work, Salvatore was knocked down by a horse and buggy carrying building supplies from the P.M. Moore Company. The horse stepped on Salvatore's leg, the same leg that had been damaged in the mine accident, leaving a severe wound. Some men carried him home, and Maria promptly sent for Marra Geuzeppe. She arrived, took a jar of leeches out of her bag, and used them to clean the wound. She then smeared an ointment on the wound and wrapped it. Limping and in pain, Salvatore went to work the next day, but by the end of the work day he was in excruciating pain. Maria unwrapped the wound, which was seeping puss, washed it out, and applied more of Marra Geuzeppe's ointment. It took weeks for the wound to heal, but Salvatore could not afford to miss work. If someone didn't show up, he was immediately replaced. The bike was beyond repair and so Salvatore began a lifetime of walking to work,

Brother Joe always took great pride in his appearance and even had some of his clothes made by a tailor in Youngstown. When he visited distant relatives who had moved from Pacentro to Youngstown, he always returned with a new shirt or pair of pants. Now, Miss Cochran—a pretty, young teacher at Frannie's school—walked past Salvatore and Maria's house on her way home. As often as he could, Joe got home early enough to shave, slick back his hair, put on a crisp, clean dress shirt, and just happen to be sitting on the porch as the teacher walked by. As she passed, he strolled down to the gate, greeted her, and made a little pleasant talk. It never got any further than these pleasantries, however, because Miss Cochran was a Scottish Presbyterian school teacher and he was an Italian Catholic mill worker. As a teacher (and teachers were nearly always single women), she was not permitted to live alone. She had to board in the home of one of the school's pupils. At that time the school board forbade teachers to live in an Italian or a Catholic home. Salvatore knew this, and felt bad for his brother. He didn't want to see him get his hopes up when it could never go any further. But Joe wouldn't be dissuaded. He never talked about the teacher to his family, but he was faithfully there, dressed and on the porch when Miss Cochran came down the street and passed by.

Everyone in town knew everyone else and everyone's business as well. There was a tight community bond, and for entertainment families visited each other, usually without prior notice or without waiting for an invitation. Automobiles were still rare, so on a pleasant evening an entire family might go for a walk, stop at a friend's house to visit, and stay into the night. On one such evening, Joseph and Rosa, and their son Charles, a classmate of Frannie's, stopped in to visit. They had moved to Aliquippa from Pacentro, and they also lived on Allegheny Avenue. Joseph owned a few horses and wagons that he used to haul coal and goods for businesses. He also rented out his horses and wagons. On this evening, Rosa brought Maria a huge box of candies and cookies. The company sat in the dining room, where Salvatore served drinks and Maria brought out the candy and cookies and some meats and cheeses. Joe began playing his harmonica, and soon two of his musician friends stopped by, one with a mandolin, the other with an accordion, and joined in the playing. Salvatore started singing with them. The Genarios from across the alley soon came over, Mr. Genario carrying some of his homemade wine, then the Ranaldis from next door came with a tray of food, and soon there was a big party with food, drinks, singing, and dancing.

Another evening, Salvatore, Maria and the children might walk to the Luccis where a crowd would build up in the same way. Salvatore was always ready to sing, though he never liked to dance. Maria loved to dance, and so Joe always got her on her feet, and they danced while Salvatore sang.

Their family was healthy and doing well. Maria was really feeling that this was home. She was no longer pining for Colorado, and then a telegram came from Phyllis. Sister Virginia had died. She had been the youngest, just twenty-one years old and had left behind a young husband and a year-old baby. "Why did she have to die so young?" the sisters asked. Life was hard. Of thirteen siblings, only six had lived to adulthood, and now Virginia was gone, too. As was so common, people worked hard and died young in the first part of the 20th century. In the days that followed, Maria and Salvatore talked of how important it is to squeeze in little pockets of joy wherever we find them. Maria sighed, "You know, Salie...I cherish the time with our children, family, and friends, because...in the blink of an eye everything can change and one of them will be gone."

Work at the mill was going so well that Salvatore and Joe were writing their brother Pasquale and urging him to come to America to work. There was a problem, however, due to the latest restriction on immigration. The earliest immigrants to the New World had come from the predominantly Protestant nations of northwestern Europe and Great Brittan. But the massive influx of mostly Catholic or Orthodox people from southern and eastern Europe in the early twentieth century frightened these earlier arrivers, and so the powers devised the Quota Act of 1921, which limited the number of immigrants of any nationality to three percent of that nationality living in the U.S. as given in the 1910 census. When the Quota Act failed to significantly reduce the numbers of immigrants, the National Origins

Act passed in 1924 further limiting immigrants to two percent as given in the 1890 census. Since hardly any people from southern and eastern Europe had immigrated to the U.S. before the turn of the century, this new quota meant the total number of Italians allowed into the country had been reduced to fewer than 4,000, while more than 34,000 were allowed from England and 50,000 from Germany, with whom the United States had just fought in a brutal war. Senator David Reed, one of the two architects of the bill, stated it was necessary because the previous bills didn't do enough to ensure that American stock was kept to the highest standard. At this time, the eugenics movement financed by Rockefeller and Carnegie Foundations was advocating the superiority of Nordic, German, and Anglo-Saxon people and fueling the argument.

Because of the anti-immigrant laws and mood of the country, there was no way to get a visa for Pasquale. After World War I ended, Italy had suffered a great depression and conditions were often grave. Starvation and diseases were wiping out segments of the population, and there was no place to turn for work anywhere in the country, or all of Europe. People desperately wanted to go to America for work. But the few visas that were granted went to scientists, or were given as political favors or bribes. There was no way Salvatore's family could even get close to someone with the authority to approve a visa.

Although Salvatore knew of people who had gotten relatives into the country through Canada, he didn't want to go this route because it was illegal. While his convictions were strong, however, his loyalty to family was stronger. He couldn't just stand idly by and knowingly let his family in Italy starve. After much agonizing, he found the name of a man who lived in Ashtabula, Ohio, and who, for a fee, would arrange for Pasquale to travel to Canada. There was no problem traveling to Canada from Italy because Canada had no quotas. Once Pasquale was there, a Canadian connection would notify the man in Ashtabula, who would contact Salvatore. Then Salvatore or Joe would have to go to Ashtabula and take the man to Buffalo, New York, where he would cross into Canada and bring Pasquale back. It was risky, and was going to cost enough money to put a strain on the family's meager budget, but it had to be done.

One evening early in October of 1924, as Salvatore was leaving the mill, he overheard some men talking about an accident in the section of the mill where Joe worked. There were no safety barriers on the massive machinery at this or any of the mills at that time, and injuries were common. By the time he had walked home, Maria was waiting on the porch. Officials from the mill had stopped at the house to inform them Joe was the man who had been injured. One of the huge pipes being formed at the tube mill had broken loose and rolled off the conveyor and onto Joe. He had been taken to the Jones and Laughlin Hospital on Pittsburgh's South Side. Maria had sent Frannie to get Christy who told Salvatore a friend, who owned a car, would take them to the hospital.

When Salvatore and Christy arrived at the hospital, they found that Joe had been severely burned all over his body from the hot pipe, plus several of his ribs and other bones had been broken. He was in a ward with other seriously injured men. The staff had drugged him with as much morphine as they could, so he was not coherent. Salvatore tried talking to him, but got no response. The men stayed into the night, but before dawn, the driver told Salvatore he had to get the car back to Aliquippa and go to work; Salvatore also had to go to work. They returned to Aliquippa in time for Salvatore to get his lunch pail, kiss Maria goodbye, and rush to the mill.

That evening, he went from the mill straight to the Woodlawn station and took the train to Pittsburgh, then walked from the station to the hospital. When he got to the ward, Joe's bed was empty. A nurse came up to Salvatore and told him bluntly that his brother Joe had died just a few hours before. Salvatore sat down, put his hands over his head and wept for his young brother who would never have a chance to marry, have children, or do all the things he had dreamed of and shared with Salvatore. Life felt cruel. How could God have taken this young innocent boy so full of hope and plans, so full of life?

As was customary, they had Joe's body at home for three days of viewing. He was in his best tailored suit with his harmonica by his side. A constant stream of friends, neighbors and coworkers filed through the parlor each day. Relatives and friends from Youngstown came. Even Miss Cochran, pale and visibly shaken, quietly walked through the parlor, shook Salvatore's and Maria's hands, offered her sympathy, and left.

Salvatore had always wanted the best for his brother. The St. Titus Church in Woodlawn had recently opened a Catholic cemetery out in the country beyond town, but Salvatore knew it would be too hard to get there for visits because there was no public transportation to that location. St. Joseph's Church used the Union Cemetery, which was on a hill above the town of Monaca in an area called Moon Township. While that was six miles away, there was train service to Monaca, and they could walk from the train station.

Salvatore purchased a plot, and a simple headstone on which he insisted that his brother's real name, Giuseppe, be engraved. As was customary in Italy, he also had an oval picture of Giuseppe cemented onto the face of the headstone. On the day of the funeral, the pallbearers carried Giuseppe to the church where the new Pastor, Father Zauner, said a funeral mass. Following mass, the local Darroch Funeral Home provided a shiny, black hearse drawn by two stately horses adorned with black plumes on their heads. The family walked behind the hearse, and the Sons of Italy Orchestra played a solemn dirge as the family and friends processed through town to the tunnel. Once at the tunnel, everyone got into cars borrowed from the few people in town who owned them and the family rode to the cemetery in Monaca.

After the interment, everyone was invited back to Salvatore and Maria's house for a meal that their friends and neighbors had prepared. Later that night, when everyone had gone home, Salvatore sat at the kitchen table and wrote the hardest letter he ever had to write, telling his family in Italy that young Giuseppe was gone. Salvatore told of how much he would miss his brother, and Maria felt as though she had lost a younger brother, too. They always remembered his smiling face under that shock of unruly hair and his harmonica playing and the dancing. The children would miss the uncle who played with them, throwing them into the air and rolling on the floor with them more like an older brother. Miss Cochran didn't walk by the house as often anymore.

Giuseppe was still in their life. Every Sunday that Salvatore had off, he and Maria, and the children went to the cemetery to visit Giuseppe. First they went to mass, then they walked across town, through the tunnel, and up to the train station, where they took the train to Monaca. Once there, they walked two miles, across the train tracks and up a long hill to Monaca Heights, a small neighborhood above town with a scattering of houses and three small stores. Then they crossed open fields to another hill in Moon Township. This was where Giuseppe had been placed at rest. Maria often packed a lunch. Salvatore cleaned around the grave and the children quietly played while their parents sat as though visiting with their uncle. After their picnic lunch, they walked back down to town for the train ride back to Aliquippa.

* * *

The day came when Salvatore received word that Pasquale had arrived in Canada. He promptly went to see the local contact in Aliquippa, and after negotiating a price, took the train with this man to Ashtabula, where he was introduced to the next man in the chain. The first man collected his fee and returned to Aliquippa, and Salvatore went on to Buffalo with his new contact. Here he had to wait in a shabby little hotel while the Ashtabula connection crossed into Canada to retrieve Pasquale and bring him across the border into New York.

The wait was stressful. Knowing what he was doing was illegal, Salvatore was feeling guilty. But what else could he do? His family in Italy needed his help, and he also had a family here to support. Unable to send money home, he could help in this way. He also feared for the safety of his brother. He had just lost Giuseppe. He couldn't lose Pasquale. And he had the added fear that if he were caught smuggling his brother into the U.S., he could go to jail. Then what would happen to his family? It was too stressful. The room seemed to be closing in on him.

To get out of both his anxiety and the drab room, he decided to go out for a little air. He walked down the street and stopped into a bar for a beer. The bartender looked familiar, but he couldn't place him and Salvatore certainly didn't know anyone in Buffalo. He kept looking at the man; trying to make some connection. Suddenly, as the man was handing Salvatore his drink it came to him.

"Hey, Gino. What's the matter? Don't you speak to old friends?"

The bartender looked at him. "I'm sorry, my man. Do I know you?"

"I'm Salvatore. From Starkville."

A look of shock, then recognition swept over the bartender's face. "Oh, my God! Salvatore! How many years has it been? What are you doing here? Have another drink. This one's on the house."

It was Gino Patino, the man who had disappeared after stabbing Alfredo with his miner's pick in a fight over the card game. The two men talked for a long time as Gino told Salvatore how he'd run away, fearing jail (or worse), and worked his way north and east, ending up in Buffalo, New York. Salvatore told Gino how the men had dropped Alfredo into the well, not knowing that he wasn't dead. He also talked about the mines closing and his move to Aliquippa and how he had come here to get his brother. Talking with an old friend calmed a hard time for him.

The next morning, the Ashtabula connection received the rest of his fee, and hastily he left after turning over Pasquale. The brothers embraced and Salvatore wept bittersweet tears for losing one brother and gaining another. Here was the two-year-old baby he had left in Italy, now a man. Pasquale was a bit taller than Salvatore and stockier in build. He had the same skin coloring with dark slicked back hair, better dressed than Salvatore when he arrived in the new country, but still an obvious foreigner. Salvatore was eager to get away from Buffalo and any chance of being found out by the authorities, so they kept their reunion short.

Safely arrived in Aliquippa, Pasquale was warmly welcomed by Maria and the children. Christy brought his family to meet the cousin he had never known, as he had left Italy before Pasquale was born. Other families also came to welcome him and, as usual, meetings turned into parties with singing and eating and drinking.

The mill was working at full speed. An article appeared in the *Woodlawn News* announcing that the entire steel industry was working at ninety percent to full capacity and employment managers at the plants were seeking workers. Not even during the war had labor been in such demand, and yet the tight restrictions against immigrants were still being enforced. Salvatore had no trouble getting Pasquale a job, however, because no one seemed to care where he had come from or how he had arrived. No one asked to see papers or proof of residency, and they didn't care that he couldn't speak English. They were happy to have a warm body to put to work. He would be on the labor gang, and you didn't have to speak English to handle a pick and shovel.

Pasquale was not the warm, enthusiastic person that Giuseppe had been. He didn't like to dance or sing, he didn't play an instrument, and he didn't frolic with the children.

No, Pasquale was sullen and suspicious of strangers, a hard worker with little joy in his heart, somewhat like his father Antonio. Salvatore didn't know what made him that way, but he and his brother were strangers.

For some time, Maria had been complaining of severe pain in her side. The cures provided by Marra Giuseppe had not been working. Their frustration peaked when Marra Geuzeppe had her drink turpentine and she became violently ill. Outraged, Salvatore insisted that Maria must stop this silliness and see a real doctor. Having resisted this because of the expense, she relented due to the severity of the pains, and they went to see Dr. Armstrong in Monaca. A surgeon who had been recommended by a friend, the doctor diagnosed her problem as gallstones and said she would have to go to the hospital for surgery. The nearest hospital was ten miles away in the town of Rochester.

Gallbladder surgery was considered very serious then, and Maria and Salvatore knew people who had gone into the hospital for it and not returned. Everyone was worried now. Maria asked Mrs. Genario to watch the children while the men were at work. It was also agreed that Mrs. Genario's mother would walk the children to school, meet them at noon, walk them home for lunch, back to school, and home again in the evening. Carl, at two years of age, was the only child not in school, so the principal permitted Frannie to bring him to school with her if he promised to behave, which, of course, he did.

Before she left her fearful children, Maria gathered them around her and said she would be fine if they would pray for her. Ever the serious worrier, eleven-year-old Frannie quickly stepped in as "mother" and got everyone organized. She took the statue of the Blessed Mother and made a little altar in their bedroom, and every evening she, Mauggie, and Leo would kneel at the altar as she led them in saying the rosary. Carl was too young to take part, but, seeming to understand, he knelt quietly next to them through the rosary with his hands folded. On school days,

Frannie dressed Carl and took him by the hand to school, where he sat obediently at her side all day.

One week later, with seventeen gallstones removed, Maria came home again, exhausted and weak. Once in her own home, however, she rebounded quickly with the assistance of Mary Lucci, Mrs. Genario, the other neighbor ladies, and, of course, Frannie.

Soon life was back to normal and running smoothly. Salvatore and Pasquale were working steadily, and Salvatore was actually able to go back to saving a little every payday. Maria was feeling better, and Theresa Rubino insisted she needed some enjoyment, so the two women went on a shopping trip into Woodlawn, something Maria had never done on her own.

Salvatore was grateful to have his wife back safely from the hospital. He admired how artfully she worked around the house, managed the family, and helped others in the neighborhood. They had been together a long time and survived much, yet he knew she still missed her family in Colorado and evenings filled with Giuseppe's music, his harmonica, and dancing. He knew how much she loved music, and had seen a gleaming new Victrola in the window of Carl Brothers Hardware store on Main Avenue. After thinking about it for a few weeks, Salvatore decided to buy the Victrola. But when he went into the store and asked about it, he was shocked to find that it cost $100. That was out of the question. Didn't they have something less expensive? Determined not to lose a sale, Mr. Carl told Salvatore he had another Victrola in the back room that might be more to his liking. He left and returned with an old, 1912 table-top model that he obviously had been unable to sell. He offered it to Salvatore for $10. That was more like it, but he didn't have the ten dollars. Mr. Carl said if he could put one dollar down, he would hold it and allow Salvatore to make time payments.

Salvatore gave this some serious thought. He was against credit, but perhaps this wasn't credit because he would not take possession until it was paid in full. "Okay," he said, "It is a deal," and they shook hands. After five months of payments, Salvatore proudly walked into the house with a surprise for Maria: an oak box with a felt roll on top over which cylindrical records could be slid, a crank on the side, and a large curving horn on top. Two doors in the front of the Victrola opened to storage shelves for the cylinders. Maria had her very own Victor Talking Machine, and a recording of the song, "Take Me Home to Colorado."

Thrilled, she hugged and kissed Salvatore, then took her new Victrola into the parlor and gave it a place of honor on the table in front of the window. The children gathered around excitedly, waiting to hear what this marvel would say or sing. Maria slid the cylinder onto the roller, cranked up the machine, placed the needle on the cylinder, and sat down to listen. She smiled as tears began to run down her cheeks. The children seeing her cry, also began to cry, which made Salvatore feel terrible. *Why had he chosen that song?*

"Thank you," Maria said as she kissed him and calmed the children. "It's beautiful."

It was soon evident when Maria moved the writing table into the living room that when no one was around, she was going into the room, playing her music, and writing to Maggie and the others. She could often be found there, sitting with a letter from Colorado in her hand, weeping. But she understood she had to stop this behavior the day she received another letter from Sister Maggie. She took it into the parlor, put on the music, and proceeded to read news of the family. There was no work in southern Colorado. Cousins Phyllis and James, Martin's sister and her husband, had moved to Detroit to find work. The Starkville homestead was almost gone. When Leo came up to her sitting alone in the room and crying, he put his arm around her and said, "Don't cry, Mummy. When I'm older, I'm going to get my own car and I'll take you back to Colorado."

She smiled, and hugged him.

Frannie, who was now thirteen and in the seventh grade, started asking Maria questions about courtship and marriage. In those days, people didn't speak in public about such things, so Frannie's questions presented a challenge to her mother. Frannie had been in class with Charlie since first grade and had a crush on him. He seemed to be paying a great deal of attention to her. And so Maria knew it was time to start the talks.

Pasquale was not happy about the attention Charlie was paying Frannie. Pasquale had always favored her over the other children, and on payday, he always brought a little treat for her. At the same time, he was abrupt with the other children. Maria didn't care for the attention he was showing Frannie and mentioned it to Salvatore. When Pasquale began to voice his opinion about Charlie, Maria insisted it was none of his business. Salvatore was trying to figure a way to smooth things over when Pasquale made an announcement that seemed to solve the problem.

It had been three years since Pasquale's arrival from Italy. He had been working hard and sending money home regularly, but now he felt it was time to marry and start a family. He told Salvatore he was going to return to Italy to find a wife. Salvatore told his young brother, "Eh, Pasquale, there are many good women right here in America. Why go back to Italy?" He added, "You know that because you come into this country against the law, when you leave, it will be a problem to come back." But Pasquale would have none of it.

"American women are loose and wild. I am going back to Italy, to find a pure, innocent girl whose father keeps her under his eye until she could be married, not like the women here who are allowed to hang out with boys before they are even of a marrying age." Clearly that last was intended to be a criticism of Salvatore and Maria's supervision of Frannie.

Salvatore turned on him quick, "You sound like Papa with his blind eyes to what is in front of him. I found my

Maria here in America, a wonderful woman. You could do no better." Pasquale said no more, but soon left the room and before long, left the country for Italy.

* * *

Though sad to see Pasquale go, with the household back to just Salvatore, Maria, and the four children, life in Aliquippa was calm and pleasant once more. On Sunday evenings in the summer, the family often went for a stroll around the few blocks that made up their little village, stopping along the way to talk with neighbors. The children didn't care much for the adult conversations that slowed down their walk, but they were usually rewarded with fresh roasted peanuts from the machine in front of Theil's corner store. On really special evenings, they might forego the peanuts for an ice cream cone at Richmond's. After dinner on cold winter evenings, Salvatore lit a fire in the living room stove and the family gathered around to listen as he read one of the stories of his favorite Italian hero, Ercolino. The children howled with laughter when Leo pranced about, acting like the hero, until Salvatore threatened to end the story right there and Leo sat down with a grin.

There were times, when he was working the day shift, when Maria permitted the children to walk two blocks to the corner of Main Avenue, where they could wait for Salvatore to emerge from the tunnel. He would allow Leo or Carl to carry his metal lunch bucket, although Carl could barely lift it off the ground. Salvatore always kept a piece of uneaten fruit or cake or a cookie so the children could rummage through the bucket and eat the treat on their walk home.

While the children were allowed to walk to the corner of Main Avenue, they were not permitted to cross the street or venture any further. They kept trying to convince their parents that they were responsible enough to be trusted, but that corner was the limit, especially when the carnival came to town. The rides and game booths were set up along

Erie Avenue, directly across from the freight yard, and nearly all the children started running down the street to enjoy the excitement. But Maria and Salvatore insisted that their children could only go with them. They explained this by saying that some of the carnival people were gypsies, and while they were a colorful spectacle, there were always rumors that gypsies stole children, and Maria would take no such chances.

In May of 1927, Charles Lindbergh made the first solo, non-stop transcontinental flight across the Atlantic Ocean, from Long Island, New York, to Paris, France. His success caused quite a stir around the world. In August that year, there was an equal stir in Aliquippa. Lindbergh was touring the country with his plane and had stops in Pittsburgh and Wheeling, West Virginia, where he either gave a speech or rode in a parade. The buzz in Aliquippa was that although Lindbergh himself would not be there, the *Spirit of St. Louis,* his plane, was going to be taken through Woodlawn on a trailer on its way from Pittsburgh to the streets of Wheeling.

Salvatore felt there was no need for girls to see an airplane, but the boys begged to go. They were ecstatic when he consented to take them to Woodlawn to see the *Spirit of Saint Louis* as it rode up Franklin Avenue on its truck bed. On the big day, Salvatore and the boys took the bus to the "wye" in Woodlawn, the intersection at the main gate into the mill. Here he and his sons stood wide eyed and joyous at that intersection with a crowd of people as the flatbed truck draped in bunting and carrying the famous plane passed by, accompanied by the high school band and a car filled with town dignitaries.

The town was in a festive mood, and Salvatore stopped in one of the bars for a drink and some conversation with his friends. He bought the boys a bottle of Yaky soda pop made in Aliquippa, and then they started for home. Back at home, Salvatore told Maria that the talk in town was that the long rumored merger of Woodlawn and Aliquippa was about to happen, although there were many people who were not happy about the decision.

There had been rumors for some time of merging Aliquippa with Woodlawn. Since the Jones & Laughlin Company had built the mill and employee housing in Woodlawn, its population had long surpassed that of Aliquippa. Because the J&L plant was named the Aliquippa Works, however; the two towns' names caused confusion. In early 1928, the merger became official. Woodlawn became Aliquippa, and the original Aliquippa became West Aliquippa, even though it was northeast of old Woodlawn. When the Pittsburgh and Lake Erie Railroad changed the name of the Woodlawn station to Aliquippa, it renamed the former Aliquippa station the West Station because it was next on the east-west line to Youngstown, Ohio. This merger of towns made the new Aliquippa the largest town in Beaver County.

Salvatore was doing well in the late 1920s. They had their home and a healthy family. A relative who lived in Youngstown wrote to tell him there was a good investment opportunity, as Youngstown was growing rapidly due to the expansion of its steel mill. There was a farm just outside town, the relative said, that was being broken into building plots in anticipation of being annexed to the city. Salvatore had always believed land was the best investment. On a day off, therefore, he took the train to Youngstown and met his relative. Together, they walked around all the land that was for sale. Based on what he saw, he decided that purchasing land would be a good investment, so he bought two of the lots. He also joined the Sons of Italy so that he could purchase a $400 death benefit. Now he had land in Ohio, a house in West Aliquippa, a beautiful family, a steady job, and life insurance. But he still was not satisfied. He had never really liked Aliquippa where the houses were too close together, the lots were too small, and the air was filthy from the smokestacks of the mills. It was not his idea of paradise. What he wanted was a big piece of land farther out of town where the air was cleaner, where he could have enough room for a nice garden and animals, and make his private paradise.

Still looking for land, he went to Woodlawn and took the trolley to the end of the line, to an area called New Sheffield. This was a little village consisting of a small wooden church, Mt. Carmel Presbyterian, a gristmill, a little park, and a lot of land for sale. Although the land looked nice, he felt there might still be pollution from the mill. It just didn't feel right to him.

When the family went to the cemetery in Moon Township above Monaca to visit his brother Giuseppe's grave, Salvatore would look out over the countryside from that hill. One day a house sitting out in an open field caught his eye. He commented to Maria that he thought it was a perfect setting. On another Sunday visit, he persuaded her to walk past that house with him on their way back to the train. On their walk to the station, they always stopped at Chambers grocery store, where they bought Eskimo Pies for the children. On this Sunday, Salvatore asked the owner where that house was in relation to the store and how to get to it.

There was no street to the house; just a path running alongside a row of electrical wires. Three houses were set along the path. They came to a little cottage surrounded by acres of flat land. The cottage was empty, and the land around it was overgrown. They looked in the windows and walked around the grounds. When they walked back to the store, Salvatore got information from the proprietor to locate the owner, who, as it happened, was very interested in selling the house.

Salvatore really wanted that little farm. He began thinking of nothing else. Maria, however, had come to like Aliquippa, where she had a close-knit circle of friends who had come to replace her family. She didn't mind the soot either having grown up in Starkville. Salvatore told her the people in Aliquippa were not as friendly as those in Starkville and he had never felt that Aliquippa was home. He told her that the men in town were big card players and spent a great deal of time drinking at the club, and, even though he had joined, that was not what he wanted. "I am not a card player or a drinker." He touched her arm, and said, "Maria, when I first see this house I know right away I find my paradise." Smiling at her, he said, "Maria, there are three acres of land with that house! I can make a nice garden and have animals. Some chickens. A cow. This is what I've always talked about. The houses where we live are on top of each other. The air isn't clean with the mill hanging over us. And you know, there is not enough room for our big family."

"But, Salie," she replied, "that house has only four rooms. It's small, too. There isn't enough room there for our family."

"Ah, but Maria, with all that land, we can make more rooms. I can make a beautiful place for you."

"My friends are all here," she said. "I felt so alone after leaving my family in Colorado, and these people have been good to us. They've made me feel welcome and are my family. I can't leave my family again."

"Maria, Monaca is not so far. You can visit anytime you want. We go to the cemetery every Sunday. You can come to Aliquippa just as easy."

She wasn't ready to give in. "But the children," she said. "They will be leaving their friends, and school, and...."

At that point, however, Salvatore was finished negotiating. The discussion was over. "Eh, *signora*, in nineteen and two, I come to this country alone, a little boy. Don't talk to me of how hard the children will have it. For the young, everything is easy. We talk of you and me and how we do this. That's it."

A few days later, speaking a little more calmly, Salvatore finally won Maria over. Or maybe he just wore her down. She consented, and he set about making an offer.

The owners of the house he wanted had bought the house and land in 1922 for $1,900. With the country going strong now in 1928, the owner wanted a good deal more. Salvatore was finally able to negotiate a purchase price of $4,450. The sellers would hold the mortgage on the house. As much as he didn't want to go further into debt, Salvatore now had two mortgages, one on his house in Aliquippa and now this new one. He was also paying on the land in Youngstown. But times were good, and he was so sure that he could make it all work, he went out and bought himself a nice, broad-brimmed hat. The soft cap he wore was what the *contadini* wore in Italy. Men of position wore hats. From now on, he would wear a proper hat.

Frannie was devastated at the thought of moving. She didn't want to leave Charlie. Mauggie didn't want to leave, either, because she had become close to the Lucci girls and the social life in Aliquippa. They would, the girls knew, be moving out into the country with hardly any neighbors. Salvatore agreed the girls could come back to Aliquippa for the festivals and stay with the Luccis. This was a huge concession on his part, allowing the girls to stay away from home overnight, but the Luccis were considered family, and he knew Mary wouldn't let them out of her sight.

The two boys liked the idea of living in the country where they could run and play in the open fields and the nearby woods.

Once the decision was made, Maria put every effort into making the move a positive one. She got the girls involved in planning what they would do with their new room. She talked about how much she had enjoyed the animals as she was growing up in Colorado. She tried to weave exciting stories about the coming move. The day would soon come when they were to leave and start a new chapter in their lives. Mary and Frank Lucci invited the family to their house for dinner, and when they arrived, they found all the neighbors and friends had pitched in to make a huge block party and picnic out on the street. They had closed off their block and turned it into a town party.

There were games for the children and food and music. But the fellowship and celebration made it all the harder to say goodbye.

On moving day, the Luccis, the Genarios, and most of the other neighbors came to help. Charlie's father, Joseph, brought one of his trucks. The men loaded all the family's belongings onto the truck, and the women and children were loaded into the Luccis' car. Everything was ready to go. Salvatore went inside to see why Maria was not outside with the others. He found her upstairs walking through the rooms. Carl had been born in that room. When Leo had the bicycle accident that permanently damaged his vocal cords, the doctor had tended him in this room. Frannie and Mauggie had built their altar to the Virgin Mother in their room.

Downstairs, she looked one last time at the bathroom Salvatore had built after the priest had walked in while she was giving the girls a bath. She brushed the stoves with her hand as she walked past them, recalling all the times she lovingly polished them. She recalled the day the dinning room furniture had arrived. The room was now empty, the pictures all gone. The parlor was bare, too, with no Victrola near the window. Just memories.

Maria looked down the street at the church where they had gone every Sunday, holidays, saints' day, and funeral, where Carl had been baptized. She stood quietly until she felt the pressure of her husband's hand on hers. Finally, they stepped into an automobile that Christy had procured for the occasion and rode down the street and through the tunnel.

Maria vowed to herself, "This will be my last move."

West Aliquippa, Pennsylvania 1909

West Aliquippa, Pennsylvania c. 1920's

Monaca, Pennsylvania

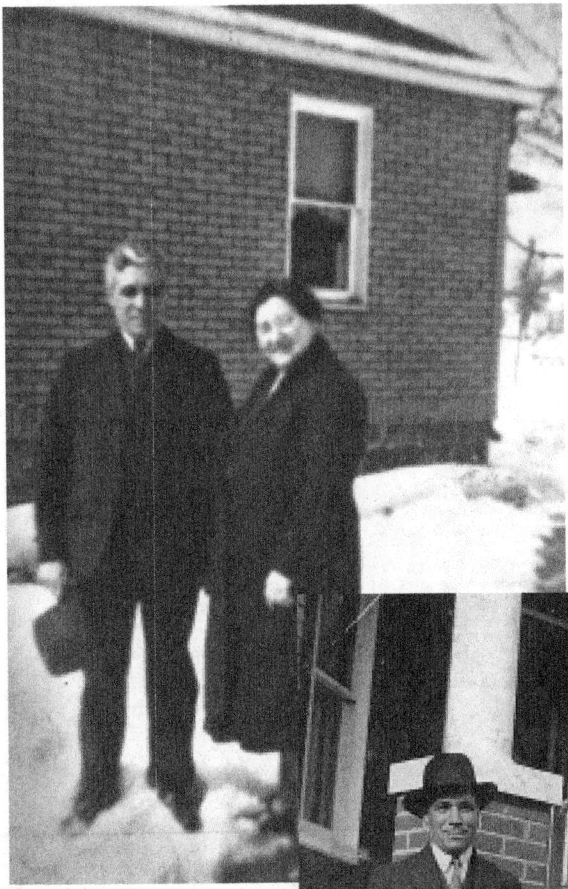

Salvatore and Maria before family home in Monaca, c. 1939

Salvatore and Maria with son Sam at Minnie's house in Detroit, 1938

Part III

Paradise and the Great Depression, War, & Loss

Family gathering in Monaca house, Easter, 1947. Front: Frannie with baby, Salvatore and Maria amidst grandchildren. Back: Paul's brother and wife, Paul and Mauggie, Carl and Bets, Charlie and Rosie. *Note the photo of Pietro Grosso on wall right.

They arrived in Monaca at their rustic four-room cottage with clapboard siding, one porch running across the front, and another along the back. It sat on three acres of land and was the last of only three houses on this dirt lane. Inside were a living room and a side bedroom. Directly behind the living room was the kitchen, with another bedroom behind the first one. Out the back door and past the back porch sat the water pump and a path that led to the outhouse, a small barn, rabbit pens, and a chicken coop.

Almost immediately, Salvatore and his friends, self-made carpenters, set about expanding the house. They tore down the front porch and dug a basement over which they built a new living room and a new bedroom; then they built a porch along the width of the new front. On the side of the house, they added stairs and an outside door leading into the basement. They enclosed the back porch, creating an entryway with a pantry on one side and the bathroom on the other. Planning ahead, they outfitted the bathroom with a tub, a toilet, and a sink, though no water was piped into the house yet in 1928. It would still be necessary to get the water at the well and use the outhouse.

Across the front of the property, at the edge of the road, Salvatore planted four sycamore trees. He also planted two more in the backyard, one by the water pump, the other beside the path to the barn. He found two ornamental trees and planted them in the front yard on both sides of the walk that lead to the front porch. He was creating his vision of paradise.

By 1928, people were buying gas stoves for cooking. Salvatore didn't want Maria using a wood or coal stove in the kitchen any longer, but there was no gas to the homes on their lane, so he went to the gas company to request service. They told him they would lay the pipe if he dug the ditch for it from the main road down the lane and all the way to his house. He talked this over with his two neighbors whose houses also lay along the lane, and they agreed to his plan. Each man would dig a ditch to his house. The first neighbor on the lane would dig the ditch from the main street to his house, the next neighbor would dig from the first house to his house, and Salvatore would finish the job by digging from that house to his. Everyone on the lane would now have gas, and Salvatore planned to buy Maria a new gas stove.

Maria liked the popular Craftsman design she had seen for house kits in the Sears catalog, and so Salvatore had copied the design. Inside, they now had a living room, a dining room, a kitchen with a pantry, three bedrooms and a bathroom. It was a warm and cozy house.

The house in West Aliquippa they kept and rented it to a family that had moved there from an Italian village near Pacentro. Things were going well. Salvatore now owned a three-acre farm, a rental house in West Aliquippa, and two building lots in Youngstown, Ohio. He bought some chickens and enlarged their coop, caught a few rabbits, extended the pen around the chicken coop to the barn, and bought two pigs. During the year, as he could, he enlarged the small barn and created new housing for the pigs under it. Then, after some searching, he found a cow that a farmer wanted to sell for $125. That was a lot of money for a cow, but it was pregnant. Feeling he would be getting two cows, making it worth the money, Salvatore bought the cow.

Because he would have to get the cow from the town of Freedom to Monaca, Salvatore asked Joseph if he could help with his truck. The truck was committed for a long period of time, but Frank's son had a car. He offered to take Salvatore to the farm. Once there, Salvatore paid for the animal and then walked the miles back home with her. It was like his tending the family cow back in Italy. With a pregnant cow, this was a very slow and difficult walk that took the entire day. They had to walk seven miles down into the river valley, proceed along the side of a highway and across the bridge over the Ohio River, then go up the hill to the cow's new home. As Salvatore told Maria, "The cow she would not cross the bridge with a wooden plank floor. She sees the river below through the slats. I had to pull her then push her across that bridge and up the long hill. But look, Maria, we now have a great cow!"

Maria and the children were kept busy working on the house. She had the girls making new curtains for the windows. She also ordered floral wallpaper for the dining room and hung it herself when it arrived. Then she put the large oval picture of her father on the wall and, as before, set the framed family photos across the buffet. A bit later, she took the boys into the woods with a wheelbarrow to search for large, smooth, round stones, which they used to line the driveway. They whitewashed both the stones and the bases of the sycamore trees which Salvatore had planted to line the street.

Salvatore dug a flower garden around the base of each ornamental tree, and Maria lined these miniature gardens with more whitewashed stones. After Salvatore found a number of flat rocks, he laid a walk from the back door to the outhouse, then planted a grape arbor over the walkway. He also made a wooden bench and set it beside the well, next to one of the little sycamore trees. Beyond the well, he built a trellis and planted Rose of Sharon bushes around its base.

They kept one acre as pasture for the cow to graze and dedicated the other two acres to the house, the outbuildings and a huge garden. During the year Salvatore would plant strawberries and rhubarb for Maria's pies, tomatoes, lettuce, potatoes, onions, garlic, beans, cabbage, and squash—everything that would sustain them through the winters. At harvest time, Maria taught the girls to can all their vegetable riches, and Salvatore built wooden shelving along one wall in the basement, which they filled with enough canned goods from the garden to last until the next harvest.

Salvatore taught Leo to milk the cow. When he was milking, Carl liked to stoop over, open his mouth and allow Leo to squirt in milk. Mauggie liked the warm milk, too, but used a tin cup. Frannie had made a pet of the cow, naming her Daisy, and taught her to take an apple out of the pocket of her jacket for a snack. The family were each a part of a living paradise now.

* * *

Toward the end of 1928, brother Pasquale returned from Italy. No one knew how he got back into the U.S., and no one asked. He had married a young woman from Pacentro, and she was already pregnant with their first child when he left her in Italy. He had no intention of making America his permanent home, but promised to earn money and send it back to his wife for the eventual purchase of a family home.

Many Italian men came to the United States during the first half of the twentieth century to work, save, and eventually go home again. Although men from most other European nations brought their families with them, many of the Italians did not, which was unfortunate because it often resulted in split families. Oftentimes, one mate died, leaving the family forever split between two continents unless those left behind were eventually brought here. It typically delayed the assimilation process. When the reunions finally happened, the reunited family members were often strangers to each other. But Pasquale clearly intended to return to Italy. He easily got another job at the mill, no questions asked. The Ciccone family was growing, and Salvatore, Maria, the four children, and now Pasquale filled the house. Salvatore and Maria loved their paradise. The air was cleaner than in Starkville or Aliquippa, and the children were healthier than they had ever been.

* * *

Although they were enjoying their new home and the land, life in Moon Township was not like anything they had experienced in Starkville or Aliquippa. Monaca was an extremely closed community. Originally created from a land grant awarded to Colonel Ephraim Blaine—who served in the Continental Army during the American Revolution—it had been purchased in 1821 by George Rapp, founder of the German religious sect called the Harmonites, or the Harmony Society. In 1822, Stephen Phillips and John Graham purchased some of the land for their riverboat building business and named the little cluster of homes around their business Phillipsburg.

Historically in 1832, Bernhard Muller—known as the Count de Leon—broke away from the Harmony Society at the town of Economy, Pennsylvania, and moved with 250 of his followers down the Ohio River to Phillipsburg. Here they established the New Philadelphia Society and church. The town's name was changed in 1892 by the Pittsburgh and Lake Erie Railroad from Phillipsburg to an Indian name, just as they had done in Aliquippa and other stops along their rail line. The new Monaca name was in honor of Iroquois Indian Chief Monacatootha.

From the beginning the town was heavily German, Lutheran, and Presbyterian, with hardly any other ethnic groups. There was a little industry, but not enough to allow a large influx of southern and eastern Europeans, as in the other mill towns. The opening of the Colonial Steel plant in 1902 brought Irish iron workers and a few Slovaks, but Monaca was nowhere near the melting pot the other towns were. It was, in fact, ninety-eight percent white, and the governing people and property owners, without exception, had names like Schule, Acker, Speyerer, Forstner, Herkenreider, and Chambers. Darker skinned people with last names that ended in vowels, or contained no vowels at all, were not part of the community. Furthermore, there was a division between the people living in town and those living on Monaca Heights or in Moon Township, as it was then called. Everyone just referred to the heights as "the hill," and you either lived in town or "on the hill." Typically townspeople looked at those on the hill as country bumpkins, whereas people on the hill thought the townspeople were snobs. And no one seemed to like "foreigners."

The problems for Salvatore's family began when the children started school. Not knowing where the school was, Maria talked to a neighbor who offered to have her child show the way. On the first day of school, Frannie, Mauggie, and Leo said goodbye to their mother and followed their new neighbor on a one-and-a-half-mile walk, cutting through pastures and walking along roads until they reached the Marshall Road School.

Leo, who was small for his age, had started first grade in Aliquippa when he was five and a half years old. He had been ready for fifth grade at the end of the last school year, and therefore, upon arriving at the Marshall Road School, went directly to the fifth grade classroom. But the teacher told him he was too small and too young for fifth grade. He would have to go back to the fourth grade. When he argued that he'd already finished fourth grade, she told him to go to the principal's office. Instead, he walked out of the school and played in the woods until it was time to go home.

The next day, the children walked to school together again. When they reached the school, Leo again went to the fifth grade class. This time, the teacher personally took him to the fourth grade. When the fourth grade teacher tried to seat him, he refused to stay in the room and left the building. That evening, Mauggie brought home a note from the principal asking to see one of Leo's parents. On the third day of school, Maria took Leo to school and met with the principal, who told her Leo would have to go to fourth grade. Maria politely told him that her son had finished fourth grade with excellent marks. With determination she asserted that he most definitely should be in the fifth grade. After a lengthy discussion, and seeing her determination, the principal relented and agreed to allow Leo into the fifth grade, but on probation. The problem was resolved when Leo soon shined in the classroom. Salvatore and Maria's children were all settled into school now, but the problems had not ended. It was not uncommon for Leo or Carl to come home with a bloody nose or torn clothing from fighting because someone had called one of them a "dago."

Maria did not like the fighting. She told them they had to overlook the name-calling because they were new in the community. As people got to know them, she assured them, the names and other insults would taper off and eventually go away. But Salvatore told them they were never to *start* a fight, but if someone started a fight with them, they were to make sure to *finish* it, regardless of the size of the other guy or how many guys got into the fight.

Then one day Mauggie came home very upset. She said the girls in school were not friendly. Maria told her it would just take time, but Mauggie was not appeased by that reasoning. She told her mother that a girl in her class had written an essay that the teacher said was exceptionally well written. The teacher had called the girl to the front of the class to read it aloud. The topic was "How Italians Live." The girl proceeded to read to the entire class—and to Mauggie's mortification—that Italians ate sheeps' brains, gave their children wine to drink, and hung garlic in their kitchens and around their necks, stomped grapes with their bare feet, and kept animals in their houses. As she read, Mauggie reported, the other children kept looking at her and snickering. As the performance ended, the teacher, showing complete insensitivity toward Mauggie, praised the girl for a very well written paper.

Maria sat down with the children and told them that people thought these stories were true because they did not know any Italian people. "Once they get to know us better," she assured them, "they will realize that we're no different than anyone else." Then she suggested, "Why don't you girls invite some of your classmates home for cocoa." She had just bought a hand-painted cocoa pot and cups from the Jewel Tea man, and thought it would be a nice gesture to have a cocoa party.

Mauggie listened respectfully, but she vowed, "Mommy, I know you mean well, but I will never allow that girl who read that insulting paper to ever step inside our house. I just won't. I have nothing to prove to people like that." Maria listened and nodded.

By now, there was a third neighbor down the lane. All three neighbor families were pleasant and cordial, if not a little curious, about the Italians with their strange customs. The men watched Salvatore closely, observing with interest how he planted and maintained his garden and tended his animals. Every Christmas Eve, they came by to wish him a Merry Christmas and enjoy a few glasses of his homemade wine, though the wine was not to the delight of their wives. This practice started their first Christmas in Monaca, when Maria asked Frannie and Mauggie to take some of her cookies to the neighbors as a good will gesture. Salvatore walked along with them. At the first house, the husband, Jim, invited Salvatore in to have a seat and enjoy a little Christmas cheer. The holiday punch was made with Jim's homemade moonshine. Not accustomed to hard liquor, and especially moonshine, Salvatore returned home and was extremely ill. Maria had him sit outside in the back while she put cold towels to his head. When he threw up, she scolded him for drinking the moonshine. The next year, the girls were sent alone to deliver the Christmas cookies. Missing Salvatore's visit, and knowing he had bought a wine press, the neighbor men decided to stop in on him with a holiday visit, and of course, Salvatore offered them some wine. Soon these Christmas Eve visits became a tradition.

While Salvatore was establishing his Christmas tradition with the neighbor men, Maria was trying what she had suggested to Mauggie and invited the women on the street for afternoons of hot chocolate. While they occasionally reciprocated, Maria was never to know the easy in and out neighbor visits which she enjoyed in Aliquippa.

In downtown Monaca there were a few shops and restaurants, a pharmacy, a five and ten cent store, and the post office. Even though it was over a mile down the hill and into town, the girls liked to walk there when they had the time and to wander through the shops, dreaming of the day when they might be able to own some of the beautiful merchandise they would see. They also enjoyed watching the people in town. The boys were more interested in a stream in the woods where they went to skip stones and hunt for crawfish. In the winter, they went ice skating and played hockey on the pond at Harttenbaugh's farm near the cemetery. And Salvatore kept his promise. He allowed the girls to make overnight visits back to West Aliquippa to the Luccis for the saints' day celebrations, plus other times during the year. These visits delighted Frannie because they gave her an opportunity to see Charlie again.

The local bus company started a regular schedule of trips from Monaca to Aliquippa to accommodate the large number of men who were now commuting to work in the mill. Bus service proved less expensive than train tickets, and the buses ran more regularly. Some days when the children were in school and Salvatore and Pasquale were at work, Maria treated herself to a bus ride to West Aliquippa. She got off across from the train station and walked through the tunnel into West Aliquippa to visit Mary. Afterward, she usually walked to the church to stop to pray, and then she walked past their old house, stopping to visit with Mrs. Genario or Theresa Rubino, on her way back to the bus stop. She always timed her return so she was home for the children's arrival from school, and in time to begin preparations for dinner.

All was not easy at home. Pasquale was not at all pleased about the freedom his brother gave to the children and to Maria, often voicing his disapproval and, on occasion, disciplining the children himself. This usually led to a quiet bedroom argument between Maria and Salvatore with the door closed and after the children were in bed. Pasquale's interference was harsh and unnecessary. Salvatore was a kind, but stern, caring disciplinarian, though the children often felt he was unyielding. He was a man of few words, but when, for instance, the children began to act up at the dinner table, he might just reach over and bop them lightly on their heads with the handle of his knife. This always restored good manners at the table. When he made a decision, whether the children liked the decision or not, there was no negotiating. He also didn't believe in a lot of free play time. He required all the children to work around the house and in the garden, and help tend to the animals. His motto was "Work is honorable and idle hands only lead to trouble."

Unfortunately, Salvatore was experiencing some difficulty as landlord of his house in West Aliquippa. The family renting from him often fell behind on the payments, and so it became standard practice for him to stop at the house to collect it in person. But there was always a reason why the money would be late. The woman of the house began to wring her hands and plead with him to be understanding. Her plea would then be followed by a complaint. The toilet wasn't working, or there was a leak somewhere.

On his off-time, therefore, he went to the house to repair the toilet or work on whatever the current complaint was about. Through these visits, and from what he was told by men at work, he discovered that his tenant was renting space to boarders. While he was working on the toilet one day, one of the boarders arrived and began to talk to him. He told Salvatore in addition to his landlady (Salvatore's tenant), the husband, and their three children, she had nine boarders in the house—all nine of them in one bedroom. Three beds with two men at a time in each bed, and since they worked shifts, as one got up and went to work, another came home and took over the bed. "No wonder the toilet is broken," the boarder complained. "It never gets a rest. As soon as someone flushes it, someone else is on it. It's the same with the beds. They never get a chance to cool down."

When Salvatore questioned his tenant, she denied it and protested that she did not have that many boarders. The boarder was a liar, she said. He never paid on time. She needed boarders, she added, because Salvatore's rent was too high. She had trouble paying him on time because these men were all lazy. They drank all their money away and were always late paying her. Salvatore listened, and reluctantly continued to tolerate her late payments.

When Salvatore arrived home that day, he found Pasquale in a very good mood. He had just received a letter from Italy. His wife had given birth to their first child, a son. He had also decided to break with tradition. Instead of naming the new baby after his father, he would name his first-born son Giuseppe, in honor of their deceased brother.

While Maria was happy for Pasquale, she was also feeling a little blue. She had received a letter from her sister Mattie. Although times were good for the family in Monaca, they were not as good in Colorado. The mines were still opening and closing by design of the owners, leaving the miners' future uncertain. Mattie's family was finally at a time in their lives when they had been able to save a little. If they were ever going to move forward with their lives, Mattie wrote, something had to be done now. With no future in southern Colorado or the mines, the family decided to move to Bakersfield, California, where they had the opportunity to rent a dairy farm and start a new life. Maria shared her sister's happiness, but felt a loss that there was hardly any family left in Starkville.

* * *

As 1929 opened, things were going well. They were able to get to the next payday with a little left over. Everyone in Salvatore and Maria's family had drifted into a routine that allowed for bits of leisure time. Frannie was fifteen, Mauggie was twelve, Leo was ten, and Carl was seven. Maria occasionally permitted the girls to walk to Rochester to see a matinee at the movie theater. Pasquale, of course, was still not happy with the freedom the girls were given. Sometimes when they went out on their own, he followed them at a distance. Mauggie was completely oblivious to what her uncle was doing, but as they were walking, Frannie would quietly say, "Don't make it obvious, but look over your left shoulder into the woods. See Uncle Pasquale hiding behind that tree?" While his behavior amused Mauggie, it frightened Frannie, and infuriated Maria. She told Salvatore, "You must stop your brother's following our girls when I've given them permission. It's not right."

This situation came to a head with two incidents. First, Pasquale bought Frannie a new crank-up Victrola for her birthday that was better than the old model Salvatore had bought Maria. This one, which looked like a little suitcase, had no horn and played record disks that were made of laminated fibers coated with shellac. Maria did not like the special attention he was giving Frannie and thought the gift seemed far too lavish. A few days later, while Salvatore was at work, the boys got a little rough and loud while they were playing with each other. Pasquale jumped up, grabbed the boys, and started hitting them. Maria quickly pulled him away. "If you ever touch one of my children again," she told her brother-in-law, "I'll break your neck." He backed off because she was bigger than he was, and very strong.

That evening, in the privacy of their bedroom, she told Salvatore, "This is the last straw. No one touches my children but me or you. He has gone too far. I want him out of here."

Pasquale was outraged at the way Maria talked to him. A bit later, he told his brother, "Salvatore, you cannot control your wife, and this is what comes of marrying an American."

"Stop!" shouted Salvatore "I run my own family as I please, and I decide how the family should act. Pasquale, I am forced to say, if you don't like it, you can leave."

It wasn't long before Pasquale contacted friends in Farrell, Pennsylvania, who told him it would be easy to get work in the steel mill there. He packed his belongings and moved out.

Salvatore regretted this unpleasantness with his brother. He was family, and family didn't fight, and he would miss the camaraderie as well as the help with the animals and garden. However, the boys were becoming more helpful, and he had more than enough work to keep him busy. He would not dwell on the difficulties with his brother. Now that Pasquale had left, Maria began to help with many of the tasks he had assumed. She and Salvatore enjoyed working alongside each other in the garden. Until the boys were big enough to handle some of the load, she also helped Salvatore trim the trees and move the cow to different feeding spots. She was a strong woman who could even hold a pig by its hind legs while he slaughtered it.

Sam Celeste, a friend of Salvatore's who had come from the same village in Italy, had left the mill and bought a tavern in downtown Monaca. When he moved his family to an apartment above the tavern, there was now more than one Italian family in town. Soon after, another family opened an Italian *groceria* down the block from the tavern. The community was slowly changing. Occasionally, Salvatore walked into town, stopped at the bank to make a deposit, picked up a few items at the *groceria*, and finally stopped at Sam Celeste's tavern for a drink, which he referred to as "fuel to get me back up the hill."

The families soon began to visit each other as they would in Aliquippa. And then suddenly their world changed more than they could ever have imagined. Everyone would remember October 29, 1929, Black Tuesday, when the stock market crashed. In the mid-twenties, when the stock market was experiencing an unprecedented surge, a friend had advised Salvatore to buy stocks rather than put money in traditional savings. Although Salvatore didn't feel comfortable buying stocks, which he didn't understand, he bought a few shares of U.S. Rubber stock. As the Great Depression began, his fears came true: his stocks were now worthless. Although he didn't like losing hard-earned money, he was glad he hadn't bought more stocks and that he still had his job at Jones & Laughlin. There were stories in all the papers and on the radio about people committing suicide because they'd lost everything. Salvatore and his family were grateful they still had their properties and their work.

The changes were gradual at first. During the winter of 1930, the mill had been cutting back on hours. Having lived through many years of mines opening and closing at will, losing a few hours a week didn't seem too alarming to Salvatore. However, by spring, there were days when he was sent home after being told there was no work for him that day. By mid-1930, the loss of pay was enough that Salvatore and Maria decided they would start selling eggs and milk to make up for his loss of income. This was nothing new, of course. They had done it in Colorado. They could do it here. Instead of the galvanized metal, one-quart pails they used in Colorado, however, Salvatore now bought glass bottles that he would fill with milk and sell milk for seven cents a quart.

Just as their mother had done before them, the girls delivered the milk and eggs on their way to school. As they walked home, they picked up the empty bottles, which Maria washed and refilled, ready for the next day's delivery. The income from the eggs and milk was not enough.

Around this time Frannie became terribly ill. She was doubled over with pain. They took her to the doctor, who told them she would have to have her appendix removed, forcing them to come up with the money for the operation. Frannie had always wanted a vanity like those she had seen in magazines, but there was no money for such luxury. While her daughter was in the hospital, Maria picked up some orange crates and stacked them in a way that made a vanity. By using some chicken feed sacks with a pretty floral pattern, she created a skirt around the vanity. When Frannie arrived home, she spied her beautiful vanity, and sighed, "Oh, mother! It's beautiful." Then she went outside for a little walk. The rabbits and their cage were gone. That was how they were able to pay for the operation. Frannie cried. She had named and made pets of these rabbits, and now it was her problem that caused them to be gone.

Money problems were never discussed in front of the children, but the boys' bedroom was next to the kitchen. In the evenings after they had been sent to bed, Leo and Carl could hear Salvatore and Maria quietly discussing how they were going to make the necessary payments. When the boys heard soft sobs, they knew another hard time was presenting itself.

Salvatore put it off as long as he could, but the day came when he had to tell Frannie she would have to quit school. They needed another person in the household working, and she was the oldest. He and Maria had agonized over this decision for some time because they felt that education was the key to a better life for their children; this was a loss that echoed their own youth. They simply needed more of them working so the family could survive. If he had to choose, the boys would stay in school and get the education they needed to get better jobs that paid enough to support a family. At the time, with the exception of domestic work or teaching, women were rarely in the workforce. And Frannie was the only one old enough to quit school. Dutifully she told them she really didn't mind and would be happy to be able to help. She really meant it. A friend of hers at school had an older sister who was doing housework in nearby Beaver to help her family. The girl had told Frannie her sister knew of another family that was looking for a girl.

Beaver was the county seat, and home to many attorneys, judges, county politicians, business owners, and professionals who worked in Pittsburgh and commuted by train. It was a beautiful, genteel community with a luxuriously broad main street lined with tasteful shops that opened onto a grand central park. The county courthouse dominated the office buildings that surrounded the park, in which there were a charming gazebo and a band shell. The streets off the main square leading to the river were tree lined and adorned with large, stylish, Victorian houses with wraparound porches and turrets and lush lawns overlooking the Ohio River. At this point of its route, the river was still pristine and peaceful, as there was no industry along this stretch. Walking along the banks, one could feel peace at being miles from the industrial soot and clamor that proliferated upstream all the way to Pittsburgh.

But Beaver was more closed to outsiders than Monaca. It was populated almost exclusively by white, Anglo-Saxon Protestants. It was also a dry town and would remain so after Prohibition was lifted and into the future, even though it was said that the best stocked bars in the valley could be found in the privacy of those lofty homes. Somehow the tentacles of the Depression didn't seem to reach into this fair community.

Dressed in her best (and only) church clothes, Frannie went to Beaver with the address clutched in her hand. She walked from the bus stop down a beautiful, tree-lined brick street to a house larger than any she had ever seen before: a grand, three-story, brick Victorian with a wraparound porch. She walked up the steps to a sparkling, beveled glass door with beveled side windows, pulled on a brass door bell, and held her breath. She was frightened and nervous, yet she also didn't know places this beautiful even existed.

A stately woman wearing clothes better than her mother's good church dress, plus jewelry and high heeled shoes, answered the door. This was Mrs. Alenbaugh, whose husband owned a small fabricating plant in the next town, a place where the soot it created would never reach the clean, shining streets of their Beaver home. Mrs. Alenbaugh explained that her previous "girl" had gotten married and had to quit. She was at her wits' end, she said, trying to manage the household, cook, clean, and care for the children. Even though two of the children were in college, she was still overwhelmed with the work. She wanted a girl who could live in, but Frannie said she couldn't do that. Her father insisted that she live at home. After some hesitation, Mrs. Alenbaugh said that since she was in a bind, she would hire Frannie. She was to work six days a week, with Sundays off. And she was to arrive at the Alenbaughs' house by eight thirty in the morning, after Mr. Alenbaugh had left for work. Her first task was to wash the breakfast dishes and those from dinner the night before, and then clean the kitchen. Next, she was to make the beds, clean the rest of the house, do the laundry and ironing, and set the table for dinner. Mrs. Alenbaugh would prepare the meal, but Frannie was to serve cocktails when Mr. Alenbaugh returned from work. She would also serve the meal before she left, which would be around seven in the evening. For this, she would receive four dollars a week.

Frannie was elated to have this job and be able to help her family with her earnings. Back home, she went into great detail describing the house and furnishings, Mrs. Alenbaugh's elegant dress and jewelry, and all the beautiful china, silver, and crystal in the house. Maria cautioned her, "Oh, Frannie, do be careful when cleaning. Whatever you do, don't break anything."

While it sounded exciting, Mauggie was sad that her sister had to do so much work. She (Mauggie) still had to deliver the milk and eggs on her way to school, but Leo was old enough to help with that now. She wanted to do more. Because so many were having it hard, the movie theaters started doing promotional activities to encourage people not to give up going to the movies. Mauggie learned that the Oriental Theater in Rochester was having a talent contest, and the prize was a basket of groceries. Like her father, Mauggie had a beautiful singing voice—a crisp, clear soprano of operatic quality. She wanted to enter the contest at an upcoming Sunday matinee. She was confident she could win the groceries, and in that way, do her part to help her family.

It took some convincing, but Maria persuaded Salvatore to allow Mauggie to go. It was decided that Frannie would go with her since she was off on Sundays. Mauggie decided to sing "My Isle of Golden Dreams." They had a recording of Charles Harrison singing this song, so she played that recording and sang along over and over every day until it was time for the contest. The girls walked to the theater, and Mauggie sang as they went down the hill, across the bridge, and up the street, all the way to the theater. To everyone's pleasure, she won first prize. Overjoyed, she and her sister carried that basket of groceries home.

The next day, a strange man walked up their drive, and asked to see the man of the house. He explained that he had been at the talent show and heard Mauggie sing. He was a talent scout, he said, and he wanted to work with her to get her into a career in music. He said he could get her lessons from a professional singer in Pittsburgh and soon they'd be able to set performance dates. He was confident that Mauggie would have a successful singing career. Salvatore, however, swiftly escorted him off the property. He said his daughter was a good girl, and she was not going to go on the road in such a dubious adventure. He remembered the offer once made to him in Colorado to play and sing with a band. His distain for show business was as strong now as it had been before his daughters were born.

In the heat of August 1931 Salvatore was working in his garden when he saw Christy and Sam Celeste walking up to the house. He knew immediately that they were bearing bad news. Crossing himself, he asked, "Who died?"

Pasquale had died. On an unusually hot day, while he was working next to the stiflingly hot furnace in the mill, Pasquale had complained of a headache and an upset stomach. He'd finished his shift, they said, and stopped on his way out of the mill to drink a large amount of cold water. He'd fallen to the ground. The company doctor said it was heat stroke. Salvatore was inconsolable. He had promised his mother he would take care of the family, and now both brothers under his charge were dead. He felt responsible and still felt guilty because of the way Pasquale had left his home. There must, he kept thinking, have been a better way around that situation...but it was past, and now all he could think about were a widow and a child in Italy without a father. They needed his help. How could he ever make good on his promises to his mother? How could he help Pasquale's family in Italy when there was hardly anything coming in for his family here in Monaca?

They had Pasquale brought back to their home, where he was laid out in the parlor for three days. A steady stream of friends and relatives came from Aliquippa, Youngstown, Farrell, and Pittsburgh. On the day of the funeral, Bachelor's Funeral Home supplied the hearse. Family and friends gathered at the home, and processed down the hill to St. John the Baptist Catholic Church. When they carried the casket from the hearse up the steps to the church, however, they found the door was locked and there was no priest in sight. Salvatore and Christy walked around back to the parish house and knocked and knocked. After a long wait, Father Canova came to the door. He told Salvatore that he refused to say a mass or conduct a Christian burial for Pasquale because he had no record of his attending mass or contributing to the church. A shocked Salvatore tried to explain, to no avail, that Pasquale had been living and working in Farrell, but he wanted him buried in the Monaca cemetery near his brother.

At this point, Christy took Salvatore by the arm, told him he would reason with the good father, and asked him to go back to the front of the church with the others. Father Canova had been born in Italy, and as Salvatore walked back to the front of the church, he could hear Christy speaking to him in Italian.

It wasn't too long before Christy and the priest appeared at the front of the church. The doors were unlocked, and Pasquale received a hurried, but Christian, burial.

"How did you do this?" Salvatore whispered to Christy.

"I asked him to be reasonable and do this for a fellow Italian...And I gave him twenty-five dollars. That always works," Christy replied with a wry smile.

*   *   *

By 1932, the situation all over the U.S. was dire. Many mornings, Salvatore arrived at the mill to find the gate closed. Management came to the gate accompanied by guards to inform the waiting workers that not everyone was needed. They then proceeded to read off names of the men who would work that day. The rest were sent home, only to return the following day to wait and hope their names would be called. Because there was no money, Salvatore stopped taking the bus. He walked the seven miles to the mill, waited to be called, and walked the seven miles back home. Salvatore walked to the plant every day of 1932, but he was only called into the mill to work for four days the entire year. People tried to tell him that he had to change his voter registration to Republican. It was, they all said, because he was a registered Democrat that he was not getting called in to work. The management was Republican, and every elected official in town was Republican. But he emphatically refused to change his registration. He told them "Eh, in 1912 President Taft, a Republican, he called the militia on the coal miners in Colorado. Now this President Hoover, another Republican, makes us lose our working. I will never ever give in to this," he said. "I swear I will never vote for a Republican."

Christy tried to change his mind. So did Frank, who said, "Look, Salvatore. I changed to Republican, and I get called in while you get sent home."

"No! I never do that. This America is a free country and I'm a Democrat."

"So you register Republican," said his friend. "When you are in the booth, you can vote for whoever you want. No one will know how you vote."

Salvatore shook his head. "No! These men, they pick you up in their car and drive you to the polls. They tell you to vote straight Republican and stand outside the booth while you are in there. If you take too long, they report you for voting Democrat. Why waste time to play their game?"

"So don't take long. You vote the straight Democrat ticket. They'll never know."

Salvatore stood his ground. "But I know. I don't keep a secret from nobody what I feel. I am Democrat and that is it."

As in every situation of principles in his life, he refused to compromise his values. He continued to walk that seven miles to work every day. But when he wasn't called in, he would look for work anywhere he could find it.

Mr. LeGoullion had a coal tipple near the rail bridge at Fourth Street. Sam Celeste told Salvatore that Mr. LeGoullion wanted to enlarge his tipple, and was looking for a few men to dig out the hillside for another loading area. Salvatore hurried to the coal tipple and was hired to do the job for a few dollars. Soon he began selling vegetables from his garden along with the milk and eggs. But he also needed feed for the animals. Everywhere he turned, there was something that required money, but the money wasn't coming in.

He was still paying the bank on the mortgage on the house in West Aliquippa, he was paying the balance on the farm directly to the people who had sold it to him, and he was paying the farmer for the lots in Youngstown. In desperation, he met with Mr. Kopecky, the man he had bought the farm from, and persuaded him to allow him to make payments on the interest without paying on the principle until he could earn more. Then he tried the owner of the land in Youngstown. He was down to fifty dollars left to pay, and the owner wanted it all right away. But there was no money. He just couldn't do it. So for the want of fifty dollars, Salvatore lost the two Youngstown lots.

When he went to the bank to discuss the mortgage on the house in West Aliquippa, the bank would not compromise or make a deal. So he went to the house to confront his renters about the need for them to pay him. They had not paid their rent in several months, but now he had to have the money. When he got there, he found the house empty. The family had moved without telling him or paying any back rent. As he walked through the house, he found they had broken the toilet, ripped the sink off the wall in the bathroom, and left holes in the walls and broken windows. Anything that was not attached had been stripped out of the place. And they had left garbage everywhere.

Salvatore could not pay for the repairs to his house, nor could he afford to legally go after the renters for the money. And he could not make payments on the taxes. He explored all avenues, but with no luck. When every possible solution had been exhausted, he surrendered the house in West Aliquippa to the bank.

In these hard times, working-class families became resourceful, using ingenuity and cooperation to get by. Salvatore and Maria were old hands at this. Their children's clothes were wearing out and there was no money to buy anything new. They still kept a trunk of Pasquale's clothes in the basement. Maria went through it, found usable clothing, cut down what she could for the boys, and also altered a few things for Salvatore. In the 1930s, chicken feed sacks and flour sacks were made of print fabrics. Maria used these to make dresses for the girls, and then used some that were not flowered for shirts for the boys. She looked at pictures of the new clothing in the Sears catalog, then drew her own patterns on newspaper and cut them out. Using these homemade patterns, she created new clothes for her family.

The O'Keeffe family lived in a small shack behind their property. Mr. O'Keeffe, a widower with seven children, drank heavily, and so the children were left to care for themselves. When Maria made soup, she often made a big pot so she could send some to the O'Keeffes. One son, Jimmy, was a friend of Carl's. When Maria was making shirts for Leo and Carl out of some striped chicken feed sacks, she also made one for Jimmy and told Carl to give it to him. When Jimmy got that shirt, he came to see Maria, and through tears, hugged and kissed her. He and Carl would remain lifelong friends.

Using plain feed sacks, Maria made the girls new dresses and dyed them black to make them look more fashionable. But through washings, the black dye eventually faded to a washed-out greenish gray. Mauggie came home from school one day furious because the Cavanaugh girl, whose father was the bank manager, had made a snippy comment. The girl was always dressed in the latest fashion, and she even drove a little horse drawn carriage to school. On this day, and in front of several of her friends, she laughed at Mauggie and said, "I just love your green dress. Is that a new color this season?" to which all the other girls broke into laughter.

Mauggie said she would not go back to school. Salvatore said that was fine. She could look for work, too. The boys could then stay in school and graduate. He believed that the ideal would have been for all of his children to graduate from high school, but during the Great Depression, like many other fathers, he really had no choice. As soon as Mauggie said she didn't want to go back to school, she was sorry. She desperately wanted to graduate from high school. Why hadn't she controlled her tongue? But she also knew the family needed her help, and, yes, she was too proud to go to school dressed so poorly.

Within days, they received a visit from the truant officer. He explained that Mauggie was not yet at the legal age to quit school, and the family would be fined $100 if she did not return. Salvatore told the man she could not go to school because they didn't have the money to buy her shoes. How could he pay them $100 if he couldn't afford shoes for his daughter? The truant officer told them he could help solve the shoe problem. The owner of the local shoe store was offering to give shoes to children who could not afford them so that they could attend school. He gave Salvatore a voucher that Mauggie only had to give to the owner to get a new pair of shoes. Salvatore agreed she would go back to school.

Mauggie returned to school the next day wearing her old shoes with holes in the soles. After school, she and her girlfriend walked into town to the shoe store. When she gave the owner the voucher, he went into the back room and came out with an old pair of high-button shoes that had been out of fashion for years. Remembering the teasing she'd received because of her faded dress, Mauggie thanked the owner for the offer but said she had received a new pair of shoes for her birthday, and would not need these.

On the walk home, her girlfriend asked why she had refused the shoes. It wasn't her birthday, and she didn't have any new shoes. Mauggie replied she would have been humiliated to wear old-fashioned high-button shoes. When she told Salvatore what had happened, he became angry. He said she could have taken them, and he would have cut them down, or he could have taken the soles and tacked them onto her worn-out shoes. She felt terrible about what she had done, and cried until Maria told her they would work something out. Mauggie wasn't expecting what happened.

Salvatore took her back to the store and, much to her embarrassment, got the high-button shoes. When they arrived home, he sat on the floor with his metal shoe form between his legs, and cut the tops off, creating a crude pair of low cut shoes. They were too big for her, though, and so stiff they didn't bend when she walked. She wore them, but she developed blisters and her feet bled. But she was back in school. Salvatore then tacked the leather he had cut from the tops of Mauggie's "new" shoes onto the bottoms of Carl's worn out shoes, making new soles for them. Salvatore was both resourceful and stubborn.

Now winter was coming, and there was no money for coal, and so Salvatore took the boys into the woods in search of dead or fallen trees. Every time they found a tree, he cut it into manageable lengths for him and the boys to carry home, where Salvatore split the wood into smaller pieces that would fit into the furnace. They carried the cut wood into the basement, and stacked it along the walls. The three of them continued this process until they had a basement filled with enough wood to get them through the winter.

Christmas was approaching. Salvatore and Maria wanted to make it special for the children this year because last Christmas had been particularly hard. At that time, they had been trying to make all the payments on the properties they had lost during the year, so there was absolutely nothing for the holiday. Maria had been able to save one dollar, which she used to buy enough yarn to knit scarves for the children. That was all they got for Christmas last year, and there wasn't a tree. The girls had been old enough to understand the hardship, but the boys had been too young to understand, and when they'd seen those scarves, they'd asked, voices heavy with disappointment, "Is that all?" Maria had felt so terrible that she was determined that Christmas this year would be better.

Even though they were in their teens, the girls still had dolls. Maria spent hours after the children had gone to bed making new clothes for the dolls out of left-over pieces of fabric. While he was in the woods, Salvatore hunted for just the right tree branches to make slingshots for the boys. Then he made them red haw poppers. A red haw is a very small berry like a little crab apple. Salvatore found the right size elderberry bush and hollowed out some stalks to make the barrels, then whittled down sections of an old broomstick for the popper. These were used to fire the harmless red haws at targets of animals, birds, enemies, or each other.

As the big day approached, Salvatore took the boys into the woods to search for a Christmas tree. They found one the boys agreed was just right, cut it down, and took it home. Maria made popcorn from kernels from the garden they had dried, and the children strung them for garlands. They also salvaged pieces of colored paper from school or thrown away food wrappers, and cut out ornaments. The boys scavenged for broken pieces of glass or colorful pieces of metal lying along the roadsides and fashioned more ornaments. The family thus had a bright cheerful tree for Christmas, one they would talk of for years to come. Maria also had pieces of fruit from the garden that she had candied and tucked into the children's stockings.

Salvatore went to the Italian *groceria* to buy the traditional fish for their Christmas Eve dinner. They had a store bill for purchases of spaghetti, olive oil, and other Italian food stuffs they regularly used. Salvatore paid five dollars on the bill and handed Mr. Taormina his list. He was told they would give him no more food on credit until the bill was paid in full. Salvatore was furious at the coldness of the grocer, and all the way home he agonized over the thought of no fish for Christmas Eve supper. But as he entered the house, he put on a happy face, and declared, "This year we eat no fish on Christmas Eve. This year we have a special meal." Maria didn't need to ask why.

He butchered the oldest chicken, which no longer produced eggs, and they roasted it for their Christmas Eve feast. The children acted like they enjoyed their treat, but they were sad to lose another animal. They also reported eating meat on Christmas Eve in confession.

* * *

Spring came early in 1933, and it was a beautiful March. Salvatore got called in to work for one day that month. The pay was $2.75 for the day, but after management had taken all the deductions, he came home with seventy-five cents, an echo of his first week in the Colorado mines. On his way home from work, he stopped at the Italian *groceria* and gave Mr. Taormina fifty cents toward his bill.

But there was always more debt. Afraid of running up too large a bill at any one place, Salvatore and Maria shopped a little at each of the three grocery stores in their neighborhood. As he received money, Salvatore went to each store and made a small payment. The shop owners, with the exception of the *groceria*, were all good about this arrangement, but times were also hard for them too with so many people buying on credit.

Mr. Delzelle, another grocery store owner, had just retired and turned his store over to his son. One day Maria sent Leo to the store to get a tin of baking soda. The store was full of people when he stepped up to the counter. The Delzelles' son refused to sell him the baking soda. Then he said in a loud voice, "You tell your mother your family owes us thirty-three dollars. There will be no more credit until the bill is paid off."

They stopped going to that store. Still, every time Salvatore got work, he made the rounds to all four stores, the one in town, and the three on the hill, and paid each one fifty cents until all the bills were paid in full. During the gardening season, he picked carrots, radishes, onions, lettuce, and rhubarb and took little bundles of the vegetables to Herk's grocery store. Mr. Herk deducted five cents per bundle from his bill.

* * *

Every time Salvatore and Maria and the children visited friends and family in West Aliquippa, Charlie managed to see Frannie. Eventually he got up the nerve to hitchhike to Monaca for an official visit. Salvatore was a strict father who did not allow his girls to date or have gentleman callers. This was not uncommon among the Italian families, and it was well known in the town that he was among the strictest of the strict. Even though Charlie and Frannie had known each other since early childhood, Charlie still had to make the required, formal visit to ask Salvatore's permission to begin seeing Frannie. As the two men talked in the living room, Maria, Frannie, and Mauggie busied themselves in the kitchen. The girls of course were not very attentive to what they were doing because they were straining to hear what was being said in the other room. Maria, doing the same thing, was admonishing the girls to stick to their tasks.

Salvatore listened with a stern look on his face as Charlie pled his case. There was a long awkward silence, and then he replied, "Charlie, I know you and your family a long time. You are a good boy, but you have some idea about my oldest daughter. I say you can come to my house to see her, but that is all. You visit here with her. That is all. And..." poking his finger at his chest, "no monkey business."

Charlie thanked him, and, sweating profusely, assured Salvatore that his intentions were honorable. And that "There will be no monkey business."

Maria then brought in some lemonade. While Frannie and Charlie sat in the living room sipping it slowly, Salvatore, Maria, and Mauggie sat in clear view and hearing range in the kitchen.

Getting mail was a rarity that often meant bad news. In the summer, when Maria received a letter from Detroit, it was different. She quickly opened it and read, to her pleasure, that it was from Minnie, her cousin James' daughter. She knew through correspondences with her sisters that James and Phyllis and their children had moved to Detroit in 1921. She also knew Minnie had married a young man of Italian heritage named Peter, who had been born in Illinois and raised in Detroit, and that they had a daughter. She had never had direct communication with anyone in Detroit, however, and now here in a letter Minnie was saying that she wanted to talk to Maria, but couldn't find a phone number. She gave her phone number in the letter and asked if Maria would give her a call as soon as she received it.

Minnie couldn't get a phone number for Maria because they had no telephone. Now Maria's pleasure turned to worry.

Why would Minnie want to talk to her? There must be a problem. One of her parents must be sick or dying or worse. Wilma across the lane had a telephone, so Maria went over there to ask if she could make a long-distance phone call. It must, she said, be an emergency, and she would pay for the call. Wilma said of course she could use the telephone, and not to worry about the cost. She then took Maria to her phone and placed the call for her.

Maria's relief in finding there was no emergency soon turned to pleasure when Minnie told her she had been trying to reach her because they wanted to come for a visit. Her husband, Peter, worked as a machinist in the Chrysler plant in Detroit. He was working regularly, for as bad as the times were for many people, others were earning enough to buy cars. Peter had a few vacation days coming up. Minnie's parents and brothers had moved back to Colorado, and they usually went to visit them on his vacations, but this time there were too few days for that long trip. Minnie told Maria that her husband had said western Pennsylvania was close enough to drive it in one day, and so they could have a few days for a nice visit. Maria was overjoyed. Minnie was just a few years older than Frannie, so she must have been seven or eight the last time Maria had seen her. Salvatore, who remembered her, too, thought the visit would be a good thing for Maria. The children were excited at the idea of meeting a relative from the family's Colorado days. And someone who took vacations, had a telephone, and owned a car? *They must be rich.*

Maria quickly put the family to work in preparation for the visit. The boys had to clean and trim the yard and the plantings. They also had to scrub the walls inside the house while the girls helped wash curtains, scrub floors, and bake.

The day Minnie, Peter, and their daughter arrived, Salvatore was at work, and the boys were doing their odd Saturday jobs. As the car pulled into the driveway, Maria, Frannie, and Mauggie ran out of the house to greet them, swarming round Minnie and her daughter, hugging and kissing and crying and laughing all at the same time. Chattering away, they swept Minnie and Margaret Louise into the house, leaving Peter standing alone outside. Within minuets, Maria ran out of the house, apologizing profusely as she took him by the arm and led him inside. For years he would tease her about their first meeting and his being left out in the driveway.

The first thing Maria did was to take Minnie into the dining room to show her the framed picture on the buffet of the family standing in front of their home in Starkville, with baby Minnie in a neighbor's arms. When Salvatore came home, he was soon having a welcoming drink with Peter as they got acquainted, speaking in Italian. Peter's father had lived in the same Italian province as Salvatore, and so growing up Peter had learned Salvatore's dialect. The boys were fascinated by Peter's car and full of questions. Peter made friends for life with them when he took them for a spin around the hill. The families formed an immediate and lasting bond.

* * *

Maria was a big woman. She was tall, and through the years and with the birth of each child, she had retained some weight. She always wore her dresses loose. Sam Celeste and his wife came to visit one night, and they had a pleasant evening, but as soon as they left, Maria informed Salvatore she was having labor pains. Aside from Salvatore, no one knew she was pregnant. She was forty years old and starting the change of life, but such things as pregnancy and menopause just weren't talked about in those days. They had simply never mentioned her pregnancy to anyone, and because of her size, not even the family suspected.

When the children awoke the next morning, they found a new baby brother. When the girls told the neighbors they had a new brother, the neighbors didn't believe them. But it was true, there he was. Once again, Salvatore had delivered a son. And following the tradition for the third son in an Italian family to be named for his father, the boy would be named Salvatore.

The girls were delighted. Now they had a real, live doll to pamper and play mother with. And little Salvatore was a delightful baby with clear blue eyes just like his grandmother's. The family soon decided baby Salvatore should be called Sam because it would be easier to have one Salvatore and one Sam in the house. The girls felt Sam sounded younger, a more American name. It suited Maria just fine. But even though he went along with it, Salvatore always called his son Salvatore.

In addition to helping with baby Sam, Frannie and Mauggie now did the laundry and cleaning and cooking when they were not doing other work and Frannie was not at Mrs. Alenbaugh's house. Maria taught them how to make all the traditional dishes. Leo and Carl also jumped in and tackled major cleaning and repair jobs. They started by cleaning the wallpaper. Because of the coal furnace, the walls became soot covered, and needed frequent cleaning. They bought Kutol Wall Cleaner, a soft clayish substance that they softened with their hands and rolled all along the walls. As it went along, it picked up the dirt, and the wallpaper became bright and clean. Like most children, they loved playing with this stuff, a product that eventually would evolved into Play Doh.

There was always music in the house, and Mauggie sang almost constantly. When Frannie washed the dishes and Mauggie dried, Mauggie always fell behind because she kept leaning out the open window and singing at the top of her voice. Mauggie was also a prankster and often teased her sister while they were doing chores. Frannie, the serious one, got annoyed and usually walked away, leaving Mauggie to finish the chore by herself. Carl also liked to play jokes, but he was more clever than his sister and seldom got caught. As the girls were standing at the sink and Carl was getting a drink, he might reach around behind Mauggie and pull Frannie's apron string loose. Mauggie would loudly proclaim it was Carl who would deny it, and of course, everyone believed it was Mauggie. Leo was in the middle as far as mischief was concerned, but he had a temper. When Mauggie teased him, he fought back, usually chasing her around the house. One day when she had done something to raise his anger, he began chasing her again. As she came to the kitchen sink, she stopped and stuck out her foot, kicking him just above the eye and giving him a terrible cut. Maria took after her with a wooden spoon, and Mauggie ran around the rooms, jumping over the beds, and finally out the door. By the time she came back inside, all was calm. Maria was a push-over, and the children knew it, but Salvatore was not. There was no raucous fighting when he was around. Even though everyone was overworked with not enough money coming in, and even though Salvatore was a no-nonsense taskmaster, it was a vibrant happy household.

Leo and Carl did everything together. When a relative from Youngstown was visiting and it grew late, Maria invited him to spend the night. Carl and Leo were supposed to be asleep in the bedroom next to the kitchen, where the adults were sitting around the kitchen table. The boys overheard their conversation. Salvatore was saying when the relative was ready for bed, they would move one of the boys to the couch so the visitor could sleep in his bed. Later that night, when they went into the bedroom to move one of the boys, they found that Carl and Leo had tied themselves together so as not to be separated. The visitor was happy to sleep on the couch.

One day, as Maria was preparing lunch and Salvatore began teasing her, she jokingly told him to stop or she would beat him up. He joked back that he could take her in a fight. Then he wrapped his arms around her, and they began playing at wrestling while the children squealed and laughed. Suddenly they lost their footing and, arm in arm, fell heavily to the floor. When they landed, there was a loud cracking sound under them that stopped all the laughter. Salvatore got up immediately and went down into the basement to inspect. They had cracked one of the floor joists. He and the boys went into the woods a bit later, and he choose a straight, solid-looking tree, cut it down, and brought it home. He wedged it into place under the cracked joist, where it supported the kitchen floor for years.

Later that year, when the young ladies sodality at the church decided to hold a dance, Maria convinced Salvatore that the girls could go. Because they were working so hard, they deserved a little leisure activity. "You don't want them to grow old with no childhood...like you, do you?" asked Maria. Salvatore thought it over and agreed. Maria, carrying baby Sam in her arms, walked with the girls down the hill to the dance at the church hall.

Paolo, a young man who had just turned twenty and had come from Italy when he was fifteen, worked on the railroad in Coraopolis and had lived with *paesanos* until he got a job at the Jones & Laughlin plant and moved to West Aliquippa. He was now living in a boarding house with his father, a cousin, and a few other young Italian men. Fair complexioned, blond, handsome, and a dapper dresser, he loved to dance and was a street wise, fast mover whom everyone in his crowd called Paul. He and a few friends decided to go to Monaca that evening to the sodality dance.

The men were standing along the wall and sizing up the potential dancers when Paul spotted Mauggie walking into the room. He asked, "Hey, who's that pretty girl?"

One of the friends from West Aliquippa knew the family. He cautioned Paul, "You better stay away from her. She's Salvatore's daughter. You don't mess with her. He's very strict. They never go to dances alone. You see the mother with her?"

Paul never took his eyes off Mauggie. "I'm going to marry that girl," he announced.

His friends laughed. "You don't even know her," someone said.

But he was not one to be laughed at. "I know enough," he said as he crossed the room and asked for Maria's permission to dance with Mauggie.

Paul was a smooth dancer and a smooth talker. And on the way home, he was all Mauggie could talk about. Maria smiled to think her daughter was smitten, but she also thought it would go nowhere. She could see this man was much too fast and too experienced for her daughter.

Paul checked on Salvatore at the mill and asked around town about Mauggie and her family. The following weekend, he was at the door and asking for an audience with Salvatore. He made the same request Charlie had made, but with all the right words, as one would in Italy. He was from the same province as Salvatore and spoke to him in the Abruzzese dialect. Salvatore enjoyed speaking with him in his native dialect, but was not softened. He gave Paul the same cold look he had given Charlie and the same sermon about "no monkey business." Then he agreed to allow Mauggie to have Paul as an occasional visitor and possible suitor.

* * *

The Presidential election of 1932 had become a free-for-all with seven candidates, including the incumbent Herbert Hoover for the Republicans, Franklin Delano Roosevelt for the Democrats, Norman Thomas for the Socialists, and four more. Roosevelt swept into office with a landslide, carrying forty-two states and 472 electoral votes to Hoover's 59. He also carried with him a Democratic House and Senate. Roosevelt's overwhelming victory did not, of course, usher in a quick solution to the Depression. 1933 was worse than 1932, with an official unemployment count going over twenty-five percent. A third bank panic occurred that year, resulting in President Roosevelt declaring a bank holiday, which closed all financial institutions in an effort to stop a run on the banks. There was no work to be found anywhere. People were even buying less milk and eggs.

Mauggie was now sixteen and legally able to quit school. As much as she wanted to stay and graduate, she had no choice. Things were just too bad, so she left at the end of tenth grade and got a job cleaning the house of the banker whose daughter had laughed at her faded, feed sack dress. The banker's house was a grand, three-story Victorian on Atlantic Avenue with a round turret on one end and the porch wrapped around the other. The back of the house overlooked the river. The job was only for one day a week, but because hardly anyone could find work at this time, Mauggie felt fortunate to get the job. The daughter was still in school, the father worked at the bank, and the mother was busy with charity work. Mauggie was to arrive early, strip the bed linens, do the laundry, clean the entire house, remake the beds, and start preparations for dinner. Her earnings were $1.25 for a full day's work. The banker came home every day for lunch, but his wife was never at home. She left her husband a prepared lunch and then went off to one meeting or another or a bridge group or shopping.

One day during the first week, when the banker came home for lunch, Mauggie was dusting in the living room. He walked in to greet her and asked how her day was going. He slyly put his arm around her waist while he was talking to her. Mauggie was quite naive, but she knew that behavior was not right. It made her very uncomfortable. From that day forward, when the banker arrived home, she always made sure she was out on the porch sweeping and washing the steps. She worked vigorously outside until he had eaten his lunch and returned to the bank. He jokingly told her they must have the cleanest porch in town. Mauggie laughed, but that was how it went as long as she worked there.

Meanwhile Mrs. Alenbaugh's daughter was getting married. She told Frannie she needed an extra girl to help through the preparations. Wedding gifts were being sent, and they had to be unwrapped and displayed in the living room. There were also parties that required extra cleaning and ironing. And someone had to watch the other children while all this was going on. Mauggie wanted to get away from that house on Atlantic Avenue, so she jumped at the chance to be the extra help in Beaver.

When the wedding was over, the neighbor behind the Alenbaughs approached Mauggie for a job cleaning their house. She had been impressed by what she'd seen of her work. Now both girls were working in Beaver and went to and from work together. Rather than pay the ten-cent trolley fair, they saved money and walked both ways. The time of their commute flew by as they chattered about Charlie and Paul.

The money the girls earned helped the family, but Salvatore was getting only one day a month at the mill, so the family was still struggling. The neighbors told Maria they were getting free butter and sugar from a food station set up in town by the government. Vowing never to repeat the humiliation of the shoes, however, Salvatore refused to go or to let anyone in the family go, declaring, "We are a strong family. We never take charity and we work for everything we have." President Roosevelt had unveiled his WPA, public works program, by this time. One of the projects was to build a stone wall along the hillside on Fourteenth Street, which was the main artery from town up the hill to Monaca Heights. Salvatore got a job on that project, and for his work he also received the supplies that were being given out. This way he was working to earn the free supplies.

When Carl and Leo got home from school, they had work to do with the animals and garden. The cow had to be chained in the field so that she could graze, and the chickens and pigs had to be fed and given water. Then the eggs had to be collected. After these chores were done, the boys had to clean out the pens and carry everything to the compost pit, gather up new straw and spread it in the pens and chickens' nests. These chores didn't always run smoothly. There was the day the boys put the cow out to graze, but when they went back to move her, she was missing. The boys searched and searched until they finally found her in the neighbor's apple orchard eating the apples hanging in the trees. By the time the boys got her home, she was enormously swollen. Salvatore said he had seen this happen in Italy. The cow was filling up with gas, which needed to be relieved or she would die. He ran into the house, got one of Maria's long hat pins, and after walking around the cow and studying her, stuck the pin into her side. He hit the proper spot, a huge rush of air blew out of her, and she was relieved. The only problem was that her milk tasted like cider for several days, so they couldn't sell it until it returned to normal.

One day Frannie came home from work and told her brothers that Mrs. Alenbaugh's neighbor needed some odd jobs done. She had asked if Frannie knew any boys who would like to make a little extra money. Frannie immediately said yes, and Leo and Carl were happy to be able to work. On Saturday, they walked to the lady's house in Beaver. She looked them over and commented that they were not very big for the work to be done and that Carl seemed awfully young. They assured her they were good workers. After carefully studying them, she decided they would do, so she put them to work cutting the grass, trimming the shrubs, and raking and bundling all the trimmings. She then asked if they knew how to paint. They said of course they did, even though Carl had never painted before. She took them up to the third floor of the house and showed them a room she wanted to be cleaned and painted.

At midday, she called them down into the basement, where she gave them little tea sandwiches on rye toast with the crusts cut off and glasses of milk. They had never seen such tiny sandwiches before, and they had definitely never had the crusts cut off the bread, but they thanked her politely, ate their lunch, and went back up to the room they were painting. At the end of the day, she walked through the room, carefully inspecting their work, and said they had done a very nice job. She gave them only seventy-five cents to split between them. They thanked her and started their walk home, grumbling the whole way about what a cheapskate she was. But they were still happy to have something to give their mother.

*   *   *

Roosevelt's New Deal had energized the organizers of the unions that had suffered significant losses during the Depression. They went back to trying to organize in Aliquippa, but Jones & Laughlin used even hasher tactics to keep the unions out. Salvatore came home almost every night with stories of the intrigue around the mill gates. As in Colorado, workers who were heard talking about a possible union were fired and thrown out of company-owned houses. The organizers were beaten up and put on trains heading out of town. Because of this rough treatment, the union moved its base out of Aliquippa, and set up operation across the river in Ambridgc.

Salvatore told Maria one of the workers had been caught getting signatures for the union and had disappeared for days. The man's family finally found him. He had been arrested and taken to a mental hospital south of Pittsburgh, where he was committed as mentally ill. It was just like the mining company had done to Mother Jones in Trinidad. Maria warned Salvatore not to get involved in these activities. Her warning wasn't necessary, though. He was not getting work because he had let his political beliefs be known; he was not going to do anything more to jeopardize his family.

Other men, however, were risking everything to get involved, and the retaliations were brutal. Organizers sent word of this incident to Governor Pinchot, who ordered the man released from the mental institution. The governor also sent state police to protect the workers, and Mrs. Pinchot went to Aliquippa to deliver a speech in support of the workers. And yet several of the men who attended her speech were fired, and the managers of the plant sent guards with guns into the plant as a show of strength to quell any momentum.

While union activities stimulated a lot of talk, they were not foremost on Salvatore's mind. He had his family and their homestead to worry about. He continued to walk every day to the mill and back, and used all the creativity in his power to eke out as much as he could to stay afloat. Now that he had five children, and the Great Depression seemed deeper, Salvatore was more worried than ever. He had to get more money to make the taxes and house payments. Like most working-class families, ways of getting by had to be developed.

Salvatore decided to sell his tomatoes in addition to the other vegetables. All the Italians in West Aliquippa needed more tomatoes than they could grow in their own tiny garden plots for the sauce they would make in a year. Salvatore told the men at work he had tomatoes to sell. When it was time to pick them, he filled bushel baskets until they were heaping full and sold them for seventy-five cents a bushel. Leo continued selling milk and eggs, and on weekends he canvassed the stores in town for odd jobs. Shop owners hired him to clean out a storeroom, unpack supplies, or wash windows for fifteen cents here and twenty-five cents there. Carl took a bushel basket and walked through the alleys and side streets looking for bottles and pieces of broken glass, then took what he collected to the Phoenix Glass plant in town. They paid five cents a bushel for colored glass and seven cents a bushel for clear glass. If he came upon any scraps of iron or other metal, he picked them up to save for the old rag man, who occasionally rode through the neighborhood with his horse and wagon. He paid pennies for rags, old tires, and iron and other scraps of metal.

In the spring, Leo and Carl took two old wash tubs and went to the houses along Atlantic Avenue, where the people had money. They rang door bells and, for fifteen cents a house, offered to clean the ashes out of their furnaces and dump them over the hill by the river. They also walked along the railroad tracks on their way home, looking for lumps of coal that had fallen from passing trains. The coal would be helpful in heating the house. Doing this could be dangerous because the tracks were occasionally patrolled by armed plant guards who would shoot scavengers.

During the summer drought, Salvatore was afraid he would lose his crops of vegetables and the income they brought. Because of the drought, he couldn't use water from the well, so he had the boys take buckets down to the stream in the woods, fill them, and carry them home to water the plants. They did this until the drought ended. That was also the year when his grapes didn't yield enough to make wine, so he and the boys picked all the wild berries they could find, and Salvatore made berry wine that year. It wasn't very good, but better than no wine at all.

* * *

Mauggie and Frannie were seeing Paul and Charlie regularly now. One evening while the couples were visiting in the parlor, Sam Celeste came calling on Salvatore with friends from Beaver Falls. Salvatore welcomed Rosa and her son and asked them to join him at the kitchen table, where he poured everyone a glass of wine and Maria set out a plate of biscotti. Once the pleasantries were concluded, Sam explained that Rosa's son was interested in Mauggie. The custom back in the old country was for the parent of the son to visit the parent of the daughter with a proposal to work out an arranged marriage.

Sam Celeste thus came as the neutral party to introduce the interested family to Salvatore. Rosa was from Salvatore's village in Italy, and as they were being introduced, Salvatore mentioned that he remembered her as a child. Now widowed, Rosa presented her proposition to Salvatore. Her son had his own business, and she owned several houses in Beaver Falls. Rosa said that Mauggie would be very lucky to marry such a successful man and into a family that was fairly comfortable during these difficult times. Rosa knew that Salvatore would have no dowry to present, but she was willing to accept that sacrifice for her son's happiness. In fact, she would provide one of her houses for the newlyweds.

Salvatore replied that her offer was most generous, but Mauggie already had a suitor, Paul, who was in the parlor with her this very minute. Rosa responded that she was aware of Mauggie's suitor, for she had had Mauggie's situation thoroughly investigated before deciding this was an acceptable arrangement for her son. This Paul, she said, was working, but he was living in a boarding house with his father and several men, none of whom had any property. He was not in a position to offer all that her son could offer. Surely Salvatore could see the wisdom in this proposed union. As a good father, she suggested that he turn away this current suitor and inform his daughter that she would marry Rosa's son.

Salvatore immediately stopped the conversation. He informed the widow that his daughter was free to choose the man she wanted to marry. Rosa complained that he was rejecting the proper way marriages were arranged in the old country. It was how she had been promised to her husband, and they had had a good marriage. It was a good custom.

"But," said Salvatore, "we are not in the old country." He had chosen his wife without any arrangements, and his children were free to choose their spouses. Her son was permitted to call on Mauggie, and after meeting him, she could make the decision as to which man she would marry. Rosa reluctantly agreed to this, and her son began calling on Mauggie. The courtship lasted a very short time. Salvatore told Mauggie she was allowed to have the two suitors so that she could make a decision, but he was not going to permit this carrying-on with two suitors very long. She had better make up her mind right away. Paul, unhappy with the competition, made sure to always be there when the other man came calling. Mauggie was still working in Beaver and walking to and from work. Now when she left work, she usually found Paul waiting on the street corner to walk her home. She was flattered and told him it was very far for him to walk, hard for him to make it from work. But he insisted this was what he wanted. He was not going to give the other suitor a single opportunity to be alone with her.

It didn't take Mauggie long to make her decision. She knew from her first meeting with Rosa's son that he was not the man for her. She also knew from that night at the dance when they first met that it was going to be Paul she married. He was delighted to hear her say this and told her he wanted to get married as soon as possible. But Mauggie told him that, as the older sister, Frannie should be married first. Frannie and Charlie wanted to marry, too, but he was earning so little that they could not afford a place to live, and Frannie was still giving all her earnings to her parents to save the homestead. And so this tradition of family order did persist.

Salvatore was determined that his sons were going to graduate from high school. The income from the girls was needed until at least Leo graduated. He was now in high school, but he was embarrassed because for the first time, he was with the students from town who dressed nicer than he did. He also now had to take gym class, where the other boys wore gym trunks, but he just had his work blue jeans. When he told Maria about his embarrassment, she found photos of running shorts in the Sears, Roebuck catalog, then found some fabric and made him a pair of the shorts. He also liked sports, but because of all the work that had to be done at home and extra jobs for pay, he had no time to become active in any school sports. Maria knew how much he wanted this, so she knitted him a varsity sweater like those they saw in the movies. She made it gray, trimmed in red, the Monaca school colors, and sewed a big "M" on it. He was thrilled and proud to go to school wearing his varsity sweater.

Leo knew his family could not afford these extra things he was getting and felt guilty. Wanting to do more to help, he found a job working the counter at the Islay's ice cream store and delicatessen in town. The job was in the evenings after school, which meant Carl had to take over more of the jobs at home and also assume the responsibility of the egg and milk sales. Little Sam was too young to assume any responsibility, but he would follow along with Carl and help where he could.

Leo enjoyed his job at Islay's, but he had to work late into the night, cleaning and scrubbing floors after closing, which took him past midnight. This made him tired the next day in school, but he didn't mind. His pay was twenty-five cents an hour, but he wasn't paid for the clean-up time after the store closed. He didn't mind the hours or the low pay because he was contributing at home. When he was working the counter, he could meet and talk to many of the town kids he had not met at the high school.

One girl in particular caught his eye and his interest, but she didn't attend his school. Emily was a perky little redhead from Beaver who spent a great deal of time visiting her grandmother in Monaca. Her father and grandfather had management positions, and so her family lived comfortably. She was a pretty, well dressed girl. Because her grandfather liked ice cream after dinner, she always enthusiastically volunteered to walk to Islay's to get it for him. Her grandmother knew she was doing this so she could see Leo and thought it was nothing more than a cute diversion. Surely this was a young girl's infatuation with a good looking man from another culture; a harmless flirtation that would not last.

Charlie and Paul were continuing their regular visits with Frannie and Mauggie, and the couples were again talking about marriage. Charlie had known Mauggie as long as he had known Frannie, and was a warm open person with a great sense of humor. He kept the visits lively, but Paul could be a hot head and extremely jealous. He did not like the attention Charlie paid to Mauggie. At the end of their evening visits, the two young men hitchhiked home together, usually getting a ride to the tunnel from someone driving to Aliquippa. Then they walked through the tunnel to their homes. One night, when they were walking in the middle of the tunnel, Paul stopped and told Charlie he had been making passes at Mauggie all night and that it was going to stop. Charlie was surprised and denied any romantic intentions. But Paul was not appeased. He threw a punch that turned into a fist fight there in the tunnel.

The next night, it was obvious there had been a fight, and there was tension between them, though no one said anything. Bothered by what she saw and figuring out what was going on, Maria invited Paul to step aside for a talk. She told him that she knew he was a good person and a hard worker. She knew he would provide well for her daughter. But she also knew he had a bad temper. "You will have arguments," she said. "All married people have arguments. But I warn you now, don't you ever touch my daughter in anger." He listened intently and spoke humbly. He admitted to having a bad temper and said that was something he was working on. He promised solemnly that he would never hit Mauggie. That was the end of the conversation.

Soon afterward, Paul made a surprise peace offering by taking Maria and Mauggie to the Stanley Theater in Pittsburgh to see a live performance of the Jimmy Dorsey Band. He knew Maria loved music, and he said that he would be pleased to take them to see other popular orchestras. Mauggie was impressed by these extravagances. Although Maria was not swayed by Paul's gestures, she was pleased. She had never traveled into Pittsburgh before, and certainly had never seen these famous big bands in person.

* * *

Although work was picking up slightly, there was such an accumulation of bills from the years when there was no work that Salvatore continually struggled to keep the house and pay off his debts. They were living almost entirely off the land, selling everything they didn't absolutely need or could live without. He used ingenuity to get work done at the lowest cost. For example, he devised a tripod and ran a chain through it with a pulley at the top. When it was time to butcher a hog, he smacked the animal in the head with a hammer to knock it unconscious. Then he and Maria carried it to the tripod. She held its two front legs as he attached the chain to the hind legs and hoisted it up. Once it was in place, he slashed its throat, drained all the blood, and then proceeded to butcher it. Salvatore and the boys made sausages and cured one of the hams for their own use, and then he sold the other ham and the prime cuts of meat.

Salvatore also collected all the fat to make lard, which could be used throughout the year for cooking. He cut the fat into chunks, which he melted in a large pot on the kitchen stove. The boys helped. One was constantly stirring while the other fed chunks of fat into the pot. Salvatore poured the rendered lard into large crocks that he had partially filled with his newly made sausages. During the year, as Maria took lard out of the crocks, she occasionally also got a few sausage links. On those days they had sausages for dinner that were so well preserved they tasted freshly made.

When his gardening tools broke through heavy use, Salvatore took the boys into the woods to look for just the right tree branches. As he had learned to do in Italy, Salvatore used a large branch to make a new handle and attached smaller twigs to make a garden rake. In the basement, they had an old wooden washing machine that had a foot treadle for working the agitator. When the large, leather, conveyer belts in the mill broke, the broken pieces were thrown into large trash bins. Salvatore went through the bins, found suitable pieces of leather, and took them home. One day, he also found the remnant of a stone grinding wheel that had been worn too small for industrial use and had been discarded. He took the wheel home, attached it to the top of the washing machine, and made a leather belt that he attached to the treadle. He had thus built a foot-operated grinder for sharpening his knives and garden tools.

Some evenings, Salvatore got his shoe form, sat on the floor with his back against the wall, and used some of the left-over leather pieces to make new soles for his children's shoes. Nothing went to waste. Everything was used or sold. However, for as dire as the family's situation was, when beggars came to the door, Maria always made them something to eat and drink, fed them, and packed a bit more for them to take along.

* * *

In 1936 Frannie and Charlie finally made the decision to get married. Since Leo was graduating from high school that year, it was hoped he would get a full-time job at a better salary. When Frannie left, there would not be such a financial hit to the family, and so she mustered up the courage to approach Mrs. Alenbaugh for a raise. She had been there for five years and was still making only four dollars a week. When Mrs. Alenbaugh heard this, however, her response was, "Frances, you know many people are out of work. I could easily get a live-in girl who would be happy to do your job for room and board. I feel I'm being most charitable just by keeping you on. An increase in pay is simply out of the question."

Paul insisted that since Charlie and Frannie had made their decision, he and Mauggie could now marry. He was not willing to wait any longer. The couples decided Frannie would marry in May and Mauggie would marry in September. Leo would graduate in June. This flurry of activity worried Salvatore. The house was still not paid off, there was debt to be reconciled, and he would be losing both the financial contributions and the help of the girls. He made it clear that Leo needed to find full-time work as soon after graduation as possible. Carl and Sam had to stay in school, he added, and the younger boys were not even to think of marriage until times got better. Meanwhile, he and Maria had to find a way to pay for two wedding receptions. When the cow had twins that year, Salvatore said the good Lord always provides. There would be one calf for each wedding.

When Frannie and Charlie were married in May, Mauggie was maid of honor with Laura Lucci as a bridesmaid, Charlie's brother was best man, and Paul was an usher. Cousin Minnie and her husband and daughter came from Detroit for the wedding. The guests also included Charlie's family, the Lucci family, and Paul's father. Salvatore butchered one of the calves for the wedding feast and used long boards and wooden horses used in his farm work to create a long table that ran through the kitchen and the dining room and on into the living room. Following the service at St. John the Baptist Church, everyone came to the house for the dinner where they feasted and toasted the couple with Salvatore's wine. One of the Lucci sons played the accordion, and Salvatore began singing favorite songs from the old country. Soon others were joining in with more contemporary tunes, and the guests began dancing. It was just like the old days. For a brief moment everyone seemed to forget about the Depression.

There was no money to even think about a honeymoon trip. From the reception, Frannie and Charlie walked to a tiny, rented, four-room cottage just blocks from her parents' house, their new home. They could barely furnish it. Because there was no money for a refrigerator, in the cold seasons they bought groceries for a few days at a time and kept milk and other perishables in a box nailed outside the kitchen window. Although life was extremely difficult, they were happy to finally be their own little family. Charlie was always up early to walk down the hill and take the bus to work in the mill in Aliquippa. Shortly afterward, Maria, and Mauggie when she wasn't working, walked to the little house and helped decorate with odd pieces from home. They made curtains and picked wild flowers and set them on tables to brighten the place. Like her father, Frannie loved gardening and was soon starting her own garden from cuttings he gave her.

Time was moving fast, and Maria was concerned for Leo. He would be the first member of the family to graduate from high school, and she wanted to make it a special occasion for him, even though his graduation would be sandwiched between two weddings. This was no problem, but there was the senior prom to prepare for. He would need a suit for both events. He had never had a suit. Growing up, the boys always wore blue jeans, which were the cheapest and most durable pieces of clothing. In the summers, Salvatore shaved their heads, and they ran around in their bare feet. They enjoyed the freedom, and it saved wear and tear on their shoes. As Leo got older, every cent he earned went toward paying off family debts, so he had very few clothes. His old clothes were passed on to Carl, and Carl's were passed to Sam. By the time Sam got the hand-me-downs, there were more patches than original fabric. Everyone they knew was living that way, or at least it seemed so. But now was different. Leo needed a suit, but a suit was an extravagance they could not afford. Even though he was embarrassed about not having a suit for these big events, he said it was okay. He did not have to go to the prom or the graduation.

Paul had a better job than anyone else in the family at this time, and he was a dapper dresser. Mauggie told him about the situation with Leo. The next day, when Paul came to call, he brought a charcoal gray, pinstriped suit of the latest fashion, a beautiful, hand-painted necktie, and a pair of good shoes for Leo, who was eternally grateful. The two men were close enough in size that everything fit well enough, and now Leo would go to the prom and the graduation. Mauggie spent the next month teaching Leo to dance (they practiced constantly in the kitchen), and somehow Maria came up with two dollars for the tickets to the prom and a soda afterward.

Leo asked Emily, the pretty little red head from Beaver, to be his date. The night of the prom, she stayed at her grandmother's house. Maria made her a corsage from flowers in their yard, and Leo walked to the grandmother's house with it. From there, they walked to the prom. Salvatore had told him he had to be home by midnight—"and no monkey business!"—so after the dancing ended, they walked to Islay's for a soda and he proudly showed off his beautiful date and his clothes to his coworkers. They were treated like visiting royalty. With his head spinning in delight, he walked her to her grandmother's home and was back by midnight. Maria and the girls were eagerly waiting for a full report of the evening.

The prom was soon followed by graduation, after which Leo worked tirelessly to find a better full-time job. Although he searched from Beaver to Pittsburgh and from Monaca to Zelienople, he was turned away everywhere he inquired. At last an opportunity finally presented itself. The Pennsylvania State Highway Department (which had been expanded in 1931 under Gov. Pinchot to include over 20,000 miles of rural roads) was hiring laborers to work on roads for the remarkable pay of forty cents an hour. There was a small problem. If he wanted the job, he would have to register as a Republican. Even though Franklin D. Roosevelt was now in the White House, the local government was still Republican biased. Being careful not to tell Salvatore, Leo registered as a Republican and got the job.

By September, 1936, it was almost time for Mauggie's wedding. And the next payment on the house was overdue. Salvatore went to Mr. Kopecky, the man he had bought the farm from, to explain his situation, promising he would continue to pay the interest if they would just give him time to get past the wedding. But Mr. Kopecky said he could wait no longer, and Salvatore was going to have to find a way to resume payments on the principal. Taxes on the property were also due. Salvatore kept this bad news from the children, wishing beyond hope that a resolution would present itself.

As was the Italian custom, Paul offered to pay for Mauggie's wedding gown, but Salvatore refused the offer. "I thank you. If this is the custom in Italy," he said, "it is not here, and I, as the father of the bride, will pay these expenses." Mauggie could not wear Frannie's gown. Mauggie was built like her mother, and Frannie, at four foot eleven, was built like her grandmother. But Mauggie could wear Frannie's headpiece and veil. Frannie would be her matron of honor and Paul's cousin would be best man. Lena Lucci was the bridesmaid and Leo was the usher.

Paul, his father, and his cousin boarded with the DiBenedetto family in West Aliquippa. Mrs. DiBenedetto was an extremely kind woman who had nine children and still maintained a clean boarding house. She treated the men staying at her house as family and always fed them well, too. Since only he, his father, and his cousin were in this country with no other family, she offered to host Paul's rehearsal dinner at her house.

That Friday evening, as they were preparing to leave for the rehearsal and dinner, they heard pounding outside the house. Salvatore went out to find a man hammering a sheriff's sale sign to the side of the house. Mauggie was horrified and began to cry. She told them it was her fault. If not for her wedding, they could have made the house payments. Salvatore held her and assured her the wedding had nothing to do with their debt. He said she should enjoy her special day and everything would be fine. There was enough time before the date listed on the sign for the sheriff's sale for him to straighten it all out. Besides, there must be some mistake. They went on with the evening's events and everyone put on a festive face, even though they were sick with fear and panic inside.

The next day was the wedding and celebratory dinner. Just as at Frannie's wedding, the other calf had been butchered, the tables built, and the last of Salvatore's wine was brought out. Minnie and Peter came from Detroit again, and everyone in the Lucci family was there, plus Paul's father and cousin, and the whole DiBenedetto family. Everyone attended the service at St. John the Baptist, then gathered for the reception dinner. Minnie brought a camera, a luxury in the family, and they took pictures out on the lawn. It was a beautiful day.

Paul took Mauggie to Niagara Falls for their honeymoon. Even though money was tight, and they had to stay with relatives who lived in the town, it was still a honeymoon. It was also the first honeymoon anyone in the family had ever taken. Upon their return, Paul moved Mauggie into a duplex on Hopewell Avenue which ran high along the hill overlooking the train tracks, West Aliquippa, and the steel mill.

Paul's brother would soon come to the United States, and he and Paul's father would move in with him and Mauggie. Paul had also built a substantial network of friends originally from his home town in Italy and who had migrated to West Aliquippa. At first, it was a hard adjustment for Mauggie, because, even though it was only seven miles from home, she was the first to move off the hill and far enough not to be able to drop in on her mother at will. She became lonely, and many nights when trains passed by, she ran out to their back porch to gaze at the trains and dream of both home and faraway places. However, Paul was entrenched in the social life of West Aliquippa, and she knew many people from her childhood years spent there. The newlyweds eventually blended into the active social life of that vibrant little community.

Shortly after Mauggie's wedding, the steelworkers became more aggressive and began taking stands against the strong-arm tactics of the mill and town management. When the elections were held, the Democrats won all the local slots. Republicans, including Leo, who had held the government jobs were swiftly fired and replaced with Democrats. That meant Leo had no choice but to explain why he lost his job, which prompted a lecture from Salvatore about having the integrity of one's convictions. Leo did not appreciate the lecture. The family was hit especially hard because in a period of five months, they had lost Frannie's and Mauggie's incomes and now Leo's, too.

At the same time, Salvatore began frantically searching for a solution to the imminent crisis. He had to save his house. He went everywhere, looking for a way to keep up the payments on the house. He went to banks and savings and loans throughout the Beaver valley, but no one would approve a loan for a man working just a few days a month and with unpaid debts and no savings. What little he had accumulated in his bank account had been long gone and the account was closed.

Paul tried to help his father-in-law by talking to a relative of his who lived in the Beaver valley and owned a successful business. Perhaps he would be able to lend a little money to prevent the sale of the house. Besides, Leo had dated this man's daughter a few times, and she was also interested in a relationship with him. The relative said he might be able to help, so Paul brought him to see Salvatore. They sat around the kitchen table and the relative questioned Salvatore in great detail about his financial situation, his income, and his expenses. Then he asked Salvatore if he had anything he could use for collateral. After a lengthy discussion, Paul's relative told Salvatore he could not help him. He also promptly forbade his daughter to see Leo anymore, saying, "That family does not have a pot to piss in," there was no way he was going to let her think of a future with a pauper.

Salvatore was furious. He believed the relative had only been interested in knowing his personal business, and had never had any intention of lending him money. Another man in West Aliquippa that Salvatore had considered a friend had frequently offered to use his influence to get Leo a job in the steel mill if he ever needed one. Now Salvatore took Leo to see this man, who was very happy to help...for a commission. He said he could take Leo into the mill that day and get him a job if he (Leo) would give the man a percentage of his wages every payday. Salvatore had a few words for this man about integrity and friendship, and then they walked out. He said if there were jobs to be gotten in the mill, Leo could get one without this man's influence. But there were no jobs.

Salvatore was really despairing now, caught between his high principles and his immediate need. How could all this misfortune be overcome? Many evenings after Leo, Carl, and Sam were asleep, Salvatore and Maria sat at the kitchen table and agonized over ways they could pull themselves out of this dilemma. He was determined not to lose their home, but all his resources seemed to have been exhausted. There was nothing left to do.

Just as they were approaching the day of the sheriff's sale, Sam Celeste came to visit. Sam said he had been talking to the man he dealt with at Monaca Federal Savings and Loan. He felt they could be successful at working something out through an FHA-approved loan. But Salvatore said he had talked about an FHA loan with the manager of a bank in Beaver, and that manager had told him he would not be eligible. Enactment of the National Housing Act in 1934 had created the Federal Housing Administration, which regulated mortgage interest rates and insured mortgages. The FHA's goal was to loosen money and encourage the banks to grant more mortgages. However, the distribution of the money was regulated by criteria that were based on the ethnic compositions of neighborhoods and determinations of whether the area was increasing or decreasing in growth reliability. On this somewhat arbitrary basis Salvatore had been rejected by the bank in Beaver.

Sam said the man he had talked to was more optimistic, and also, that Mr. LeGoullion was a director at the savings and loan. Remembering Mr. LeGoullion to be a reasonable man when he dug out space for his new coal tipple, Salvatore went to see him for help getting the loan. At the loan office, the manager assured Salvatore that Monaca Heights was not an endangered neighborhood. He shook hands with Salvatore and approved his loan. The house was saved. Salvatore never forgot the kindness of his friend, Mr. LeGoullion, and the Monaca Federal Savings and Loan. When work had picked up enough to make it possible, Salvatore opened a savings account at Monaca Federal, and kept it for the rest of his life.

* * *

By 1937, work was slowly beginning to pick up at the mill, and so Salvatore was getting more days. In addition, Leo had gotten a job driving a delivery truck for Pettibon Dairy, and Carl was in high school and getting better part-time jobs. Maria received a letter from sister Mattie reporting that they were doing so well dairy farming in Bakersfield, California, that they had decided to buy their own farm in El Monte, which was in Los Angeles County and northeast of the city of Los Angeles. Maria was pleased.

As was so often the case, however, good news was followed by bad. In February of 1937, Frank Lucci suffered a stroke and died. This hit Salvatore and Maria particularly hard because Frank had been a good friend since the two men had lived in Italy. Frank had become as close as family since their move to Pennsylvania, and the girls looked at the Lucci girls as sisters. Frank's death was a great loss.

While mourning the loss of his dear friend, Salvatore had to focus on his next family leadership issue. He had been keeping the family back in Italy informed of the slight improvements to the economy. Now it was decided that his sister Virginia's son, John, would try to get a visa and come to the United States and live with them.

Soon they received word that John was on his way. When he arrived, he moved into the family's house. Salvatore was happy to be helping his sister, and Maria was happy to have more people in the house to soften the lonely feeling resulting from both daughters leaving. When Salvatore approached his boss at the mill about a job for John, the man was cool and noncommittal. Tensions were extremely high. Even though the Wagner Act of 1935 provided for the recognition of the unions and the right to collective bargaining, Jones and Laughlin remained insistent that unions were not going to operate in Aliquippa. A group of workers had recently met to revive the old Lodge 200 as the base of the emerging Steel Workers Organizing Committee (SWOC). The men who attended the meeting were fired, and the SWOC took the issue to the Supreme Court, which handed down a landmark decision upholding the Wagner Act, and ordering Jones and Laughlin to reinstate the fired workers.

Aliquippa workers went to Pittsburgh to meet with Jones and Laughlin management, seeking formal recognition. The workers accused management of using stalling tactics, and at 9:00 p.m., on Wednesday, May 12, 1937, five hundred men set up a picket line at the tunnel entrance to the mill. Paul and Charlie joined the picket line. When it was time for the 11:00 p.m. shift change, workers came out but none went in. The crowd had swollen to more than a thousand when local police and state troopers arrived with tear gas. Each group started carefully watching the other. The next day, the Governor of Pennsylvania arrived at the site, and the day after that, only forty hours after it had begun, the strike was over. Jones and Laughlin would recognize the union,yet this did not mean an immediate end to strife. Workers were still carefully watched, and reasons—like issuing a poor work notice and other contrived reasons that were hard to dispute—were found to send them home without warning.

About this same time on the home front, Maria began having trouble with her teeth. There was no money for the dentist, and so she just lived with the pain. Then several teeth became abscessed, and it developed into a major problem. One blustery winter day, while the men were at work and Carl was in school, Maria decided something had to be done. She bundled up Sam, wrapped a scarf around her mouth, and the two of them walked down the hill into town to see Dr. Todd. Her teeth were so bad that he pulled thirteen of them, all during that one visit, and sent her home. As she and Sam walked back up the hill, she was in excruciating pain after significant blood loss. As soon as they entered the house, she attempted to begin preparing supper. It was in the kitchen near the stove where Salvatore found her, in terrible condition and barely conscious. He immediately sat her down, ministered to her, and completed the cooking.

John eventually got a job, but didn't care for mill work at all. And then he hooked up with a gang of wild men. Salvatore sat him down for a talk and set some ground rules for living in the house. After that, John started going to Youngstown on his days off to stay with friends and relatives. He would get back late, barely in time to make it to work, and soon began receiving poor work notices and was often sent home before the end of the work day. Finally, after several months of this, he was let go. He just hung around for a while, then decided to move to Youngstown. He said he was forever grateful to Salvatore for getting him to the U.S. and letting him live with them, and he loved Maria like a mother, but the fast-paced life in Youngstown held too strong an appeal for him. John visited the family often, but he soon met a girl, married her, and made his move to Ohio permanent.

Work at the mill and unemployment fluctuated a great deal in the late 1930s until Germany invaded Poland in September of 1939. Fearing an imminent war, the U.S. government started building a military arsenal, which caused an increased need for steel. And so steel workers started working more regularly. The average annual salary in the U.S. in 1939 was $1,850, but for steel mill workers it was only $939. Although Democrats were winning the elections for public office, management at the steel mills was still Republican. Records show that Salvatore, insisting upon staying registered as a Democrat, worked a total of thirty weeks in 1939 and earned $550. By contrast, Paul and his father, both registered as Republicans, worked fifty weeks, and earned twice as much. Nevertheless, this was Salvatore's best year in at least a decade. Things were, in fact, picking up for everyone.

Carl was more outgoing than Leo, and even though he had just as much work to do outside of school, he managed to keep an active social life. At school events, he noticed a pretty girl with dark, shiny hair, a fair complexion, and a bright smile. He became interested in getting to know her better. Betty or Betts, as he called her, lived downtown in a house with a large front porch that was perfect for courting, and right on the main street. Carl would walk Betts home from school, spend a little time on the porch swing with her, and still get up the hill to take care of the farm animals before his father got home from work.

On days he had to get to one of his part-time jobs, Carl found a way to pass her house, either on the way to work or coming home. That way, they could spend more time talking on the porch. Soon he was devoting as much time as he could to being with her, yet he still had to be home in the evenings by ten o'clock. When Leo gave up his varsity sweater, Maria freshened it up and gave it to Carl who wore it on dates.

While times were getting better, there was still a lot of work required for the family to get out of the hole created by the Depression. Carl would be graduating from high school and looking for full-time work in the spring. Young Sam was in grade school, and Leo was thinking that if the U.S. got into the war, he would enlist. He also remembered the promise he had made to Maria years ago that he would take her back to Colorado, and that promise was weighing heavily on his conscience. If this trip was going to happen, it had to be soon.

When Leo told his mother he was going to take her to Colorado that summer, she smiled and said that would be nice, still not believing it would happen. He talked with Salvatore about it, but Salvatore said that now that he was working regularly, he could never afford to leave his job that long, and he also had animals and the garden to care for. He would not go to Colorado. Leo continued to plan, but Maria did not want to go without Salvatore. One evening as they were alone having their usual talk at the kitchen table, Salvatore told her she should go. He said they would never be able to afford the trip, but Leo really wanted to do this for them. Besides, if the U.S. entered the war, their son would surely be drafted. So this might be the only chance she would have to do something special with their son. Maria wanted Salvatore to go, too, because their life together had started in Colorado, and if they had the opportunity to go back, it should be together. Then she thought about how much she wanted to see her sisters. This would be her only chance. Yes, she would do it, she would travel west with Leo.

* * *

As soon as Sam was out of school, Leo sold his 1933 Chevrolet and bought a 1937 model. Then he, Maria, and Sam left for Colorado. On the first leg of the trip, Maria was quiet; she felt guilty for leaving Salvatore and Carl behind, but knew they couldn't leave their jobs or the animals. Each day, as they got closer to Colorado, she became more animated, and once she started talking, the stories flowed. She described Starkville in vivid detail. She told stories about the house they had lived in and the people she had known...everyone, family and friends, just as though she had just been there yesterday.

They received a royal welcome. Maria and Maggie hugged so tight they could each have broken a rib, and they confessed that twenty-two years ago, when they'd promised they'd see each other again, they had never really thought it would happen. And here they were, a family together. Tony embraced Maria and welcomed her, then led her and her sons into the house she had lived in as a child and a married woman. A bit later, she took the boys to see the school, the church, the dancehall, and what had once been the Grosso compound. They walked up to the remains of the coke ovens where Salvatore had worked. These ovens had been closed in 1918 and never reopened. From there, they could also see the remains of the mine tipple which had been closed in 1921. Starkville was nowhere near as populous or active as it had been two decades earlier, but Maria recognized people here that she hadn't seen in twenty-two years. They all talked to each other like it had just been last week.

She and the boys also went into Trinidad and saw the church where she had been married and the children baptized. Next, she visited the graves of her mother, her baby daughter, and other relatives in the Catholic cemetery. Then she went to the Masonic cemetery where her father lay buried. Each brought tears and prayers.

Sister Phyllis and her husband Joseph had moved to Fredrick, north of Denver, where he was mining and sculpting statues for churches. When sister Mattie came in from California to see Maria, they all traveled to Frederick to visit Phyllis. The family fawned over little Sam, who enjoyed the attention from aunts he had never met. It was a wonderful reunion. There was a constant stream of friends and family coming to see them, and Maria, who was radiant, joked and told stories. She had been the tomboy and jokester when the girls were younger, and they were delighted to see how she hadn't changed. There was a lot of reminiscing, talking, laughing, and crying. "Oh, the time has gone too fast," lamented Maria echoing the sentiment of all. Soon they were saying their sad goodbyes and not promising to see each other again this time. There was no fake joviality this time, either, just tight hugs and tearful kisses. And then they were on their way home to Pennsylvania. Maria was quiet, her head spinning with memories that she would tell Salvatore about and other, long-forgotten memories that had resurfaced. She had received the one thing that she had been too afraid to hope for all those years: the chance to see Starkville and the family she loved one more time. Leo sent postcards to the family back home from every stop on the trip.

They hadn't been back home long when news came that Japan had attacked Pearl Harbor on December 7, 1941. Like almost everyone else in the U.S., the family sat around the radio and heard President Roosevelt talk of that "day of infamy" as he proclaimed the United States' entry into the war. The mill was soon back to full shifts, working around the clock. As men were being called to serve in the armed forces, for the first time, women were beginning to fill the job vacancies they left. Carl had graduated from high school, and was working in a labor job at the Pittsburgh Tool Steel Wire Company in Monaca. Leo was eager to get into the war, and when he wasn't drafted soon enough, he enlisted in the Army Engineers.

Maria was shaken by Leo's enlistment. Knowing that the tragedies of war were so life-changing as to be almost unthinkable, she couldn't imagine how this new war would change her family or her life, but she knew it would. Salvatore silently cried as he watched his son walk down the driveway and down the street into a dangerous and uncertain future, but he hid his grief from Maria in an effort to give her strength.

Carl, who also wanted to get into the war effort, secretly went to Pittsburgh to enlist. He was extremely disappointed when he failed the physical. On the long ride home, thoughts swirled through his head. While he felt bad about not being able to go, he also did not want to needlessly worry his mother, who was already worried about Leo. Besides, he knew production at the steel mills was important to the war effort. Some of the men at the mill, who were older and had children, were exempt from the draft. Since Carl had been in his job at the steel mill only a short time, he was too young to be in this draft-exempt group, but he decided he would tell the family he was exempt from the draft because of his work at the mill. They were so relieved, they never questioned it, and he never revealed the true health reason.

Maria was already feeling the sting of loneliness. The girls had their own families and were having children. Mauggie and Paul moved to a new house in the suburbs of Aliquippa, eight miles away, though it somehow seemed much farther. Frannie and Charlie built a bungalow farther out in the country where his father had purchased a large tract of land and built his own house while giving a plot to each son. The sons built on their plots, creating a little compound. Frannie's new home was a charming two-bedroom cottage similar to some she had admired in magazines. Just as her mother had done, she quickly set about making curtains, crocheting doilies, and making the cottage warm and cozy. It had a fireplace in the living room around which she arranged her furniture, mimicking romantic scenes from movies. It was their little piece of paradise. But while it wasn't as far away from home as Mauggie's new house, the girls still were no longer close enough to run in and out every day.

Maria helped out when each of her grandchildren was born. Mauggie had the first grandchild at home, and Maria assisted the doctor and stayed for a few days after the delivery until Mauggie got on her feet. Maria always continued to help where she could.

The girls came to their parents' house to visit on days their husbands were off from work. Frannie and Charlie continued to come home for the traditional Sunday dinners, yet because Paul worked rotating shifts, it was not possible for him and Mauggie to make every Sunday. The rest of the week, when no one was visiting, the house was empty and too quiet. Sam was in school, and Salvatore and Carl were usually working, and when Carl wasn't working, he was spending all his free time with Betts. Now that almost everyone was out of the house, Maria began to feel that no one needed her anymore.

It was a Saturday morning when Salvatore and Carl were at work that Sam was awakened by a banging in the kitchen. He came out of the bedroom to find Maria taking the wood doors off a large cupboard that was built into the kitchen wall. She turned and saw him. "I have always hated these bulky cupboard doors," she said. "I'll give you some breakfast, and then we are going to make them beautiful." She and Sam carried the doors into the basement where she found a hand saw and asked him to help her cut the thin wood panes out of their frames.

"What are we doing?" Sam asked.

"We're going to surprise your daddy, and put glass in these doors and make that cupboard look like a built-in china closet."

Maria and Sam went out to the barn and found old pieces of glass from a window that had been broken. Salvatore had replaced the glass with isinglass—a transparent sheet of mica, though he had probably used a cheaper version. The old glass had been lying in a corner in the barn for some time. Other pieces of glass from windows in the house were also stored in the barn. Maria picked out pieces of glass until she had enough for her project. Then she found Salvatore's glass cutter and cut and fitted the glass into her cupboard doors. Next, she and Sam glazed the glass, painted the wood, and rehung the doors. When he saw this major construction project had been carried out while he was at work, Salvatore just shook his head. Maria loved her new built-in china closet. For her next project, she started painting faux grain on the wooden floors from the edges of the carpeting to the walls, another technique she had seen in a magazine. There was no stopping her; she would work her way through her sorrows.

Before leaving for the Army, Leo had been seeing Emily from Beaver regularly. She didn't want him to go, and they had a tearful goodbye. He was soon stationed in California and wrote to his family at every chance. Then the letters stopped for a while until one day there was a phone call. It was an ecstatic Leo telling his parents that Emily was standing right beside him. She had gone out to California to be with him because she just couldn't bear to be away from him, and time was so short before he would ship out to Europe. They had decided to get married. Even though Emily wasn't Catholic, Leo had insisted they marry in the Catholic Church. "We're calling from our honeymoon, Mom. I have a three-day leave, and we're staying in beautiful Long Beach."

A series of postcards followed from Laguna Beach, Tucson, and then Louisiana, where he shipped out to the front in Europe. Shortly afterward, Emily returned to Pennsylvania and moved in with her grandmother in Monaca. She occasionally visited Maria, Mauggie, and Frannie and told them how her parents didn't understand what she was going through. She couldn't live without Leo. Her life, she said, was meaningless without him. This went on for a time, and then suddenly, Emily stopped visiting.

Meanwhile, Carl and Betts were also planning to marry. Because pay for a laborer at the mill was so low, Salvatore and Maria offered to let them live at the family house until they could save enough for a place of their own. They were married in November of 1943 at St. John the Baptist Church. Minnie and her family came from Detroit; including her younger sister, Margaret, who had gone to Detroit from Colorado to marry Pete's brother.

Carl and Betts went to Niagara Falls for their honeymoon. Upon returning, the newlyweds moved into the front bedroom, and Salvatore and Maria moved one bedroom back. Maria was happy to have activity in the house again.

Soon Carl found a new, better paying job as a surveyor with the Michael Baker Engineering firm, and he and Betts were able to get a place of their own on the hill. The house was quiet again, and Maria was now worried sick over Leo. Being in the Corps of Engineers, he was in the front lines, building bridges and preparing the route in advance of the troops as they moved forward. It was extremely dangerous. Everyone anxiously waited for any news from him. It took a long time before his letters got to them, and when they did arrive, they were heavily censored V-mail. These letters had to be given to the commanding officer, who would read them and black out anything that might reveal the person's location or give other sensitive information that could help the enemy if the letter were intercepted. The letters were then put on microfilm, reduced to about one third in size, and then printed on glossy photo-type paper to be mailed. By the time they were received, usually so much of what he wrote was blacked out that the letters barely made sense. But at least his family knew he was alive.

Maria felt she had to snap out of her depression if she was going to be any good to the rest of her family. One day while Salvatore was at work and Sam was at school, she decided to get dressed up, and take the bus to West Aliquippa for a visit with Mary. She put on her church dress and walked down the hill and into town to catch the bus. Once she was on the bus and anticipating a pleasant day with her friends, her spirits began to lift. Suddenly, she was at the stove preparing dinner. Sam was home from school, and Salvatore was due any minute. She had no recollection of her visit to Mary. She remembered nothing after the bus ride to West Aliquippa. No memory of getting off the bus. No memory of the visit. No memory of her return home. The day was completely lost. She was extremely tired and confused, but she told no one about this mystery of a lost day.

* * *

Mauggie and Frannie had both tried to call Emily on several occasions, but she was never home. Mauggie and the children were riding the bus to Monaca to visit Maria one day while the men were at work. They had to get off the bus in downtown Monaca, so Mauggie decided this would be a good time to stop by Emily's grandmother's house to see how she was doing. The grandmother answered the door and briskly told Mauggie that Emily had moved back to Beaver with her parents. Then she closed the door in her face. This certainly did not seem right.

What the family did not know until he returned from the war was while Leo was going through the most dangerous part of the war, he received a letter from Emily informing him that she would be seeking a divorce. It was too difficult for her to go through her life every day not knowing if he were dead or alive. Frannie and Mauggie found out through gossip that Emily had been seen with another man. She had gotten a job in the office at J&L Steel, and a "wonderful man" at work had been consoling her. He had a high-level supervisory job and often stopped in her office to see if he could cheer her up. Through these talks, they had grown fond of each other and begun dating. He wanted to marry her. It was only fair, she said, to let Leo know that, if or when he returned from the war, he should not try to reconcile with her. She was moving on with her life, and he should, too.

Leo never alluded to any of this in his letters home. He wrote about what was happening in Europe, at least as much as could pass the censors. What kept him going was his optimism, or perhaps it was denial, or perhaps fantasy. Later, he would tell family he was sure he could fix it all when he returned. She would relent once she saw him, and they would be back together again. Their love was strong, and she was acting this way to prepare for the worst if he should not survive the war. He claimed that this refusal to acknowledge reality had kept him going through the war.

Although the war and Maria's ailing health made these times stressful, Maria and Salvatore continued to maintain a happy home for the children. It was a real saving grace to have young, active Sam in the house. Now there were grandchildren, too, for whose visits Maria continually prepared. Occasionally, they were allowed to stay for a few days of "vacation" without their parents. Maria read to them, baked bread and cinnamon rolls, and made dishes their mothers did not, like creamy, succulent risotto. No one made bread quite as good as hers. For a special treat, if there were no cinnamon rolls, she would put a slice of bread in a bowl, sprinkle it with sugar, and pour milk over it. Her grandchildren thought it delicious.

A good friend of Paul's had a brother in the Italian army who had been captured and was being detained in a military prison in New York. The prisoners were allowed visitors, so Paul's friend, another brother, and Paul himself, plus their three wives decided to make a trip to New York City to visit the imprisoned brother. Mauggie took her children to Monaca to stay with Maria and Salvatore while they were on this trip. As Mauggie was walking down the driveway on her way to the bus, the children began to cry. Maria told them not to cry or she would begin to cry, too. She told them to go into the house with her because she needed some help baking bread.

While the children missed their parents, they loved staying at their grandparents. Sam, who was not much older than the oldest grandchild, enjoyed playing with all of them, especially teasing them. Maria had enameled metal bowls that she used for breakfast cereal. The bowls were red, blue, green, and yellow. Everyone wanted the red bowl, so Sam always fought them for the red, and the loser had to go for the blue, then the green, and the youngest kid would end with the yellow bowl. Maria would let some of the teasing go on, but she eventually stopped it by making Sam yield to his guests. Her discipline was soft and gentle, for she enjoyed watching the children play, and was happy to see Sam joining in with them. Being the youngest and with his brothers and sisters out of the house, life had to be lonely for him. Having young children in the house made Maria feel good, too. She enjoyed having a little girl around again so that she could do little things like wash her hair and wrap it in strips of cloth to curl it.

The grandchildren loved to run and play on the farm. They helped their grandfather feed the chickens and collect the eggs. After dinner they walked down to the pen to feed left-over scraps or carrots to the pigs. They also laughed as the pigs snorted and gobbled their food. By now, the cow had died. She had not been replaced, and the kids liked to play hide-and-seek in the barn and in the tall grass of the field. The tiny sycamores Salvatore had planted were now huge, and he let the kids climb and play tag in the largest one out back between the house and the barn. Visiting the grandparents was a real treat. The only negative thing was using the outhouse. No one wanted to be in there long; definitely not when the toilet paper ran out, for the only option was the Sears, Roebuck catalogue, especially when all the soft pages had been used up.

Everyone was now working full time, and life was good...except for the war hanging over everything. There was a constant search through the papers and listening to radio broadcasts for information on the progress of the war. But at the same time, now that there was finally money for groceries, there was also rationing. Numerous goods were rationed, such as rubber, nylon stockings, and gasoline, because the materials were needed for the war. Sugar, butter, and meats were rationed. Each family received a book of ration stamps, and they could only buy the amounts listed on the stamps. Grocers were not permitted to give change back from ration stamps, so the government made ration coins that the grocers could give if there was a balance on a stamp. Goods were tight and closely monitored through rationing boards set up in every town. But everyone in the Ciconne family was used to making sacrifices. They had never known a time when they didn't have to do so. The whole country was doing it, and everyone complied with the rules unquestioningly as an act of patriotism.

As people read about the brutal bombing England was enduring, talk turned to the possible bombing threat to our country. Maria had to buy blackout blinds for the windows. There were air raid drills. When the fire siren blew, everyone was to close their blackout blinds. They also turned out all lights and then peeked out from behind the blinds to watch the neighborhood go into complete darkness. But Salvatore laughed at the drama. He pointed out, "You know a pilot can see the flames of the open hearth at J&L from a hundred miles in the air." He smiled, "A little house light in the country like this is not going to get the enemy's bombs."

No matter what was happening, he continued to make improvements on his paradise. He now was able to have water brought into the house and had a hot water tank installed, which he felt would make life a little easier for Maria. She would no longer have to pump water and heat it on the stove for baths, washing dishes, and doing laundry. They could also put away the pail and dipper on the kitchen sink used for drinking water. Best of all, indoor plumbing meant they could stop using the outhouse. Salvatore also removed the pump from the well and built a covering over it, then he created a patio area between the back door and his favorite bench under the elm tree. In addition, the road to their house was extended and additional homes were being built nearby. There was now a little automobile traffic passing their home, though it was still a quiet area.

Occasionally on a hot summer holiday—Memorial Day, the Fourth of July, Labor Day—all the family packed into Carl's and Charlie's cars, the children sitting on parents' laps, the trunks filled with food and drink, and they went on a picnic. They rode out into the country to a quiet spot along Raccoon Creek and laid blankets along the bank. The men and older children played ball while the women and younger children waded in the creek and picked wild flowers. For lunch, there was fried chicken, sandwiches, and potato salad, plus beer for the men and soda for the women and children, and then watermelon for everyone. The men might play a little *morra*, and eventually Salvatore would begin to sing, soon to be joined by the others as the crowd mellowed.

As dusk began to close in, they packed up and started for home, the children always falling asleep on the way. Invariably, either on the ride to the picnic or on the way home, Charlie's car heated up or lost power going uphill. Everyone piled out of the car to push. Maria, who had difficulty with the heat, remained sitting in the front seat to get a bit of air from the little fan at the windshield while the rest of the women and the children walked and the men pushed the car to the top of the hill. Recalling the jitney from Trinidad to Starkville that also needed encouragement to get over the hill, Salvatore and Maria laughed.

The family was very close and celebrated every event together: birthdays, baptisms, first communions, confirmations, graduations...everything, and with all the family members present. Oftentimes, Paul's father, brother, and eventually his brother's family and in-laws were included. There were also events where Charlie's brothers and their families, or Betts' family members joined the festivities. Whenever cousins from Detroit, Youngstown, or Pittsburgh visited, the family also came together for food and drink and celebrations that always ended with singing and toasting.

In 1944, when Minnie's in-laws were celebrating their fiftieth anniversary, a big celebration was planned and the entire family was invited. Salvatore and Maria and their children and grandchildren took the train to Detroit. This was an overnight trip with everyone sleeping in their seats in coach. In Detroit, they were picked up by family and friends and taken to Minnie and Pete's house, which was a big, two story, brick house in the Highland Park section of

Detroit. The women and girls had the bedrooms upstairs, and cots were set up for the men and boys in the living room, dining room, and enclosed porch. For meals, the cots were taken up, and replaced with long tables running through the same downstairs rooms. These precious times were felt to be just natural, everyday life for the family. But they were not to last.

The day came when Maria could no longer keep her failing health a secret. She had gone down into the basement to do the laundry when another stroke seized her. She fell to the floor and was unable to get up. When Sam came home from school, the house seemed to be empty. He called out and thought he heard something in the basement. He went down to find his mother still lying where she had fallen hours before. They got her to a doctor, who said she had had a stroke. Until then, when she complained to the doctor, he always said she was just going through the change of life...and "those things happen." This time, though, he gave her a strong medicine, but it made her sick. They went through a series of medicines...and possibly a few more minor strokes that seemed to go undetected, except for a noticeable decline in her overall health. Sam often got home from school to find her sitting in the kitchen with a far-off look on her face and her housework undone, but she always immediately brightened up when she saw him and asked about his day. She was good at fooling everyone, at least for a time.

Carl's job as a surveyor required him to travel a great deal, which meant he and Betts were not happy being separated so much of the time. Her father worked as a butcher at the Howard Meat Market in Beaver Falls and was able to get Carl a job as an apprentice meat cutter. Carl jumped at the opportunity, and they were soon settled into a more pleasant routine of work and home.

Every time a major news event occurred, a man ran down the street waving the newspaper and yelling, "Extra! Extra!" Sam, or whoever was around, ran out to buy a copy, praying it would be an announcement of the end of the war. Back inside, he read the headlines to Maria. The invasion of Normandy on June 6, 1944. The death of President Roosevelt on April 12, 1945. VE Day on May 8, 1945. Then, in quick succession, the dropping of the two atomic bombs, first Little Boy over Hiroshima on August 6, then Fat Man over Nagasaki on August 9. Finally, the one "Extra!" they had been waiting for: VJ Day on August 15, 1945. The tragic war was at last over.

Leo was returned to the U.S. and discharged. As soon as he could he came home. Eager to surprise the family, he walked into the house. Maria, who was home alone, did not recognize him, and he was devastated to see her in such a deteriorated condition. In all the letters he had received, there had never been a hint of her poor health. Through the worst of the fighting in Europe, he had dreamed of the day he would run through that door to the smell of bread baking and his mother's welcoming smile. And she didn't even know him. It was a terrible blow. Worse, it was a double hit to not have his wife waiting for him. With no time to recover from either shock, he tried to reconcile with Emily, only to be faced with the divorce papers and her refusal to see him.

As Leo was going through the finalization of the divorce, Maria had another stroke that left her paralyzed and bedridden. The girls went as often as they could to care for her while Salvatore and Leo were at work and Sam at school, but they lived too far away to be there all the time. No bus service existed in the country, and Frannie didn't drive, so she could only go when Charlie was off from work. Mauggie and Paul had no car, which meant she had to take two buses and walk the mile up the hill to get to her mother. Carl and Betts helped when they could, but they were both working.

Even with all this effort from everyone, it was not enough. Salvatore did all the cooking and cared for Maria. He had to manage the bed pan, lift her to change her position in bed, wash and rub her back with ointments in an effort to prevent bedsores, and more. She needed constant care.

Young Sam began coming straight home from junior high school to a quiet house. He always went immediately to the bedroom to give his mother a drink of water and ask if there was anything else she needed. She always said no, and asked him to tell her about his day at school. He might get her tea or sit and talk with her until his father got home from work. Aside from caring for the chickens (all that remained of the animals), Sam did not have to deal with the amount of afterschool work forced on his brothers by the Depression. The worry of war was over now, but there was still the garden to attend to, and he had the added task of caring for his mother. There was no mother baking bread, no one knitting sweaters, no one to come to school events. He had no brothers or sisters to run and play with. Sam had been only ten years old when he first found Maria on the cellar floor. Now, just entering his teens, he had the worries of an adult. Just like his father before him, Sam had his youth stolen away from him.

* * *

Leo began not coming home from work until late at night. Instead, he went drinking with a few other men who had returned from the war emotionally damaged. While Salvatore was very sad about what his son was going through, he was also concerned that Leo was on a path to destruction. Carl tried to talk with his brother, to cheer him up and present a positive face. But Leo was not hearing any of it. He felt that no one understood what was inside him. No one knew the terrible things he had seen in the war, the death and destruction he witnessed only to come home to this.

Finally, when Leo came home early in the morning after a night of drinking, he found Salvatore sitting at the kitchen table. "Sit. It is time for us to talk. You are ruining your life. You have to pull yourself together, son. Stop this crazy business and make a life of respect."

"Pop, I have no life. Everything I cared about is gone. Everything I fought for is gone. I wish I had never made it through the war. I should have been killed there. It would have been better than what I have."

Salvatore stood up. "Hey, Mister, You have a life. You have family here. Your trouble is you feel sorry for yourself. You need to snap out of this and make a new life. In nineteen and two, I come to this country, a little boy by myself. I leave my family. I leave my mama and never see her again. I—"

"Pop, I'm sick of hearing about nineteen and two! This isn't nineteen and two. You weren't in a war; I was in a war, and now my life is ruined."

"Don't talk to me with no respect. You act like a bum. You straighten up. You have a sick mama. You have special training from the war. Stop drinking and start to make a new life. No more of this monkey business."

Leo just shook his head. "You don't understand."

"I understand plenty. You make a mistake. You try to go outside your class with this woman. It never works. So now you find a good girl in your class and make a life with her."

Leo shook his head. "Pop, I'm a divorced man. I talked to the priest. He says if I marry again, I'll be excommunicated from the church."

At that, Salvatore slammed his hand on the table, "Eh, the priest! What does he know? He's a man like you, like me, sometimes maybe worse. In Colorado, the priest comes to our house to ask for money for the church. Your mama has no money, but she makes him a sandwich. Later I see a friend who says he gives the priest money, and I see the priest under the bridge with a bottle. He's drunk and your mama's sandwich is floating down the creek. You think a man like that knows better than you?"

"It doesn't matter," Leo said. "I'm the one who insisted we get married in the Catholic Church. Now they tell me it's because Emily and I were married in the Catholic Church that I can't remarry."

"You listen to the church?" Salvatore asked. "You listen to the priest? Now you listen to me. You are a good man. God knows you are a good man. Don't waste your time with the priest. You talk to God. God knows you. The priest, he don't know you. God will tell you—find a good woman and get busy with your life."

Leo hated the way his father was talking, but knew Salvatore was right about one thing. He had to get on with his life. He was angry now, and his anger fueled his determination to end this self-pity and move forward. He had done some welding in the war, so he enrolled in a technical school on the GI Bill for more training and certification. Then he found a welding job. He also started seeing a young local girl named Rosabelle, who helped him to stop drinking. He turned the corner.

Rosabelle was six years younger than Leo, but she had already noticed him about town. She remembered going into Islay's, where he had worked, just to see him. Now they began dating, and things were getting serious. Leo began calling her Rosie, and so from that day forward, everyone called her Rosie. Except her father.

He demanded she stop seeing Leo. There was no way, he said, he was going to allow his daughter to see an Italian, Catholic, divorced man. When Rosie informed her father she would marry Leo, her father threw her out of the house and told her she could not return until Leo was out of the picture.

Leo was conflicted. He wanted to marry Rosie, but he still felt he had to reconcile with the church. He went back to talk with Father Canova at St. John the Baptist Church, but the priest coldly confirmed that he would be sinning if he remarried. He would also be excommunicated from the church. Then he curtly dismissed him. Leo was wondering if anything would ever go right in his life. This was another trauma to inflict on his family because divorce did not exist for them. They knew no one who was divorced. People in their world just didn't do this, and they never talked about it. They just didn't know how to react to divorce. Frannie and Mauggie talked every day on the phone. During one of their conversations, Frannie said she had seen Emily in town and had stopped to talk to her. She had asked about Leo, and cried while they were talking. Frannie felt badly, but Mauggie was furious. "How could you feel bad for that woman? She ruined our brother's life. I saw her on the street, too, but I walked straight past her without a nod or a word. Hell will freeze over before I talk to her." But Frannie was the one who made pets out of every animal she ever saw including strays. That was her way, and she could never change.

Leo and Rosie were married in June of 1947 in a quiet ceremony at the First Presbyterian Church. Rosie's brother gave her away. Afterward, the newlyweds and all the family went back to the house and put a small reception together. They brought Maria in a wheelchair so that she could be part of the celebration.

Maria and Salvatore always talked about how great it would be if their children would build their homes on the family's property and they could all live in a compound like Maria's family had in Colorado. They were going to divide the land among the children in their will, so why not start now? Shortly after Leo and Rosie's wedding, Salvatore told the children about this plan. Since Frannie, Mauggie, and Carl already had their own houses, Leo could begin the process. Everyone thought that was fine, and so Leo began building a house at the far end of the land, beyond the barn and in the open field where the cow had once grazed.

* * *

As Salvatore learned, Italy was nearly destroyed in the war. Now the country was filled with poverty, unemployment, and bombed-out towns that needed to be rebuilt. Reconstruction was to take many years. Salvatore's family in Italy was destitute and needed help. His sister, Bombina, had a son named Antonio who was old enough to make the trip to America. There was work here, they told her, and so he could help the family survive. The National Origins Act was still in effect, however, and the few visas issued were being given to scientists and political refugees. Antonio was unable to get a visa, so he went to Venezuela, where immigration was wide open. There he found work as a bricklayer and stayed.

Salvatore put together packages of clothing, nonperishable foodstuffs, and other items he thought his relatives in Italy would need. He wrapped each package with cloth, stitched the seams shut, and sealed them with sealing wax, then mailed them to his sisters in Italy. They had done packages like this for Maria's sister, Maggie, when Tony was injured in a mine cave-in. His pelvis had been crushed, and he was no longer able to work. Salvatore and Maria considered themselves fortunate to be able to help. Now, even though Maria couldn't help him, Salvatore made new packages for his relatives. The act was uplifting for Maria, and Salvatore involved her by telling her about everything he put in the packages.

Maria's health continued to decline. She had been gradually losing her eyesight, and now the last stroke had left her totally blind. Her daughters continued to visit her at least once a week when their husbands had a day off. Her grandchildren came in the bedroom, kissed their grandmother, and talked to her about how school was going and what else was new in their lives. But as soon as they could, they ran outside to play, digging roadways for their cars under the front porch, playing tag in the tree, or terrorizing the chickens.

Occasionally the kids snuck into the cellar to explore for hidden treasures. They found an old stereoscope, a metal and wood contraption with a handle and lenses to look through. There were also cards that had two side by side photos of the same scene. When a card was placed in the holder, and you looked through the lenses, the image appeared to be three-dimensional. The kids were fascinated by this and wondered where it had come from. They also found the old cylinder Victor talking machine and rummaged through a trunk filled with odd things like military uniforms, a German officer's knife with a swastika inlaid on the handle that Leo had apparently brought back from the war, and photos of bombed-out cities in Europe. They fantacized about the origins of these treasures. There was also the old washing machine converted into a knife grinder. They couldn't imagine how it was ever used for washing clothes. Barrels that held Salvatore's wine filled one corner of the cellar, and next to them sausages were hanging to dry. They wondered why a tree trunk was holding up the floor boards, and why the cellar was divided into two separate rooms. They explored until their grandfather called them upstairs for a soft drink. The adults gathered around the kitchen table while, two or three at a time, they took turns sitting in the bedroom and visiting with Maria until she became tired.

Sam, who was now in high school, did as much as he could to help out after school, but Salvatore was soon required to hire a part-time nurse to care for Maria all those times no one could be there. Maria was so weak and fragile that it was no longer possible to get her out of bed and into a wheelchair. Still, she was heavy for Salvatore to lift and turn, but he did it anyway. He acquired a hospital bed and moved it into their bedroom. It had an apparatus attached to it with a bar suspended above Maria. Salvatore tried to lift her enough so that she could grab hold of the bar and pull as an exercise, but even that was far too painful, and he could not stand to hear her cry out in pain. The nurse worked with her when she was there, but there was still much to be done by Sam and Salvatore.

In addition, Salvatore was still feeling the need to help his family back in Pacentro. He thought often of the widow and the son that his brother, Pasquale, had left behind. In 1949, Pasquale's son, Giuseppe, was able to acquire a visa, and with Salvatore as sponsor, he came to the U.S. Everyone in the family except Salvatore called him Joe. He moved in with his uncle, easily got a job, and helped around the house when he was not working. He soon developed a close attachment to Maria, Salvatore, and young Sam. Never having known his father, and grateful for his uncle's generosity, Joe adopted Salvatore as a father figure. Salvatore felt that by helping his nephew, he was helping the brother he had lost too early.

On his days off, Joe often traveled to McKees Rocks to visit with other relatives, and on one of these visits he was introduced to a young girl named Jane from the Squirrel Hill section of Pittsburgh. They started dating and soon were married. Jane was an only child, and so Joe and his bride moved in with her parents in the city, closer to where he worked.

The house in Monaca was once again quiet, though Maria's health was slipping more quickly. Leo was building his house himself. It was taking a long time since he could only work on it when he was off from his regular job. Rosie went to the site with him and while he was working on the house, she walked up to Salvatore and Maria's to help with the cleaning or laundry. Carl and Betts, living about a mile away on the hill, were close enough to also help out.

Young Sam was pretty much on his own now, and though he was worried about his mother, he was a young man and in need of youthful companionship. He was in his junior year of high school and had limited involvement in activities. His parents never attended a school event, Maria because she was ill and Salvatore because there was no time left in his day. Sam understood this. At the same time, he welcomed the extra help which allowed him to get a part-time job at the Phoenix Glass plant in downtown Monaca. On one of the few evenings he was free, he and a few friends went to see a movie in Rochester. He wasn't really interested in the movie, but he quickly noticed a girl a few rows away. He wanted to get her attention, so he started throwing his popcorn pieces at her, then miraculously parlayed annoyance into an introduction. The girl, whose name was Marjorie, was cute and young, with large, expressive eyes and an engaging smile. She was in the ninth grade at Rochester High School. Sam was finishing his junior year, and did not drive yet, but they started dating anyway, which meant any free time he had was now spent hitching rides to Rochester to visit "Marge."

* * *

On a warm June evening in 1951, Maria became more uncomfortable. The house was quiet. She and Salvatore were alone. He opened the bedroom window for a breeze and sat by her side. He saw that she was very weak and breathing hard. Holding her hand, he quietly began to cry. When she asked what was wrong, he told her he felt bad about how her life had turned out. He had taken her away from her family and all that she had loved. He had not been able to give her all the beautiful things he had thought he would. It was always hard work, he said, never getting ahead, one problem after another...and now this.

She reached up and softly stroked his hair. "Salie," she said, "you gave me all I ever wanted. A beautiful family and life with you. This is our family, and anywhere we were was always our home. I thank God you came into my life. I loved everything about our time together and would have had it no other way." She told him that from the time she was twelve and saw him for the first time, she knew he was the only one for her. There never was anyone else or anything else she ever wanted but the life she had with him.

He laid his head down next to her and they stayed that way through the night. He drifted off to sleep. When he awoke in the morning, he knew something was wrong. Her breathing didn't seem normal. When he called her name, she did not respond. Alarmed, he called out for Sam, but he had already left for work. Leo had moved into the house he was building, even though it was not completed. Luckily, he had already had a telephone installed. Salvatore ran to the phone and called him.

"Leo, something is no good. Your Mama, she's not right. Come quick!"

Leo dropped what he was doing and ran up to the house. As soon as he saw Maria, he called the doctor, and then he called Frannie, then Carl. Frannie and Charlie jumped into their car and drove as fast as they could. Carl called Mauggie. Paul still had no car, so Carl and Betts drove to Aliquippa to get them. By the time they arrived at the house, the doctor was walking out of the bedroom to tell them Maria had had a massive stroke. "So sorry, but Maria is gone," he said. Mauggie was distraught that she didn't get there in time to say goodbye. The family was crushed at this great loss.

After having suffered a number of strokes and being bedridden for five years, Maria passed away on June 15, 1951, at fifty-seven years of age. Salvatore sat, hopeless, crying like a child, and had to be led out of the room and set in a chair in the living room. The one and only love of his life was gone, and he didn't know what to do. The only woman he had ever known, the only woman he had ever wanted to be with had been taken from him too soon. He couldn't respond to questions, he had no idea what to think or what to say. He didn't know what to do next. Nothing mattered. His five children took over. They made all the arrangements. Telegrams were sent to Colorado, California, and Michigan. Salvatore insisted on one thing. He wanted her laid out at the house. One of his children called the Bachelor Funeral Home to handle the funeral. Maria's casket was placed in the parlor for three days while family and friends passed through and paid their respects. Salvatore never left her side

Maggie and her daughter Margaret came from Starkville for the funeral and stayed for a few days afterward. The cousins came from Detroit, Youngstown, McKees Rocks, and Pittsburgh. Family, neighbors, and friends from West Aliquippa and Monaca came. By now, St. John the Baptist Church had built a new Catholic cemetery over the hill, just beyond Union Cemetery. Salvatore bought a family plot for her interment.

Seeing their grandmother in a casket in her parlor was not only sad for the grandchildren, but strange, too. This was their first experience of death for many in the close family, and they spent most of the time sitting in the tree out back, watching from a safe distance the constant movement of people in and out of the house.

Maria had been the rock of strength everyone turned to. She had been witty and creative, a soft and gentle force, but never wavering, a foundation of encouragement for her children, grandchildren, and friends. So many had relied on her, and now she was gone.

The family would never be the same.

Part IV

The Mellow Last Years

At Martin's Cavern in Colorado 1961 after Martin's death...Tony and Salvatore center with Tony's family surrounding.

Following the tragic loss of Maria, the children were doubly concerned for Salvatore's physical and emotional health. He had lost a considerable amount of weight and became listless. His coloring was poor. He just wasn't looking good. When they insisted he see a doctor, he resisted for some time, but eventually he was feeling so bad that he finally gave in. The doctor found him to be anemic. Through all the years of lifting and turning Maria, Salvatore had also developed a double hernia. He had to go into the hospital for an operation.

Mauggie begged him to stay with her after the operation until he was strong enough to return home. He was too weak to argue. At Mauggie's he and Paul had a good rapport, and Paul had a dog, chickens, and a large garden to tend. Salvatore felt better walking around the garden, collecting eggs, and talking to the dog. He and Paul had an ongoing competition over who had the better garden, whose tomatoes were the biggest and who made the best wine. They enjoyed goading each other about the quality of one's zucchini, or the size of their hen's eggs.

The other children came often to visit. On one visit, Mauggie saw Salvatore smiling seeming to be his old self. She put on some music, and he appeared to be enjoying it. Everyone was joining in a loud, pleasant talk when they noticed that Salvatore was crying; "Ave Maria" was playing, and he was shaking his head and saying, "My Maria, my Maria, she is gone." The room got quiet. Charlie tried to tell a joke. Mauggie turned off the music and the visit went on.

The next day Salvatore announced he was going home. He had been away long enough. Although Mauggie and Paul told him it was too soon, he needed more time to get his strength back, he just shook his head and said, "No. Sam, my dog, and my chickens, they need me." Mauggie replied that Sam was busy working for the summer, and her brothers were all chipping in to take care of the land and the animals. "No," he replied, "I go back to my *paradiso*. It's too long I'm gone. I go back to my *paradiso* now." Despite all he had endured, it remained "my paridiso." And as always, once he made a declaration, there was no arguing. Salvatore went home.

It was a lonely house for young Sam. He went through his senior year and graduated from high school, but the excitement and anticipation most young people feel at graduation were missing. There was no direction in his life, nothing to plan for. He was seeing Marge regularly, but she had two years of high school left. His job with the railroad at Conway Yard didn't seem to be going anywhere. A few of his friends were talking about going into the military. That sounded like as good a plan as any, so in December, 1951, Sam made his decision and joined the Navy.

Salvatore was now utterly alone for the first time in his life. His color was still bad, and he wasn't gaining any of his lost weight. His children insisted on another visit to the doctor. This time, the doctor told him there was nothing physically wrong with him. It was the loneliness that was pulling him down, the doctor told him. "You need to retire," he said. "You should remarry." Salvatore was furious at the doctor's comments. Maria had been the only woman he had ever known, and she would remain the only woman in his life. He told the doctor, "You listen to me now. It is better you mind your own business!" And with that he left the office.

Without telling anyone, Salvatore began walking to the cemetery regularly to visit with Maria. He first stopped at Union Cemetery to see Giuseppe and Pasquale, then continued on over the hill to his Maria. When his children found out that he was doing the several mile walk, they told him how worried they were, but he waved them away. From that day forward, they began taking turns driving him to the cemeteries. They also worked to ensure that he wasn't alone for long stretches of time. Carl often stopped after work to have a drink and visit with him. In the evenings, Leo walked up from his house and they sat on the bench under the tree. Salvatore offered him a beer, which he called a little *cichette*, and they talked with Salvatore telling tales of Colorado, his life there, and of Maria. Again and again, Salvatore told them, "Me, no, I am not ready for retirement."

Everyone continued to gather at Salvatore's house for the holidays, and even extended family members paid their respects at Christmas and Easter. Christmas Eve always began at Salvatore's with light food and a grab bag of presents for the grandchildren. The entire gang then went to midnight Mass, after which they returned home for drinks and more food. The little ones fell asleep on the beds and were carried home to awaken on Christmas morning in delightful search for what Santa had left them. On Christmas day, when Salvatore's children were at their homes with their children, his nephews and their spouses always stopped by to visit him. There was a great deal of activity, but Salvatore missed young Sam. And he never stopped thinking of Maria.

On one occasion when the children were visiting, Salvatore announced that since J&L had increased the number of its employees' vacation days, he would be using his days that year to visit his cousin Tony and family in Colorado. This came as a surprise to the family. Taking a vacation was something he had never had the time, the money, or any desire to do. Aside from the novelty, however, everyone thought it was a good idea. Leo and Carl were working and could not leave their jobs, so Salvatore asked Frannie and Mauggie if they would like to go with him. As neither of them could leave their children, he decided he would go by himself. While everyone was further surprised by this decision, they were happy to see him planning something. They were also hopeful the trip would lift him out of his funk.

The night before he left, everyone came to the house to say goodbye and wish him well, and Carl took him to the train station in the morning. For the second time in his life, he was traveling alone and heading west toward Colorado. Watching the passing landscape, Salvatore fell into his memories of traveling this same route more than fifty years earlier. This time there was no billowing smoke, and he was moving a great deal faster under the speed of the new diesel engine. This time, he was not filled with anticipation, fear, and excitement. This time he could see in his mind's eye where he was headed and where he had been. Good time and memories lay ahead.

At the sight of the sign announcing Trinidad, Colorado, he shook his head as if to clear it of his reverie. Looking out the window, he saw a small crowd awaiting his arrival; some faces he knew immediately, whereas others were new. There were Maggie and Tony with some of their children and grandchildren, nephews and nieces. It was as though he were an arriving celebrity.

After hugs and kisses and introductions, they all piled into cars and drove to Starkville, where they were greeted by more relatives and friends at the same house where he and Maria had started his married life. They talked and talked, reminisced, ate, sang, reminisced some more and at times cried and laughed. After everyone had finally gone home, Salvatore went outside and walked around. He looked across the stream over which they had crossed on the rope bridge so many times. The rock still embedded in the basement wall reminded him of the flood that had taken so many lives. Every stone and blade of grass seemed to hold a memory.

Every day during his visit, he and Tony walked around town. Much had changed. The mine was gone, and many of the houses and buildings in the lower town had been washed away by the last big flood. With the mine's closing, there had been no reason to rebuild. Even the saloon where Salvatore had begun singing was gone. They walked to the upper part of town where the only saloon remained and went in for a drink. But there was no pool table or potbelly stove, no stuffed stork gazing down on them, and none of the old-timers. No one was playing music, and the few people inside were younger. They were all strangers living in what felt to be a ghost town.

One day, Tony's son-in-law drove them to the canyon where they visited with Martin Bowden. He had become distinguished looking in his old age and now sported a neatly trimmed, shining white Van Dyke beard that made him look every bit the artist. He showed them the carvings of wildlife that he had made and painted in precarious places along the walls of the canyon. Although he proudly pointed out the snake and the cowboy, he would not talk of the only woman in all his carvings, and he never said who she was. On the drive back to town, they stopped at the cemetery, where Salvatore walked past all the Grosso family graves and stopped at the grave of baby Frances. He wiped away a last tear, then said he was ready to leave.

Back on the train Salvatore was heading east and feeling even sadder than before. So much had changed, so many people were gone. Most of all, his Maria was not there to share this visit with him. All the times they had talked about returning to Colorado, he had always known they never would, but he'd kept up the charade to lift her spirits. In the end, they had returned, but not together. The experience left him feeling empty and alone.

At the house in Monaca his children gathered to greet him and asked him to tell them about the trip. Who did he see? How was everyone? Did it still look like it had when he'd so many years ago? Salvatore just smiled and said his vacation had been wonderful. He told them about Maggie and Tony and his visit with Martin. He talked about the trip as he thought he should have, but they could tell.

All spring and summer, Salvatore worked in the garden on his days off and into the evenings. Now that the cow and the pigs were gone, he had only a few chickens to tend. The dog, which he called his *companero,* was constantly by his side. In the fall, he cleared the fields and made his wine and sausages with meat he now bought. There were always visitors. His nephew John often drove in from Youngstown, usually to show off a sporty new car. Nephew Joe came in from Pittsburgh with his wife and, it seemed with each visit, a new child.

Though his children wanted him to get a gas furnace, he was still using coal to heat the house. On the days a coal shipment arrived, he had it all shoveled into the basement before the boys got home from work, despite their begging him to wait until they could help.

When Marge graduated from high school, she and Sam became engaged. His ship was temporarily assigned to Philadelphia, which was close enough to Monaca that he could get home on leave to be with her. Sometimes, when Leo or Carl drove to Philadelphia to get him, they would take Salvatore and Marge along. It was a good diversion for Salvatore, who always enjoyed the days when Sam came home, even though he spent most of his time with Marge.

* * *

In the fall of 1954 Salvatore received word that his sister's son, Antonio, would be coming to the United States from Venezuela. The Immigration and Nationality Act of 1952 had loosened some of the restrictions on certain groups of people while tightening them on those from countries deemed to be communist-leaning. The new regulations signaled the acceptance of skilled workers and relatives of U.S. citizens as long as there was no evidence of pro-communist thinking or activity. Salvatore was pleased to help Antonio. He would be able to do something for his sister and was looking forward to having his nephew's company.

January 1955 was an eventful month. Antonio was due to arrive, and Salvatore had finally retired from the steel mill. After thirty-six years of service, he was recognized and given an engraved gold wristwatch. On the day of his retirement, he wore a suit and tie and had a picture taken with his superintendent for the company newsletter. He felt great pride for his years in the mill and also felt honored by the attention given to him on this special occasion.

One cold day before Antonio arrived, Rosie called out to Leo that something was not right at Salvatore's house. From her kitchen window she could see black smoke billowing from his windows. Leo immediately ran up to the house. Smoke was pouring out the doors and windows. He ran into the house and, choking on the smoke, called out to his father. But there was no answer. Leo opened the basement door and ran down the stairs to find that the main pipe to the chimney had come apart. Smoke and flames were lapping at the floor boards above. Salvatore was trying to smother the flames by shoveling ashes onto them which was causing more choking smoke. Ignoring Salvatore's protests, Leo took hold of him and pulled him out the basement door, and sat him down on the grass. Then he ran back inside to douse the flames with water. Once the fire was out, they sat side by side, coughing and gasping for fresh air. Rosie ran to them with a bottle of gin. After the men each took a few swallows and regained their breath, they all went inside to begin a mammoth clean-up job. Salvatore's children protested his being alone. Then insisted on the issue of a gas furnace again, but Salvatore held them off.

When Antonio arrived a few days later, activity returned to the house. By now, Sam and Marge were talking about setting a wedding date. Frannie and Charlie bought a bigger house on the hill just three blocks from Salvatore. Carl and Betts were living in their house a few blocks in the other direction. Leo and Rosie were just next door. With the exception of Mauggie in Aliquippa and Sam in the military, Salvatore's family was close by.

As the months went by, Antonio became acclimated to his new country. He soon found work and started dating a girl named Julia, whose father had come from the same province in Italy as Salvatore and owned a tavern in town. Antonio and Julia were wed by August.

Salvatore had a health scare that summer while he was working in the garden. He was taken to the doctor, where through testing, they found that his heart was enlarged. He had gotten into a routine of walking down the hill and into town once a week, but now the doctor was telling him to cut back on heavy garden work and stop walking into town because the walk back up the hill was not good for him. Salvatore's activities were all putting a strain on his heart. The doctor also repeated his advice, "Sam, you need a wife. This living alone is not good for your health."

When the doctor left, Salvatore just shook his head. "What does he know? He's just a doctor. I know my body better than he does. Stop working in my garden and stop walking up that hill, and I'm finished. He reads books about these things, but I know my body." And that was the end of the discussion.

It was not the end of the subject of remarriage.

Christy and Sam Celeste, also worried about Salvatore's health, decided the time had come to take action. One day Salvatore was surprised to see them at his door. He welcomed them, sat them down at the table, and brought out beer and wine. After a little small talk, they brought up the subject of their concern. Their old friend Rose might be right for marrying. He protested, but his protest was far milder than it had been in the past. "Eh, I know this woman. I knew her as a child in Italy. She's a good person. But I do not betray my Maria. Ever."

In September of 1955, young Sam and Marge were married at Saint Cecilia Church in Rochester, with a reception at the Sportsman's Club built on property directly behind Salvatore's farm. It was a great occasion for celebration, but again Salvatore's house was empty. Even though his children were all nearby, and more grandchildren were being born with everyone visiting him regularly, it remained a lonely house. Christy and Sam Celeste came again, and now he agreed to meet with Rose.

Sam Celeste had spoken earlier to Rose and her son about his idea that she should marry Salvatore, and they had agreed to a meeting. Sam invited Salvatore and Rose to his house. They discussed the possibility of a marriage. Salvatore was straightforward. He said that he remembered Rose from Italy and felt she was a good person, but he had had a special relationship with his wife. "My Maria will always be the only love of my life," he said, but he might agree to marriage only if Rose understood it was solely for companionship.

Rose agreed. In fact, she said, it would be the same for her. But she didn't care for living "in the country," as she referred to Monaca Heights. She also thought his wooden house was weak, whereas she had three strong brick houses in excellent condition in Beaver Falls. They should live in one of them. Salvatore immediately stopped the discussion. "Look signora," he said, "when you come to my house to ask for my daughter to marry your son, I tell you I don't care about your houses. I tell you again. I don't care about your houses. My place is my *paradiso*, and I don't leave it until they put me in the cemetery. You think about that, and you make a decision." And with that, he left.

A few days later, Sam Celeste came by again. Rose would agree to Salvatore's terms.

Salvatore's sons had known these negotiations were going on. They were in favor of the marriage because they felt the companionship would extend his life and give it more quality. Mauggie, however, was crushed. She didn't say anything at the family meeting, but back in the privacy of her own home, she fretted and cried. She and Frannie talked about it. They both felt that by doing this, he was betraying their mother, but Frannie was much more accepting of the marriage. Every time she took the bus into town for shopping, Mauggie got off at St. Titus Church to say a few prayers. Now she was feeling such despair that she just had to pray about it. The church was empty, and as she knelt and prayed and cried about the terrible feeling she had about the pending marriage, something profound happened. Mauggie and Frannie still talked every evening on the phone. That evening, Mauggie couldn't wait to tell her sister what had happened. "Frannie," she said, "you know how terrible we've been feeling about Daddy's getting married. I don't want him to be alone, but I couldn't get over this feeling that by doing this he was being unfaithful to Mommy. Well, today I stopped in at the church and was praying. I was so sad and, well, damned mad. Then all of a sudden I felt a cool breeze on my neck, like someone opened the door and came in, but I was alone. Then this voice said to me, 'You're only thinking of yourself. You need to be thinking about your daddy. I never wanted Salie to be alone.' Frannie, it was Mommy. No one ever called Daddy Salie but her. I know it was her talking to me."

From then on, a certain calm settled over Mauggie. She and Frannie were fine about the marriage. In November of 1955, Salvatore married Rose and they settled in at the house on the hill. The house was no longer a lonely place. Now, in addition to his children and grandchildren, and soon-to-be great grandchildren, nephews and nieces, there were also her children and grandchildren, plus friends and relatives. It was a constant stream of visitors. The increase in activity and the companionship were good for both Salvatore and Rose. His children could see the difference in him. This marriage had most likely extended both of their lives.

Early on, the couple's children were concerned that the increase in activity resulting from the merging of two families would be tiring for Salvatore and Rose. They began to stagger their visits. One of the children would drive Salvatore and Rose to the family host house, which meant they didn't have to contend with preparations for the crowd but could still enjoy the family holidays. Salvatore would sit and gaze at the large group before him on visits, then he would raise his glass as if to make a toast and say, "Look at all of this, what I started. In nineteen and two, I come to this country. I'm little like that bottle," and he would point to a wine bottle on the table to emphasize how small he was at the time, "and now look at all this. I do this."

He still enjoyed listening to his visitors discussing politics or world affairs. He usually listened to their complex arguments for awhile, but then he had to speak up. "I think this is like when my cow would...and I would..." It was always such a simple example of a common sense solution that it made their complex discussion seem silly. Salvatore used simple, uncomplicated examples from nature and animals and gardening to express on any number of issues. On raising children, for example, he might say that raising a child was no different from planting a tree. "You must feed it and water it, pamper it as it takes root. But you must also prune it, and if it begins to grow crooked, you must stake it and train it to grow straight. If you do these things, it will grow straight and strong and bear good fruit. If you don't do this, it will grow wild and weak, maybe crooked, and the fruit won't be good. You wait too long before trying to bend it back, it will have become rigid and won't bend; it will break. The child is the same."

He often ended his comment by singing a refrain from a folk song or an operatic aria that had a moral that was relevant to the conversation. Other times, he might raise his glass in a toast that always ended with, "God bless America. God bless Mr. Roosevelt." Someone who didn't know better might ask, why bless Mr. Roosevelt? Salvatore's response would come loud and clear. "I'm born with nothing. In nineteen and two, I come to this country with nothing. Mr. Rockefeller, he give me a bum leg for my old age. Mr. Jones and Mr. Laughlin, they give me this nice gold watch for when I don't need to know the time, but it's pretty nice. Mr. Roosevelt, he give me Social Security and help me save my *paradiso.* So now I have my *paradiso* here. I have a good healthy family, a nice watch, and Social Security. So I say God bless America and God bless Mr. Roosevelt. I even say God bless his wife. Even though she's *bruta*, I still say God bless her, anyway."

And that was that. No discussion.

* * *

As major events unfolded in the world, Salvatore became more of an observer than a participant. He and Rose built a good relationship together. He never stopped his weekly visits to Maria, and Rose respected that. Her sons continued taking her to the cemetery in Beaver Falls for visits to her husband's grave. They built a good, life together of mutual respect and understanding. They maintained a tidy house, and each was gracious to the other's family. They created little traditions of their own. Salvatore and Maria had never been financially able to give gifts, but now he and Rose could afford to give little gifts. Every Christmas when their family visited, Rose always went into the bedroom and came out with three or four handkerchiefs wrapped in tissue paper for the men, and Salvatore handed each woman a box of *torrone*, the traditional Italian nougat candy. Sometimes when he was going on at length telling a story that he finished with a song, she smiled and nodded toward him. "*Ubriaco*," she said. Drunk.

Hearing this, he lifted his glass to her and with a raised eyebrow replied, "Eh, signora." Then they both laughed. They were developing their own style of living together as a couple.

In 1958, Salvatore received news that shook him when he received a call from cousin Tony in Starkville saying his dear, old friend Martin had died. Martin's nephews had been worried about his being alone out on the rim of that canyon. The Colorado winters could be severe, and they worried that since his brother had died, he was more vulnerable all alone with only his dog for company. People in the area had heard about his carvings and began to call the place Painted Canyon. Young people were beginning to hike out to the canyon to see the carvings and paintings. Martin always enjoyed their visits and walked them around, showed them his carvings, answered questions, and told stories. While these visits invigorated him, however, his nephews were afraid he would fall victim to a hostile visitor. Martin scoffed at that kind of thinking. He had his dog and his rifle. He could take care of himself. But there was something he could not control, and that was his health. After hearing his health complaints for some time, his nephews took him into town to see a doctor. A series of tests confirmed that he had cancer of the throat and it was too far advanced for successful treatment. Now they really wanted him to leave the canyon and move in with them, but he grew more insistent that he was going to finish his life on his own piece of paradise. The pain seemed to have become too much for him. He worried about the fate of his dog if it were left alone if he died and his body was not immediately found. When the nephews arrived with supplies one week, they found Martin had shot at his trusted dog, but only nipped off its ear, and then turned the rifle on himself with a shot in the mouth. He was now at peace, and Salvatore bid him farewell.

In 1961, Salvatore received a call that Maria's sister, Maggie, had gone outside to get water from the well. She had slipped on the ice and fallen, hitting her head on the stone well. She had died of a concussion. He announced that he would leave immediately for the funeral. "Maggie, she come to Monaca for Maria's funeral, and now I go to be at Maggie's for Tony." Rose was determined not to go, however, and his children were worried that he should not go alone, and so Leo went with him. He knew everyone there from the time he had taken Maria. This visit was not bittersweet like the last one to Colorado. It was sad. Salvatore and Tony spent long hours talking. Salvatore's Maria was gone, now Tony's Maggie was gone. All the relatives that had been part of their lives in their generation were dying. They also talked about Italy, about Starkville and the mines, and of their foray into New Mexico. Their long conversations wound through all the family members, places, and events that had touched their lives. But they spoke very little of the years after Salvatore and Maria had moved east.

Before Salvatore left for home, they decided to go out to the canyon. Tony's two daughters and their families took them. Martin's cabin was just as he had left it. They walked down the path along the canyon wall and passed the carvings. There was a haunting and yet peaceful feeling there as they retraced Martin's steps. Leo took a photo of Salvatore and Tony together at the canyon.

But it was now time to go home. Salvatore knew this would be the last time he would ever see Starkville, a place that had meant so much to him. This was where he had met his Maria and made the life that became theirs together. So many people gone, places gone.

Before they left, there was something he had to do. He asked Leo to take him to Ludlow. He wanted them to go alone, no one else. When they arrived, they read the lonely plaque commemorating the men who had died in that horrible massacre. All their names listed. Salvatore just shook his head as he did when something was too painful to talk about. Then he turned to Leo and said, "Now we go to the cemetery."

They went back to Trinidad and walked through, stopping at the graves of all those who had meant so much to him and his early life in the United States. His last stop was at the grave of the daughter he and Maria lost too soon. He stood silently for awhile, then turned to Leo and said, "I finish with this place. Now we go home." It was as though he had said goodbye to everyone and everything in this very special place in his heart. On the trip home, the silence was deafening as Leo and Salvatore sat looking out the windows, each lost in his own thoughts.

For some time after his return from Colorado, Salvatore was rather mellow, but he continued along in his usual routine. He worked in the garden, tended the chickens, and took breaks and sat under his sycamore tree with his dog. He made his weekly trips into town, stopped at the bank, stopped at Sam Celeste's bar for his *cichette*—his fuel to get back up the hill—and he enjoyed visits from friends and relatives. People continued to come for advice and help, which he never stopped dispensing. In 1965, another call came: Tony had died at the age of seventy-nine. Now there was no one left in Colorado and no one left of his generation of his family in America. Rose's company became more important than ever. They kept each other going while their children maintained a vigilance over both of them.

Meanwhile, Salvatore's family was growing and doing well. Frannie and Charlie had three boys who were happily involved in activities in Monaca and Charlie had a good job at J&L. Mauggie and Paul had a daughter, another who was stillborn, and two sons. Paul was working as a crane operator at J&L, and now the family owned a car in which they drove to visit Salvatore once or twice a week. Leo had started his own welding company. He and Rosie, who had two daughters and a son, were settled in their house on the property. Carl was head butcher in charge of the meat department of the supermarket. He and Betts had two sons and had bought a nice piece of land nearby, where they built a new house, planted grapes, and made a garden. Sam was working at the St. Joe Lead Company. He and Marge had two sons, and now lived in a house on the hill just blocks away from Salvatore. Salvatore and Maria's children were gathered tightly around their father.

Frannie walked to her father's home several times a week to see if she could help Rose with any housework. Carl often stopped on his way home from work for a little *cichette* and some conversation. Sam, who jogged every day, passed his father's house and usually stopped for an update. Leo walked to visit his father after dinner each night, and the two of them sat under the tree and reminisced about Colorado. Salvatore's grandchildren also came to see him, and as they grew older, married, and had children of their own, they began taking their children to visit their great-grandfather.

Salvatore still had a full head of bright white hair and all of his own teeth. When people commented on a man in his eighties having such a beautiful head of hair, he replied, "Eh, you know I lost all of my hair once in my twenties when I had typhoid fever. So this hair that you see is only sixty years old." He was consistently witty and pleasant. In 1969, when he saw Armstrong and Aldrin land on the moon he marveled at all the advances that had been made in his lifetime. He said, "Eh, at thirteen years I crossed the Atlantic to a new home when the Wright brothers they were just making their first flight."

In good weather, visitors usually found Salvatore sitting on the bench under his tree with his dog at his side. He still wore his hat every day, and upon seeing the visitor's car pull into his drive, he stood up, smiled, gallantly removed his hat and bowed with a sweeping motion almost like one of the Three Musketeers. He was gracious and conversant with everyone, including the paper boy, who always came to the tree and chatted while delivering the paper. Even salespeople and Jehovah's Witnesses who stopped were offered a seat and conversation. He especially enjoyed friendly, often devilish banter with the Jehovah's Witnesses and anyone else with strong beliefs different from his, even if he might agree with them. He talked the same with everyone, young or old, never condescending or angry, always pleasant. Sometimes he would be teasing the young ones about their clothing styles, haircuts, or choice of music, but always in a kind and warm manner. His grandchildren enjoyed talking with him, and often asked questions about Italy, Colorado, and days of his youth. He was always good for a story and so family and history were passed on.

But Salvatore seldom talked about Italy, other than to remark on the beauty of the mountains and how he had enjoyed taking care of the family's cow and singing with the shepherds. Occasionally, he spoke of the kindness of his mother, but when he began to tear up, he would move on to other topics. What he never tired of was talking about Colorado, his early days in West Aliquippa, and their settling in Monaca. Although he and his family had endured hard times, he talked about those days with a fondness and reverence that led his listeners to believe they had been special, wonderful times. Sometimes he pulled out a box of old photos (there weren't many) of his family in Colorado. He showed the photos to his grandchildren and told stories about the people in them and the events he had experienced. Eventually, if someone showed a particular interest in a photo, he would give it to that person, passing on a legacy, a little piece of inheritance.

In his conversations and stories, Salvatore often inserted sage advice. To the young ones, he insisted that they pursue their education as far as they could. He felt good that his sons now were living better than he had and attributed their success to hard work, but also their graduating from high school. He encouraged his grandchildren, the paper boy, and other young people to take their education seriously. "Things you have can be lost in the blink of an eye," he always said, "but no one can ever take your education away from you." Having left school early himself, he had learned most from experience.

As he sat with his sons under his tree, the conversation always came around to Maria, his one and only love. He often paused, then said in a quiet voice, "Some day soon I will see your mama." That bothered the boys, and they told him not to talk like that. But he said it with no remorse or sadness. It was a fact, and his sons could see the smile on his face and the hint of anticipation in his voice.

In early spring Salvatore was working out in the garden when the air seemed to change. The leaves on the trees were turning upward in a way he had never seen before. Then all was still. He noticed that in the distance, the sky had changed to a dark black with a strange orange glow around the edges. Then it began to rain. As this massive dark cloud approached, there was a powerful roar like a train engine. Salvatore dropped his hoe and ran into the house, calling for Rose. They ran into the cellar, where they felt the house shake and creak and strain. Suddenly it was over. All was quiet.

Salvatore and Rose came upstairs and walked about the house, checking for damage, but all seemed fine. Then he looked out the front window and his heart sank. One of the beautiful sycamores he had planted along the road had been completely uprooted. He walked out the front door. Some branches had reached the porch, but there didn't seem to be any damage to the house. Walking around back, he found another tree down. The tornado had swept across his property, taking the front tree and the back tree, but jumping over the house itself. Within minutes, his sons rushed to see how Salvatore and Rose were, then began to clean up the debris. They cut up the trees and cleaned the area. As he watched them, Salvatore kept repeating, "God was with us, keeping us safe through the storm." Yet he and Rose were both visibly shaken by this event and seemed somehow older.

On his eighty-sixth birthday, Salvatore's family was gathered around him. They all raised their glasses and shouted, "Happy birthday!" and Charlie added, "Here's to many more."

But Salvatore shook his head. "No," he said. "This is my last birthday. Next year, I celebrate with your mama." Even though everyone protested and his daughters began to cry, he held fast. "No. This year be my last."

Spring came early that year. In late April, Salvatore went out to plant his onions. But something was wrong. In a panic, Rose called Leo, who rushed over. He found Salvatore lying on the ground, surrounded by Rose, the paper boy, and the neighbors. He had been planting his onions when he went down. The paper boy had found him there. He had had a stroke, but was trying to say something. Leo asked everyone to be quiet as he tried to make out what his father was trying to say. They finally realized he was angry because the people were walking all over his garlic plants.

He was taken by ambulance to the hospital in Beaver Falls. When his children held his hand and talked to him, all he could do was squeeze ever so lightly, but he did not speak. They felt he could hear them, and was acknowledging that fact, but according to the doctor, he never regained consciousness. The doctor's assessment meant nothing to daughter Mauggie. She knew he was hearing her and answering by his squeezing her hand. This she felt was their saying goodbye.

Three days later, on May 1, 1975, just thirty days before his eighty-seventh birthday, Salvatore Ciccone died with all of his family gathered around him. On the very same date, seventy-three years earlier, he departed from Italy, heading for the new world and a new life. Now he had departed from this world on his final journey.

The viewing was held at the Bachelor Funeral Home for the traditional three days. There were no relatives left to come from Colorado, but they came from Chicago, Detroit, Youngstown, Pittsburgh, McKees Rocks, West Aliquippa, Aliquippa, and many other cities. Friends old and new came: old coworkers from the mill, the manager of Monaca Federal, the paper boy who had found him, and other young people from the neighborhood.

The day of the funeral, the people in attendance spilled out onto the street. The church was also filled, and cars were parked in three rows across the road and for blocks down the street. The crowd was witness to the influence this unassuming man had had on this slice of the world around him, which he called *paradiso.*

At his funeral his life was recounted.

Here was a man who had never gone beyond the second grade in school, but he had taught himself to speak three languages and read and write in two. He never had a driver's license or drove a car, but he traveled halfway around the world at age thirteen and crossed the North American continent six times. He never held a political office, but helped countless people get a new start in a new country and supported them until they could survive on their own.

Salvatore worked hard and had brushes with danger all his life. He lost homes and loved ones before their time and was never to get ahead financially. But he always thanked God and his country for his good fortune. He raised a caring family and taught his children to respect people of all beliefs and values. He believed in honesty, integrity, and justice and was not judgmental, biased, or accusing. What excellent lessons those whose lives he touched learned from him and from the life he led.

Salvatore knew progress was slow, but one should never stop trying. While his formal education ended at the second grade, his children got to high school. His three sons graduated, and Mauggie, who had had to drop out of school and work, persisted and earned her high school diploma at the age of seventy-one. His grandchildren went beyond high school and received technical training and bachelors' and graduate degrees. Three generations later, college and a profession are no longer unreachable goals for this family. While Salvatore's life was consumed with a struggle to survive, he created a world where advancement and security and comfort were possible for others.

While not born in this country, he consistently praised America for the opportunities it provided. He was proud that two of his sons and several grandchildren served in branches of the armed forces. He always praised them for doing so.

* * *

And though my grandfather's story may never get into the big history books, his life was the substance of which true history is made. We search for heroes among sports figures, movie stars, and politicians, and our search becomes harder. We usually become disappointed, often disillusioned. We need look no further than within our own families for stories of heroic struggles and the accomplishments of people who worked hard to overcome nearly insurmountable odds to provide for their families and to make a better world.

This is the heritage my family has received from Salvatore and the long life which he lived and shared.

Epilogue

Salvatore in his beloved garden. c. 1970

It has been over 112 years since Salvatore stepped off the train in Trinidad, Colorado. His stories, and his memory live in the minds of his descendants and those whose lives he touched. My wife, Joyce, and I spent a month in Italy tracing the path of the villages of my ancestors' origins. We found that the impoverished Pacentro that Salvatore left behind is now a charming, prosperous storybook hill town of 1,300 inhabitants and full of admiring tourists. Many visit to see the town where the grandparents of the famous singer Madonna with the same last name were born. Others visit for the beauty of a quaint Italian hill town. We went to see where our family story began. The ruins of the *castello* have been restored and colorful medieval pageants are held on the grounds. The people are warm and welcoming.

On a separate visit to Trinidad, Colorado, we found the dirt streets that greeted Salvatore are now paved and lined with trendy boutiques and antique shops. The Holy Trinity Church still stands, its stone exterior bright and clean. A statue out front is dedicated to the miners of the area. In this town of ten thousand residents, a glitzy visitors' center is also filled with tourists. The jitney no longer runs to Starkville, where my mother Mauggie was born. Fewer than sixty people are living in this old mining town. Up in the Plazzita, the vacant train station stands in disrepair, its shingled siding falling off and letters missing from the sign that no longer spells Starkville. The few buildings left are empty and surrounded by weeds, windows are broken and boarded up. It's nearly a ghost town. We walked down the hill and crossed the stream where there is now only a hillside.

The houses, taverns, and church were all swept away by floods before the dam was built in 1978 to create Lake Trinidad. The house where Salvatore, Tony, and their families lived is gone, along with everything else. The mine tipple and coke ovens are now only a memory. We walked through the huge weeds in the shadow of Interstate 25, which now runs straight through what was once the town. It was possible to find a few stones that were once part of the foundation of the old homestead where my mother, Mauggie, was born. But the land is silent now, without a story to tell or a hint of what has been.

Driving out to the rim of the Purgatory Canyon, we found the remains of Martin's cabin. The carvings are visible, too, although the paint has faded as he had predicted years ago. Vandals have camped at the site and damaged the cabin and a few carvings, and the current owner of the land has added fencing and a locked gate, though he was kind enough to give us the key.

West Aliquippa, Pennsylvania, is now a mere shadow of its former self. Nearly half of the town was torn down in the late '60s and early '70s to build the largest, most modern, continuous casting mill in the country. But this too has been dismantled. The mill that employed over 14,000 and stretched seven miles along the river bank, the steel industry that had been the powerful life blood of the county has become acres of empty, weed-strewn, unusable ground, an American tragedy.

The house on Allegheny Avenue still stands, but its siding is falling off, as are the roof shingles. The once proud little yard is overgrown. The company houses that were next to it have been leveled and the land vacant. The neighborhood stores are closed and boarded up or torn down. The Sons of Italy building is now an empty lot, and the church and school are closed, too. The tunnel was filled in years ago, and a bridge that was built to accommodate large truck traffic into the now gone mill remains the only way in or out of this once vibrant town. People visit there mainly for lost memories.

Downtown Aliquippa, like so many steel mill towns, is a deserted, neglected relic of a time when work was good and people lived and worked in every street, building, and house. Where more than 27,000 people once lived, fewer than 9,000 remain. The buses that filled the main street, carrying workers and shoppers no longer run. They were once filled to capacity as they took my father to and from work, and me, my sister and brother to and from high school. There are no signs of the four theaters that once graced the main street, and the five-story Pittsburgh Mercantile Building has been converted to low-rent housing and is half empty. A "for rent" sign in one window looks older than the building itself.

The magnificent granite and marble library built by the Jones family of Jones and Laughlin Steel stands as a lonely sentinel over this vast nothingness. It is still in operation, and inside, the cool marble walls and elaborate chandeliers provide a peaceful haven. The beautiful gothic high school that I attended (which was built in the 1920s) is gone, stately architectural halls of learning replaced by pedestrian "modern" monoliths with no personality.

Downtown Monaca has fared better. There is still some industry operating there. Although a mall has taken much of the business from the main street, there are several shops and a restaurant or two. Celeste's Tavern, where Salvatore used to stop for his *cichette*, continues to operate on Pennsylvania Avenue. The buildings of the town are intact, and the surrounding residences and churches remain in good condition.

The neat little house on the hill in Monaca Heights is still bright and cheery and sports new, cleanly painted siding, plus a manicured lawn. This is all evidence of the work of my Aunt Frannie's son and his family. When I drive past, however, I can still see Salvatore and his dog sitting under the tree. At the far end of these three acres stands the house Leo built, freshly remodeled by his son, who lives there. Where the barn and chicken coop once stood is a neat, brick ranch house where Salvatore's nephew Antonio's family live. Other family members and grandchildren live along neighboring streets on the hill, and the rest of this large family of Salvatore and Maria's grandchildren, great grandchildren, nephews, nieces, grand nephews and grand nieces, is spread out across the country like ripples emanating from a pebble gently dropped in a pond.

The quiet fields that surrounded this peaceful little farm are now the streets of suburbia. Beyond them, though no longer possible to see because of the tall trees, stands the hill where Salvatore and Maria sat while visiting Giuseppe's grave and dreaming of their future here. They are back there again, and they continue to be surrounded by their children; all in their own resting places.

Salvatore and Maria found and made their paradise in America, and they stayed to watch it grow.

Ciccone Family Tree

name: **Antonio Ciccone**
born: June 10 1864
place: Pacentro, Italy
married: c. 1885
death: no record
place: Italy

spouse: **Francesca Tollis**
born: Pocentrono, Italy
death: c. 1918
place: Italy

name: **Salvatore**
born: May 31, 1888
place: Pacentro, Italy
married to **Maria Grosso**
death: May 1, 1975,
Monaca, PA

name:**Virginia**
born: 1890
place: Pacentro
son **John** moves to
Monaca 1937
his death: 1952

name**: Bombina**
born: April 1892
place: Pacentro
son **Anthony** moves to:
Monaca, PA
his death: 2013

name: **Giuseppe**
born: July 1898
place: Pacentro
death: 1924,
Aliquippa, PA

name: **Pasquale**
born: 1900
place: Pacentro
death: August 1931
place: Farrell, PA
son Joe moves to Monaca

Grosso Family Tree

name: **Francesca**
born: 1877
place: Montalenghe
moves back to Italy
death: nr

name: **Mattie**
born: 1886
place: Starkville, CO
married to Pampino
death: 1941, Califronia

name: **Maggie**
born:1888
place: Starkville, CO
married to Guy Garfolo
then Tony Ciccone
death: 1961 Starkville, CO

name: **Pietro Grosso**
born: Feb. 17, 1848
place: Montalenghe, Italy
death: 1923
place: Starkville, CO

spouse: **Margherita Martelli**
born: June 14, 1854
place: Castellemonte, Italy
death: Nov. 7, 1917,
Starkville, CO

name: **Maria**
born: Sept. 19, 1893
place: Starkville, CO
married to Salvatore
death: June 15, 1951
place: Monaca, PA

name: **Phyllis**
born: 1898
place: Starkville, CO
death: 1988, Boulder, CO

name: **Virginia**
born: 1903
place: Starkville, CO
death: 1924
place: Morley, CO

Salvatore & Maria Family Tree

name: **Tony Ciccone**
born: 1881
place: Pacentro, Italy
married to Maggie Grosso
death: 1965, Starkville, CO

cousin

name: **Salvatore**
born: May 31, 1888
place: Pacentro, Italy
married to **Maria Grosso**
death: May 1, 1975,
Monaca, PA

name: **Maria**
born: Sept. 19, 1893
place: Starkville, CO
married to Salvatore
death: June 15, 1951,
Monaca, PA

name: **Frannie**
born: June 19, 1914
place: Starkville, CO
married to Charlie
death: Jan. 22, 1999,
Monaca, PA

name: **Mauggie**
born: June 4, 1917
place: Starkville, CO
married to Paul
death: April 6, 2008, Erie, PA

name: **Leo**
born: Feb. 22, 1919
place: Starkville, CO
married to Rosie
death: Nov. 29, 1991, Monaca

name: **Carl**
born: Nov. 12, 1922
place: Aliquippa, PA
married to Bets
death: Sept. 1, 1995, Monaca

name: **Sam**
born: Oct. 8, 1933
place: Monaca, PA
married to Marge
death: Feb. 28, 2004, Monaca

Bibliography

Andrews, Thomas C., *Killing for Coal: America's Deadliest Labor War.* Harvard University Press, 2008.

Annual Reports of the State Inspector of Coal Mines, Dept. of Natural Resources, State of Colorado 1884–1962. Denver: Denver Public Library, Western History Upper, C622.33, C719re.

Beaver County History Online, www.bchistory.org. Beaver County Community History Index.

Beshor, Barron B., *Out of the Depths.* Colorado Labor Historical Committee of the Denver Area Labor Federation, 1980.

Brody, David, *Labor in Crisis: The Steel Strike of 1919.* University of Illinois Press, 1987

Bureau of Statistics, Department of Labor. Table 355, Wages, Hours of Labor and Employment, 1932.

Hunt, Inez and Wanetta W. Draper. *To Colorado's Restless Ghosts.* Sage Books, 1960.

Pacchioli, David, "Forged in Steel," *Research/Penn State*, Vol. 20, No. 1 (January 1999).

St. John the Baptist, Monaca, Pennsylvania 1888–1988. Commemorative publication, 1988.

Sherman, James E. and Barbara H. *Ghost Towns and Mining Camps of New Mexico.* Norman: University of Oklahoma Press, 1975.

Wollman, David H. and Donald R. Inman. *Portraits in Steel: An Illustrated History of Jones & Laughlin Steel Corporation.* Kent State University Press, 1999.

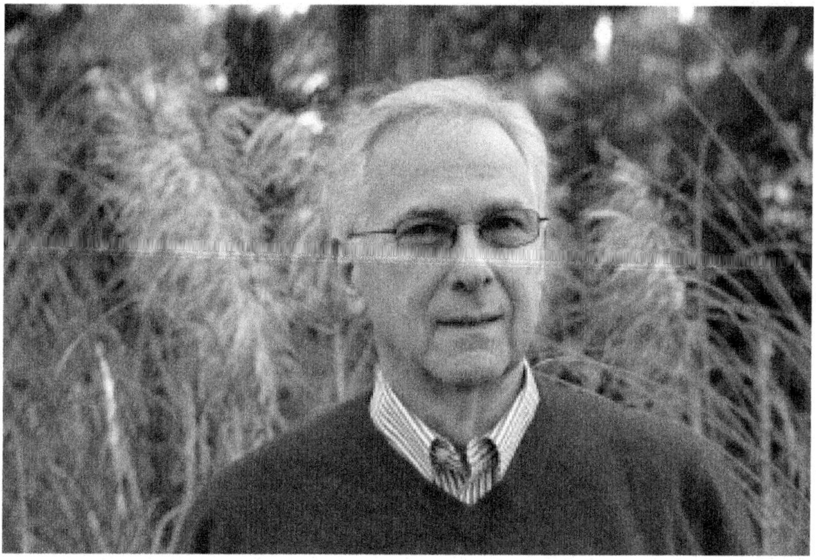

Paul L. Gentile was born in Aliquippa, a steel town in southwestern Pennsylvania where the men in his family worked in the mills. During college, he worked in the steel mill, and after graduating from California University of Pennsylvania, began a thirty-two year career in education. Paul taught junior high school and served in the U. S. Coast Guard. After a Masters Degree from Duquesne University, he was a high school guidance counselor, and eventually, after completing his PhD at the University of Pittsburgh, worked up to the position of Dean of Workforce Training and Development for the Allegheny County Community College system. Here he was responsible for Government and Industry funded worker training programs.

When the steel industry collapsed, he worked on a team that developed a program which retrained over 12,000 unemployed steelworkers. During his time as President of the Northern Allegheny County Chamber of Commerce, Paul contributed as a guest columnist to the local newspaper, writing on economic and workplace issues. He concluded his education career by helping to create the new School of Leadership and Professional Advancement at Duquesne University.

In retirement he wrote his first book, a travel memoir titled *Dolce Far Niente: Sweet Doing Nothing.* His lifelong involvement in the challenges of the working person, and years of family stories inspired him to write this story of his Salvatore and Maria's life.

Parents to three grown children, he and his wife Joyce divide their time between Pittsburgh, Pennsylvania and Hilton Head Island, South Carolina.

Bottom Dog Press

Books in the Working Lives Series

Story Hour & Other Stories
By Robert Flanagan, 122 pgs. $16
Sky Under the Roof: Poems
By Hilda Downer, 126 pgs. $16
Breathing the West: Great Basin Poems
By Liane Ellison Norman, 80 pgs. $16
Smoke: Poems By Jeanne Bryner, 96 pgs. $16
Maggot: A Novel By Robert Flanagan, 262 pgs. $18
Broken Collar: A Novel By Ron Mitchell, 234 pgs. $18
American Poet: A Novel By Jeff Vande Zande, 200 pgs. $18
Reply to an Eviction Notice: Poems By Robert Flanagan, 100 pgs. $15
The Pattern Maker's Daughter: Poems
By Sandee Gertz Umbach, 90 pages $16
The Way-Back Room: Memoir of a Detroit Childhood
By Mary Minock, 216 pgs. $18
The Free Farm: A Novel By Larry Smith, 306 pgs. $18
The Long River Home: A Novel
By Larry Smith, 230 pgs. Paper $16/ Cloth $22
Sinners of Sanction County: Stories
By Charles Dodd White, 160 pgs. $17
Learning How: Stories, Yarns & Tales
By Richard Hague, 216 pgs. $18
Strangers in America: A Novel
By Erika Meyers, 140 pgs. $16
Riders on the Storm: A Novel
By Susan Streeter Carpenter, 404 pgs. $18
Landscape with Fragmented Figures: A Novel
By Jeff Vande Zande, 232 pgs. $16
The Big Book of Daniel: Collected Poems
By Daniel Thompson, 340 pgs. Paper $18/ Cloth $22;
An Unmistakable Shade of Red & The Obama Chronicles
By Mary E. Weems, 80 pgs. $15
Our Way of Life: Poems By Ray McNiece, 128 pgs. $15

Bottom Dog Press, Inc.
PO Box 425/ Huron, Ohio 44839
http://smithdocs.net

Bottom Dog Press

Books in the Harmony Series

Salvatore and Maria: Finding Paradise
By Paul L. Gentile 268 pgs. $18
Jack's Memoirs: Off the Road
By Kurt Landefeld, 590 pgs. $19.95
Daughters of the Grasslands: A Memoir
By Mary Woster Haug, 200 pgs. $18
Wanted: Good Family By Joseph G. Anthony 212 pgs. $18
Lake Winds: Poems By Larry Smith, 218 pgs. $18
An Act of Courage: Selected Poems of Mort Krahling
Eds. Judy Platz & Brooke Horvath, 104 pgs. $16
On the Flyleaf: Poems By Herbert Woodward Martin, 104 pgs. $16
The Stolen Child: A Novel By Suzanne Kelly, 350 pgs. $18
Painting Bridges: A Novel By Patricia Averbach, 234 pgs. $18
Ariadne & Other Poems By Ingrid Swanberg, 120 pgs. $16
The Harmonist at Nightfall: Poems of Indiana
By Shari Wagner, 114 pgs. $16
Kenneth Patchen: Rebel Poet in America By Larry Smith,
Revised 2nd Edition, 326 pgs. Cloth $28
Selected Correspondence of Kenneth Patchen,
Edited with Introduction by Allen Frost,
312 pgs. Paper $18/ Cloth $28
Awash with Roses: Collected Love Poems of Kenneth Patchen
Eds. Laura Smith and Larry Smith
Introduction by Larry Smith, 200 pgs. $16

* * * *

Harmony Collections and Anthologies

Come Together: Imagine Peace
Eds. Ann Smith, Larry Smith, Philip Metres, 204 pgs. $16
Evensong: Contemporary American Poets on Spirituality
Eds. Gerry LaFemina and Chad Prevost, 240 pgs. $16
America Zen: A Gathering of Poets
Eds. Ray McNiece and Larry Smith, 224 pgs. $16
Family Matters: Poems of Our Families
Eds. Ann Smith and Larry Smith, 232 pgs. $16

Bottom Dog Press, Inc.
PO Box 425/ Huron, Ohio 44839
http://smithdocs.net

CPSIA information can be obtained at www.ICGtesting.com
Printed in the USA
BVOW08s1709100516

447446BV00001B/3/P

9 781933 964959